Hope and Courage
Across America

Life is a journey . . .

Bob Mortimer

Hope and Courage Across America
by Bob Mortimer
www.hcjourney.org

Cover Design and Page Layout by Tim Smith

Hope and Courage Across America Logo and Graphics by Tim Smith

Front Cover Photograph by Gary McCutcheon

Back cover Photographs:
Darla Mortimer, Left
Gary McCutcheon, Right

Interior Photographs:
Darla Mortimer, pp vi, 5, 48, 83, 107, 109, 146, 155, 161, 188, 202, 208, 223, 232,
238, 252, 262, 278, 293, 304, 306, 314, 324
Jeanne Oesch, pp 43, 84, 128, 172, 174, 259, 337
Gary McCutcheon, pp 11, 360
Ron Storer, pp 54, 62
Nick Burger, pp 334, 340
Todd Culver, pg 35
Azzura Photography, pg 360
Photographics Northwest pg 141

ISBN-10: 1-461-03226-1

ISBN-13: 978-1-4610322-6-7

Printed in the United States of America.

Dedication

To my wife Darla,
who has adorned my life with beauty, not just
because of the way she looks but because of the
way she sees.

Acknowledgements

I want to thank the travelers that have helped me on Hope and Courage Across America. I cannot mention you all by name but that does not mean I do not appreciate the impact you have had on this journey.

Thanks to Darla, my wife, for staying beside me all the way from "Hon, I got this really big idea!" to "I can't believe we made it."

Thanks to my kids, Nicole, Grant, and Chanel for living the message of Hope and Courage. You adapted to every change we threw at you and never asked, "Are we there yet?"

Thanks to my sister, Jeanne, for giving up your summer to take care of us from coast to coast. And thanks to your husband, Don, for letting us borrow the best person in his life.

Thanks to Mom for teaching me from the beginning to always hope for the best and keep moving forward.

Thanks to Tim Smith for your God-given talent in graphic arts. You have designed every visual aspect of Hope and Courage Across America from the RV to the book cover to this very page. Your attention to detail and extremely long hours turned the message I speak into a message that can be seen.

Thanks to David Sanford, my literary coach and friend, for coming into this book project while I was wandering in circles and guiding me to the finish.

Thanks to Jodi Carlson, The Word Chef, for your keen attention to grammar and punctuation. Your corrections and encouragement were a blessing.

Thanks to all the communities and churches from Gig Harbor to New York that welcomed us in and helped send us along our way.

Thanks to all the family, old friends, and new friends whose prayers and support made Hope and Courage Across America possible.

And thanks to God.
The message of Hope and Courage would have no meaning at all without You. Thank you for accepting, listening, and loving.

Contents

Introduction

Life is a journey. Actually, life is a journey full of journeys. Each one intertwining with other journeys to ultimately give us this great experience we call life. During the summer of 2008, I led my wife and children on a journey. We went on a little family bike ride... from the west coast of the United States to the east coast. We called our ride Hope and Courage Across America. Our message was simple: Our hope is in Christ and the courage is in us to do something with that hope.

Geographically I can tell you exactly when and where the journey began and ended. We began May 17 at City Hall in Gig Harbor, Washington. We ended September 12 at the Statue of Liberty. I can tell you we pedaled 2,500 miles in 12 states. I can tell you the roads we travelled and the towns we visited. However, the important journeys of our lives are not measured geographically. They blur the lines of distance and time. The important journeys in life always teach a common lesson: it is not about the miles, it is about the message.

... but those who hope in the Lord will renew their strength. They will soar on wings like eagles; they will run and not grow weary, they will walk and not be faint. Isaiah 40:31

Chapter 1

September 23, 2008

Amish Country, Northern Indiana. There could be no more peaceful place in America. I should know. I just spent the last four months leading my family across America on bicycles. We are making our way back home to Gig Harbor, Washington. Hope and Courage Across America – that is what we call our ride. You get a closer perspective of America when you cross on bicycles than you do when you cross it by airplane, or car for that matter. We are not on bicycles today, though. We are riding in a horse drawn cart driven by our new Amish friend, Marlin Miller. His fifteen-year-old twin sister, Marilyn, sits next to him. Our sixteen-year-old son, Grant, sits on the other side. My wife, Darla, our ten-year-old daughter, Chanel, and I fill up the back bench. Marlin loves his horse more than other teenage boys could possibly love their cars, motorcycles, or trucks. His horse is a living, breathing creature of God. Copper is not just his transportation, Copper is his friend.

"He used to be a race horse, you know," he says proudly. You can't fault a teenager for bragging about his 'ride' or his friend, for that matter.

It is a warm, sunny afternoon and the farms are beautiful. White seems to be the preferred paint amongst these Amish. White homes, white barns, white sheds, and white fences line the county road. They stand out crisp and clean against the earthy tones of the crops, pastures, and gravel lanes. I take a deep, cleansing breath and slowly let the air out of my lungs. This is therapy. There is no electronic noise, no motors, except an occasional vehicle passing us on the road. Nothing interrupts the silence but the sounds of men commanding their horse teams in the fields … and the children, lots of children, laughing and waving from the front porches. All of this is kept in rhythm by the clop-clop-clop, clop-clop-clop of the horse pulling the cart.

The farm is up around the bend where I will climb out the cart and get back into my wheelchair to enjoy the evening meal prepared by the twins' mother, Ruth Miller. I am looking forward to the home cooked Amish hospitality. Darla sees another Amish child run onto the porch to wave at us. "Oh look, he has one of our Hope and Courage badges on his shirt." I glanced quickly to see the little boy with his black-rimmed hat, suspendered pants, and a crisp white shirt waving from the porch. Our brown badge stood out on his shirt. We had given it to him in his school earlier today. He is cute. I look back at the road ahead. A truck from the local feed mill is heading toward us to deliver his load nearby. I have been watching trucks, and cars, and eighteen-wheelers pass us all summer on our bicycles. You would think I would be able to ignore them by now. But I can't. I am watching this one as it closes the gap between us. It is a different view watching over the head of a horse as opposed to the cranks on my handcycle.

The next five seconds pass clear and slow in my mind. Copper turns his head to the left and sets his eyes on the driveway across the road. He starts pulling our cart directly into the path of the truck. My tranquility is instantly replaced by horror.

The truck has no time to stop or room to maneuver. My family is being pulled into the path of an oncoming truck. I see what is happening but have no control. My hand is not on the reins. We have pedaled across this nation on one-inch tires, survived weather, bandits, dogs, and rattle snakes.

Is this how it ends, God? In a horse drawn cart in the most peaceful part of America?

I shout, "Watch out for the truck!"

Everyone snaps their heads to the front. Marlin pulls vainly on the reins. Screams are abruptly silenced as the truck hits Copper dead on and tears the horse and riggings from the cart. Marlin maintains his grip on the reins and is dragged with the horse. The impact spins and tosses the cart. Darla, Grant, Chanel and Marilyn are scattered along the road. Because I have no legs, I am jolted off the bench to the floor of the cart. The cart stops. The truck stops. The silence is not peaceful anymore.

Where's my family? Where am I?

I am lying on the floor of the cart with broken benches on top of me. I can move. *Good.* I can't find any open bleeding. *Good.*

Where's my family? I push the benches off and pull myself up.

I hear Darla say, "Grant, go check Dad and see if he is okay!"

Great. Grant is on his feet. Darla is on her feet. I look around and see Chanel standing up.

"I'm alright," I yell. "Are you guys okay?"

"Yeah, we think so," Darla shouts back.

Where are the twins? Where are Marlin and Marilyn? Marilyn is lying still on the road.

Darla starts praying out loud as she heads over toward her. "God, please help us. Please help us." Desperate prayers are simple prayers. I see Marlin up toward the truck. He is bent up and lying on the road but moving.

"Grant, let's check out Marlin."

My wheelchair is back at the farm so I am going to have to do without it. I grab a hold of the side of the cart and lower myself down on the road with my arm. My knuckles dig into the road surface as I scoot myself toward Marlin. The road is splattered with something from the horse. I reach Marlin and begin calming him down. I don't want him to stand up until we determine his condition. His arms are bent in an odd position at his side.

"Marlin, you are going to be okay. Can you move your arms? Show me if you can move your arms." Marlin sits up and blankly obeys, straightening and twisting his arms to show me.

Good. They are not broken.

"How's Copper? Is my horse hurt?" Copper lay on the road behind the truck out of Marlin's view. I watch Copper struggle to his feet. One foot has been severed at the hoof and his insides hang out of the large tear in his stomach. I am concerned the horse will panic and possibly cause more injuries to us. We are vulnerable here on this road with nowhere to hide. My fears are unfounded. Copper drops to the road, struggles to get back up, and drops for a final time.

"Copper is alright, Marlin. Don't worry about your horse." This was not the time to tell him he had just lost his best friend.

"Grant, stay here with Marlin and don't let him stand up."

"Okay, Dad."

I scoot back across the road toward Marilyn. She had come to, shuttered and went back out. Darla thought she lost her and kept praying. She regained consciousness but was not quite coherent.

I notice an Amish woman on the porch where the little boy had been standing. She has a cell phone in her hand and I hear her giving directions. I catch a few words, "A truck hit a horse and cart … several people on the road … hurt arm and legs …"

Okay, she has called 911 and EMTs are on the way.

I continue to Marilyn and check for any flowing blood but cannot find any. Darla sees another Amish woman and motions her over.

"Please talk to Marilyn in Pennsylvania Dutch to calm her." Darla knew Amish children would be better comforted in their primary language. "These are Ruth Miller's children—"

"Yes, I know. She lives down the road," she interrupted.

"Could someone contact her and let her know what happened?"

"We already have."

Where are the EMTs? I leave Darla and Chanel with Marilyn and move back to Marlin.

The truck driver emerges from his cab. He is a young Mennonite man and is visibly shaken. He stands in the grass unable to move. Darla leaves Marilyn and goes to him.

She hugs him, "This is not your fault. There was nothing you could do. Everyone is going to be alright." She returns to Marilyn.

I hear distant sirens just as Ruth comes up the road on her bicycle. She barely gets there when the first EMT pulls up in his private vehicle. He pauses to survey the scene. It is surreal. He looks puzzled. He comes toward me and I direct his attention to the twins.

"They need immediate attention." He moves off to Marilyn first. "You're next, Marlin. It'll be okay."

Marlin reaches into his trouser pocket searching for something. He finds it and pulls his hand out clutching his treasure … a brown badge that simply reads "Hope and Courage Across America: Seek · Find · Live."

The sight of the badge takes my mind home to the spring. The start of our journey seems so far away right now.

Chapter 2

March, 2008

A call from city hall. I answered the phone to find Paul Nelson on the other end. Paul is the court administrator at city hall in Gig Harbor. I had met him through my volunteering at the Victim's Impact Panel. His court was responsible for sending people convicted of drinking and driving to the panel.

"How are you, Paul?"

"I am doing fine. I have been hearing about a big project you are working on for this summer. Can you tell me about it?"

I told him about Hope and Courage Across America.

"I plan to lead my family across America on bicycles sharing a message of hope and courage. I will pedal my handcycle with my one arm while my family rides regular bikes."

He seemed truly interested, "Do you have a start date?"

I said, "May 17, 2008."

"Do you know where you will start?"

"I have a few ideas but nothing for sure."

"Bob, would you consider starting your ride from city hall here in Gig Harbor? If you do, the city would like to throw you a send-off party."

This was an answer to prayer ... I think. We had been wondering where to start the ride and what kind of ceremony we would have as we left town. We had considered our church parking lot. Pastor Andy Snodgrass would be excited to do that. We had considered some public areas closer to the route we planned. But nothing seemed quite right. Even this offer from city hall had a big red flag. You see, as an evangelical believer and follower of Jesus I have always been aware of the diversity of venues in which I present my message. I know that there are places that are not appropriate for me, as the speaker, to expound on my faith. Public schools, for example, are a place I do many programs. It is not appropriate for me to elaborate upon my personal faith in Christ in public schools. It is not illegal, it is just not practical. I need to respect other people's beliefs, especially when they are different from mine. I know not everyone agrees with my position and policy on this matter. I respect that, too.

Now, city hall would come under the same category as public schools for me. The problem is that Hope and Courage was all about having hope in Christ. Our hope is in Christ and the courage is in us to do something with that hope. That was the point of the ride, and the send-off was not going to hide that hope.

"Paul," I said, "you know I have a 'faith-based' message, don't you?"

"Bob, you've been in our community for the last fifteen years. (True.) You talk to everybody you meet. (Also, true.) We are very aware of what your message is. However, you have other messages, too. You have been speaking in our schools to encourage our youth to be their best. You have been speaking to our Victim Panels to encourage our adults to not drink and drive. For fifteen years you have been helping our community to be better. Because you do these things for us, it gives us the freedom to honor you with a send-off party. Oh, by the way, when you roll up to the microphone that day we can't legally restrict what you say."

I had to let his words sink in. First, I hadn't realized anyone noticed what I was doing in schools or panels. I wasn't doing it to get noticed. For the city to notice me and honor us by hosting our send-off was humbling. We didn't expect it or deserve it. Paul's last words had the greater impact on me, though, "... when you roll up to the microphone that day we can't legally restrict what you say." It was nice to see respect goes both ways. Yes, there are times that are not appropriate for me to expound on my faith. The start of Hope and Courage Across America was not one of them.

"Paul, we would be proud to start our ride from city hall in Gig Harbor."

Not only did we have a starting point but the send-off party was being handled by the city. God was answering prayers we had not even uttered yet.

May 17, 2008

The send-off activities were set up on the lawn outside the courthouse. There was a stage area for us to address the crowd and the band to play. Andy Johnson, the music director at Fox Island Alliance Church, put together a great set of musicians to play at the event. The local Kiwanis Club had a booth preparing pancakes, eggs and sausage. They donated the breakfast, supplies and labor to Hope and Courage. As a tribute to our bike ride, they made all the pancakes the shape of bike wheels ... round. There were tables and chairs set on the lawn. Our RV and truck were parked prominently in the parking lot. Hope and Courage Across America: Seek · Find · Live emblazoned on the side.

Our best friends, Todd and Media Culver, had come up from Oregon. We have known them since we met at a church in Cottage Grove, Oregon, twenty years ago. We had all started raising our families then. They are always ready to help us in any way they can. Todd has traveled with me to Germany and Romania several times. Media has been just as close to Darla. They were going to drive the RV for us this weekend.

We had sent invitations out to everyone we could think of on our mailing list. The city sent invitations out to their contacts. The newspapers had written articles. The Seattle NBC affiliate had filmed a feature on the ride. Radio stations had interviewed me on the air. We were getting a lot of attention and people wanted to come see us off on this epic journey. The crowd consisted of people from our church, our community, and places I had spoken. Family and longtime friends mingled with people we had never met. There were bicyclists to ride with us out of town. And bikers from the Christian Motorcycle Association roared in and wanted to roar out with us. The mayor was there along with the city judge, the chief of police and a state Supreme Court judge. We did not expect or deserve this amount of attention.

As the morning progressed, the dignitaries would go to the microphone and say wonderful things about our ride and us. We smiled politely hoping we were half as nice as they said we were. Then each of us took our turn at the microphone to say thank you to all who had helped make this dream a reality. I started by giving a brief history of the ride and a full explanation of the purpose of the ride. We were heading across America to bring a message of hope and courage to our nation. We were aware of the struggles many Americans were facing. Unemployment, natural disasters, illness, uncertainty of the future and personal struggles we could never know. We wanted to let them know there is hope in Christ and courage within themselves to use His hope to face whatever mountain is in front of them. It is a simple message: Hope and Courage.

Darla, Grant and Chanel all took the microphone to say thank you. Their talks were brief and to the point. They do not desire to give lengthy talks to large crowds. Nicole read the first of her blogs to the crowd to give them a taste of what they could expect throughout the summer. Finally, we asked Andy Snodgrass, our pastor, to pray a blessing on our ride.

We hugged our good-byes, mounted our bikes, and pedaled away from city hall. A bicycle police escort led the way, we followed, and after us came a large group of cyclists and then motorcycles. The Hope and Courage truck and RV pulled out last. We were on our way.

Pastor Andy Snodgrass sending Hope and Courage off with a prayer.

Chapter 3

The five of us stuck together as we entered the Cushman Trail and headed for Highway 16. We soon became surrounded by the other cyclists as they all wished us well. Before long we found ourselves riding with friends. Chanel rode with Rachel Polley while Grant rode with Dustin Polley. Nicole had some college age friends she grouped with and Darla and I visited with everyone. We were surprised by all the people who had started with us on our journey. Darla's brother Daryl and his sons were right along beside us. We had given them a special invitation to ride with us the whole day. The rest of the riders were encouraged to turn back after the first ten miles. Getting us started was going to be tricky enough. I didn't want to be distracted by everyone else.

I tried to concentrate on my riding. My bike was new and I hadn't put many miles on it yet. The gearing felt different. I couldn't explain how it was different; it just felt harder. Maybe it was because we didn't get out riding much in the last few months. Getting this journey started took a lot of time and energy. But here we were on our way. It was fitting that the first few miles of Hope and Courage Across America were on Cushman Trail. Cushman Trail was where the idea of HCAA was born.

Six years earlier Gig Harbor had just opened up the Cushman Trail. The paved pedestrian and bike trail provided a place for Darla and me to take a walk. Okay, Darla walked and I rolled. The trail was a great addition to our community. We would park the van at the trailhead, unload the wheelchair and enjoy the fresh smooth pavement. It was fun to go one and a half miles out, turn around and go back to the van without crossing traffic. The biggest challenge for me, aside from the three miles distance, was the rolling hills of the trail. They were only fun half the time. A wheelchair powered with one arm is not really ideal for travelling up hills. Darla would soon get ahead of me and even though we started together we didn't continue together. But it was good exercise and we appreciated being outdoors. We would go out a few times each week. I must confess though, my plan was not to continue this effort in my wheelchair. I knew there was a better vehicle for me to use. I wanted a handcycle.

A handcycle is a specialized bike designed for people who can't use their legs but have two arms. You pedal it with your arms. It is technically not a bicycle because it has three wheels. Please don't call it a tricycle. I'm a little sensitive about that. Now, I figured if a man with two arms could pedal a handcycle, I could pedal one half as well. That's simple math. That is also the story problem you will never see on a math test: "If a man with no legs and two arms can pedal a handcycle at twenty miles per hour, how fast can a man with no legs and one arm pedal the same handcycle?" You will never see that on a test. But just in case you're wondering, the answer is ten miles per hour. A man with one arm can pedal half as fast as a man with two arms.

My first encounter with handcycles was back in the early 80s. Darla and I were newly married and living in Cottage Grove, Oregon. Cottage Grove is a small town a short drive from Eugene. We lived in the beautiful Willamette Valley for the first ten years of our marriage. Eugene is a hub of innovation in human powered vehicles, or HPVs as they are called. As a community Eugene was 'green' back when the rest of us thought it was just a color. Some of the most unique bikes in the world were developed there. Commuter, tandem, recumbent, recumbent-tandem ... they were trying everything. The one that caught my eye was a three-wheeled recumbent commuter designed to be powered with both legs and both arms. It was meant as an alternative to driving a car to work. Powered by four limbs made it a quick HPV on the road. I wasn't interested in the combined power of four appendages. I wasn't deeply moved by the positive impact it would have on the environment. All I noticed was that I could pedal it with one arm. I am constantly looking for efficient and effective ways to stay mobile. Man, I wished I had one of those bikes.

And thus began a progression of thought that is common to many of us. It is a multi-stage process that takes us from desire to acquire. It begins with 'I wish.' Wishing is fine. Wishing is optimistic. But wishing doesn't get results. I needed to distinguish this bike from all my other wishes and move it to the next stage: 'I want.' There, I said it. I want this bike. But wanting is just wishing out loud. To really move forward I have to turn 'I want' into 'I need.' And 'I need' requires more than just a voice. 'I need' requires justification.

It wasn't enough for me to justify it in my mind. That would be easy. But I am a married man ... bound by heart and oath to Darla. I had to justify my need in her mind. I figured three strong reasons were better than ten weak ones.

1. I needed the exercise. This was true. We had been married over a year and Darla's cooking had a predictable effect on me. I gained weight. And with a body like mine it doesn't take much weight to be too much weight.

Pedaling would be a great combination of
aerobic and strength building activity.
2. We could ride together. Darla could get a bike and
ride along with me. It would replace those romantic
strolls along the beach that we could not do. Actually,
we had tried the romantic strolls along the beach but
if we stopped, my tires sank in the sand. It was hardly
the romantic, starry-eyed moment we sought.
3. I could travel faster than I could in my wheelchair and
feel the wind rushing past my face. The freedom and
exhilaration would lift me above the clouds. (Okay, this
was a little weak but I was playing on her emotions now.)

Either way, I justified my need to Darla and bought the bike.
It had seven gears, two wheels in the front, one in the back, foot
pedals, hand cranks, an elaborate chain path, and a seat belt.
Darla insisted on the seat belt. It was a heavy bike and very tricky
to transport. Fortunately, we lived in the country and could ride
from our house along the farm roads of Lane County. All three of
my reasons proved to be valid. I did get exercise in a way I never
had before. Darla bought a ten-speed road bike and we toured
along romantically side by side. And the wind rushing past my
face was exhilarating. After a while, we got busy and I rode less.
Eventually the bike sat in the back of the garage for years unused.
When we moved from Cottage Grove to Gig Harbor in 1992, I
left the bike in Oregon.

This brings me back to the Cushman Trail in Gig Harbor. I
wanted another handcycle but I had to show Darla I was serious about getting out and exercising. Rolling up and down these
hills week after week in my wheelchair took dedication and de-
termination. It wasn't only a ploy for a new toy, either. I really
enjoyed the exercise. I enjoyed the challenge. My wheelchair was
designed with both hand rims on the right side. One is attached

directly to the right wheel and the other is slightly smaller in diameter and attached to the left wheel through an axle. I can grip both rims with my right hand and maneuver the chair. This design has allowed me to use a manual chair instead of a battery-powered chair. I am grateful for this chair but it has its limits. A one-arm drive wheelchair was definitely not the right tool to take this activity to the next level.

It really was not difficult for Darla to see the value of a hand-cycle for me. She really wants me to be active and healthy. When I mentioned getting another handcycle she was all for it. Great.

I started my research. I was pleased to discover handcycles had come a long way in twenty years. There were several companies making cycles that were specifically for people that couldn't pedal with legs. There were handcycle associations and sports competitions all over the world. I studied the different designs to see which could be adapted for one arm use instead of two. I looked at the position of the brakes and the shifters. I tried to imagine getting on and off the bike. I settled on the cycles from Invacare. The cycles were high tech, lightweight, adaptable ... but expensive. It was the 'expensive' part that slowed me down. The cost could easily reach $2,000. Was I really serious about using this thing? Would it collect dust in my garage as a reminder of yet another 'I need' impulse? I need ... I need ... I need ... What I needed was to talk to God about this. I have learned over the years to do my best and let God do the rest. I asked God to guide me and went on with my business.

Part of my business, Bob Mortimer Motivational Ministries, is speaking in churches as an evangelist. In 2002, I traveled to Grace Community Church in Tualatin, Oregon, to present a Fathers' Day message. After the service I was lingering at the front of the church to pray with people and visit. In my conversation with one man I mentioned I was looking at handcycles. He said his friend was a representative for a handcycle manufacturer and had a demo he was interested in selling cheap.

"No kidding? What company does he represent?"

"Invacare," he replied.

Invacare? How interesting. The exact bike I was praying about made available at a reduced price in a church through a man I was praying with at the end of a service. Some people would say that was a coincidence. A grateful person would say, "Thank you, God."

I said, "Thank you, God."

By the end of July, I was able to buy the bike reasonably cheap. It was in great mechanical shape with a few upgrades. It had 21 gears, 24-inch road tires, and a banana yellow finish. The shifters were integrated into the handbrakes. I mounted the left brake in a position I could reach with my right hand, added a seatbelt (Darla's idea), bought a rack at Costco for the back of my van and I was ready to ride.

The first few times out were difficult. The Cushman Trail was my training ground. I had never had a bike with so many gears. I was convinced I was in the wrong gear whenever I went up the hills. And to this day I would like to think that was true. I kept track of miles pedaled and average speed. I was getting stronger every day. Before long I was able to keep pace with Darla as she walked the three mile trail. It had been a long time since I was able to move myself that far and that fast. By the time the winter rains forced us to quit, I had clocked more than 300 miles for 2002.

In the spring I got back on my bike. I had to reacquaint my muscles to the pedaling. It was slow to start but I knew it would get easier. It wasn't long before I could pedal faster than Darla could walk. Darla remembered her old ten-speed bike from when we were in Oregon. It was hanging on a hook from the ceiling in the garage. She got it down, we cleaned it up, and she began to ride with me. It was like old times ... only better. Since our cycling time in Oregon, our lives had changed. We were not alone anymore. We had three children now. Nicole was fifteen, Grant eleven, and Chanel five. We homeschooled the kids so they could travel with us. As many couples discover, raising a family does cut into the time you have with each other. Cycling together was great. We were riding side by side, getting exercise and having 'us' time. It wasn't long before our typical ride would be fifteen miles. Usually we would do multiple laps on the Cushman Trail but also explored other trails in the area. . Our favorite was a trail in Orting that was seven miles of pavement in one direction. We could ride fourteen miles in one lap. We rode through the summer.

I had even gotten to the point that I could load/unload my bike and ride alone when necessary. I did not prefer to ride alone but it did give me time to think, unwind and pray. Some time alone is good. It would take me a few miles to clear the noise out of my head and then I would enjoy the quiet thoughts. This was the perfect time to dialog with God. I know it makes us uncomfortable sometimes when people mention talking to God. And it can make us real uncomfortable when they say God talks to them. But the truth is I can easily and naturally dialog with God. And so can you.

Praying is a part of that. I can pray aloud with my voice, which I try not to do in public places. Believe me, I attract enough attention in public places without talking out loud to someone nobody sees. I can pray quietly with my thoughts, which is appropriate for all places. But praying is often a monologue. To have a dialog with God I need to let Him speak, also. I started this dialogue when I was a boy attending a small Mennonite church in North Lima, Ohio. I guess that is when I became a 'believer in Christ,' but actually, I cannot remember a time when I did not believe God was there. Even during those times in my life when I was far from being a 'follower of Christ,' I had no doubt that God existed and was willing to have a conversation with me. I must admit, though, I have never heard God speak in an audible voice. Others have, but not me. I usually hear God as a quiet 'voice' in my consciousness ... a voice that is in my thoughts but not my thoughts. And I hear God best when I am quiet inside. Several miles into a ride I become quiet enough inside to listen.

Spring bloomed into summer and summer faded into fall. I was out enjoying a solo ride on the Cushman Trail. I love the fall. It has been my favorite time of year all of my life. Growing up in Ohio it was the time of ripe gardens, county fairs, warm days and cool nights. The sun casts its rays from a slightly tilted angle that pick up golden hues as it filters through the atmosphere. Autumn colors replace the abundant green of summer. Okay, before I get too poetic here let me just say that I like the fall. And I was starting to take fall personally. I had just turned forty-nine. The next birthday would be fifty. Fifty has to be the end of summer and the beginning of fall in a person's life. It did not bother me to hit the big five-o. I had come to appreciate every decade of my life. And if life were measured by seasons I would expect to love the autumn of my life. I was pedaling quietly along contemplating the change of seasons when an idea interrupted my solitude. A really big idea.

God, is that You? ...or is it me?

I should probably give you a little background info here. Darla and I had been married for twenty-three years. I met her four years after I lost my limbs and we married in 1981. Later in the book, I will elaborate on both of those events. (How's that for creating a little suspense?) There is no doubt in either of our minds that we are meant for each other. I do not know if we would have matched up on eHarmony or any other cyber matchmaking site. On paper, we did not look compatible. But in real life, we fit like a hand in a glove. We had grown and matured in life and marriage together. The key word here is 'together.' We had learned our individual character strengths and flaws. I must confess though, Darla had to learn more flaws than I did. She knew I could be overly optimistic, impulsive and have a difficult time identifying the impossible. Apart, these traits are not a problem. Combined, they can be rather interesting. Knowing this about us will help you understand the next series of events.

I arrived home from my autumn ride and parked in the garage. I got my wheelchair out of the van, jumped into my chair and rolled into the house. Darla, setting the table for dinner, sensed right away that something was up.

"Hon, I got this really big idea!" She sets the last plate and turns to hear what it could possibly be ... this time.

"I was riding my bike and it came to me. I think it was God, or maybe it was me. I don't know but it's a really big idea. Listen to this. We get on our bikes... No, wait! It is even bigger than that. We get the kids on their bikes, too. Us and the kids, the whole family, we get on our bikes and we ... ride them across America!"

Now, those of you women who are married can appreciate Darla's position here. I am sure that your husband has come home with a few 'big ideas' of his own. How you handle it is your business. Now, as I said, Darla has come to know me over the years and has learned how to manage my 'big ideas.' She doesn't throw the whole bucket of cold water on them at one time.

She looked at me calmly and said, "Hmmm, going across America ... on bicycles ... with the children? That's interesting."

Then she did something that all you women do when we men come home with our 'big ideas.' (And I want you to know that it really irritates us when you do this thing.) Darla applied logic and reason to my big idea.

She said, "Don't you think we ought to try riding across a state before we try riding across a nation?"

I could feel the air slowly escaping from my big idea.

"Yeah, I guess we could try riding across our state first. That's logical. That's reasonable."

Man, she really bugs me when she does that.

Chapter 4

September 2004 we took a nine-day, 330 mile ride from Puget Sound to the Idaho border. We tested the concept we were considering for the longer trip across America. We rented a Class C motor home as a support vehicle and bike transport. Our cousin, Glynn Lamberson, drove the RV and watched the kids while Darla and I pedaled. Nicole was sixteen and dealing with a flare up from her ulcerative colitis and spent most of the journey in the back of the RV sleeping. Grant was twelve and Chanel was six. We brought their bikes but they didn't ride. We were joined by two friends on the ride. John Diezsi, a retired teacher from Redding, California, we met through our work in schools, joined us for a few days in the beginning. Doug Taylor joined us later. Doug was a new friend we met on the Cushman Trail. Doug is a quadriplegic with very high mobility. He rides a handcycle and I invited him to ride along with us.

Our first day had us pedaling up I-90 in the foothills towards Snoqualmie Pass. We were getting used to the bikes and the traffic. This was the first time Darla had ridden a bicycle on a road since Cottage Grove. We had always stayed on trails before. And this wasn't just normal town traffic. This was a freeway with cars and semi-trucks sailing by at seventy miles per hour. I watched how she would react. I wasn't sure about Darla's commitment to riding. She was torn between staying in the RV with the kids and riding out here with me. It's a mom thing. I knew the kids were in good hands but Darla knew they were not her hands.

We were moving along fine and then we heard a 'pop' and a 'hiss.' Darla got a flat. The trouble with freeway cycling is the large amount of debris along the shoulder. Motorized vehicles seem to shed all kinds of metal and glass that can puncture a bike tube. No problem. We planned for this. We pulled to the side and John, the school teacher, began his lessons on how to change a flat. I paid close attention. A few miles further and 'pop' and 'hiss.' Darla got another flat. I got another lesson. We got back on the road. 'Pop.' 'Hiss.'

"Darla! Are you trying to get flats?"

I checked our bags for tubes. We were out. I didn't think we would need three of them in the first few hours. We called the support vehicle up. It was fifteen more miles to Denny Creek Road, our goal for the day. I figured Darla would get in the RV and call it quits. John and I would finish today's ride. We can get tubes tomorrow and she can ride with us from there. When the support vehicle arrived we put Darla's bike on the rack.

What happened next will always stick in my mind. Darla pointed to Nicole's bike on the rack and said, "Get that one down. I'll ride it."

Nicole's bike was not a real bike. It was a department store bike with a big frame and big tires and a bad seat and cruddy gears. We brought it for the kids to ride in the parks.

"Hon, that's not a real bike. You can't ride it on this freeway," I protested.

"Yes I can. Get that one down. I'll ride it," she said stubbornly.

What happened to logic and reason?

Don't worry. I didn't say it out loud.

We put air in the tires, adjusted the seat, and watched as she started up the hill. I followed her all the way to the Denny Creek exit. It was a hard ride on that bike. When we pulled off the road and loaded the bikes for the evening I watched Darla climb in the RV and hug the kids. I was in awe. I never doubted her commitment to ride again.

The toughest part of the ride was Denny Creek Road to the crest of Snoqualmie Pass. Denny Creek Road is a six-mile side road suggested as the best way to the top. It was away from traffic and popular with other cyclists. John was still with us and Doug had not arrived yet. Glynn and the kids dropped us off at the base of the road. Darla, John, and I started down the road. There was no traffic and the trees and shrubs made the scenery beautiful. It reminded us of why we live in the Pacific Northwest. There was hardly any incline and we felt this could be an easy day. But feelings can fool you. We rode a mile, rounded a bend and came upon a crew of state workers. They were relaxing around their equipment enjoying their lunch break. It appeared they had been working on the wooden bridge that crossed Denny Creek. I wasn't sure the bridge was safe to ride so I rolled up to the foreman.

I gestured to the project and said, "Can we cross?"

He studied us for a few seconds. A man and a woman on a bike, not unusual, and someone with one arm and no legs on a ... something or other you pedal with your arm, very unusual.

"Yes, you can cross this bridge. But you can't come back. As soon as we finish our break we are tearing the deck off and it won't be usable for two days. There is no other road out of the area. If you cross this bridge you have to take this road all the way to the top of the pass."

He looked right at me and said, "One more thing. It's a hard road ahead."

If this was the first time we had ever faced this type of challenge we may have turned around. But we had all crossed these kinds of bridges before. Life is full of these bridges. Points of decision that can alter your life forever. You can't see the end result … the top of the mountain. All you know is that if you move forward, you can't come back to this spot and the road ahead is hard.

We slowly rolled onto the bridge and stopped. We looked at the creek tumbling underneath us. We tried to see the road ahead but it quickly disappeared around a bend. There were other options. We could pedal back to the interstate and take that route to the top. It may not be any easier than this road but our support team could reach us if we had problems. That would be safer … more sensible. I imagined the five miles climbing to the top. "A hard road ahead" echoed in my thoughts. I tried to shut them out. I concentrated on my surroundings. The sun was shining, the air was warm and birds were singing. The crew started putting their lunches away and their work gear on. Time was running out. We had to make a choice. I looked at Darla and John.

They deferred the decision to me. "It's your call, Bob. What do you want to do?"

Being the designated leader is no fun.

A hard road ahead. Okay, God, do not leave me now.

I handed our camera to the foreman, "Would you take a picture of us on this old bridge? We are going to be the last people to cross it."

The decision to take the first step is usually more difficult than the step itself.

We crossed the bridge and immediately felt relieved at the decision but we also felt very alone. Our support team was on the other side of the bridge and could not reach us if we had problems. The only thing to do was travel the road ahead. The climb started soon after we crossed the bridge and increased steadily. We all shifted our bikes to easier gears as the effort pulled on our muscles. John stood on his pedals to take advantage of his body weight to maintain momentum. He soon was out in the lead. John is a good rider. He had ridden across America before and we were taking advantage of his experience. He had already taught us a lot about highway riding and team safety. Darla found a good gear and plodded along. I shifted to my easiest gear and still slowed my pace. I leaned forward so I could use my left arm stump to assist as I pushed my cranks forward. I realized this was indeed a hard road. There were a long series of cutbacks ahead as the road climbed out of sight. I would set my eyes on the next turn and make it my goal.

The dense forest along with the Indian summer caused the air to be warm and humid. We all began to sweat as we moved ahead. Conversations came to a stop. An occasional "How ya doin'?" followed by a quick "Okay" was the extent of it. Another turn reached with another turn looming ahead. The top was nowhere in sight. I began to wonder if I had tackled a task that was too much for me.

Who was I trying to kid? What was I trying to prove?

It was hard enough for Darla and John to keep momentum up this mountain and they had two sets of leg muscles to do the work. I was quickly becoming aware of the single muscle group in my arm that was carrying my load. It is times like this that I need motivation. I need to be distracted from myself. When you are the motivational speaker, you are used to inspiring others to dig deep and overcome. But who motivates the motivator? The encouragement from Darla and John was well meaning and truly came from their hearts. Somehow it just made me more aware of how much I could not keep up with their pace. I would give them a nod and keep pedaling. My pace had slowed to a crawl.

When I decided to cross that bridge, I did not factor in the one detail that was on my mind right now. I could not get off and walk my bike. I was going to have to climb this mountain on these three wheels and these three wheels were only going forward by me pedaling or John and Darla pushing. The thought of being pushed by someone made me dig in deeper and make the next bend. However, shame is a weak motivator and was not getting me to the top.

God, I need some help here. Now, I was not using His name in vain. *Seriously, God, I need help.*

I wonder what God thought as He heard my gasping prayer. His response was not altogether comforting.

You have help. Darla and John are right there and willing to push you up the mountain. But, nooo, you have too much pride. You are going to do it on your own no matter how long they have to wait or how much it hurts. What do you expect Me to do? Send down some unseen angel to whisk you up the hill so you can take all the credit for yourself? I don't think so. Besides, you crossed the bridge. I sent the foreman to warn you, remember? 'If you cross this bridge you have to take this road all the way to the top of the pass. And it's a hard road ahead.' It was your choice. You even took a picture. (I hate it when He does this.) *However, you did ask Me to not leave you so I won't leave you. I will even help you. I promise. I give you My Word.*

Thank you, Lord. I really appreciate the soon-to-be-arriving help.

Our dialog distracted me enough to make it halfway to the next bend and I leaned into my pedals awaiting help from above.

Would it be a strong wind from behind, a leveling of the road or the crest of the pass appearing around the next bend?

No wind came … the road steepened … and as I rounded the next bend, my heart sank. The crest was nowhere near.

C'mon God, what are you trying to prove? That I am weak and You are strong? I know that. But You said You would help. So, where's my help? You promised. You gave me Your Word.

God whispered, *Exactly, I gave you My Word.*

And where is this help? You gave me Your Word.

Then came that awkward pause that happens between two friends when one says something obvious but is too worked up to know what they said.

Now say it again, only say ... it ... slower.

Okay ... You ... promised. You ... gave ... me ... Your ... Word.

Again. Just the last part, He nudged.

You ... gave ... me ... Your ... Word.

Again.

Alright, but this is getting tedious. You ... gave ... me ... Your ... Word. Ohhh! You gave me Your <u>Word</u>. I get it. Duh. The help is in Your Word. The help is in the Bible!

Bravo! There is hope for you after all.

I don't have a Bible with me. What kind of trick is this? Hold on, I am not falling for this again. He made me look ridiculous last time. I am thinking with my whole brain this time. If I do not have a Bible, I have to find His Word somewhere else. It is doubtful someone put Scripture graffiti on a tree around here but I will look anyway. Nope. No writing on the trees, rocks, or road. How about something I have memorized. The Bible refers to Scripture memorization as writing His Word on the tablets of our hearts.

Yeah. I figured that one out, God. Now, which Scripture? I haven't memorized most of the Bible so that narrows it down some. What topic? Salvation, righteous living, grace ... give me a clue, God. No. No. Forget that last plea. I bet You already gave me a clue. What was the last thing You said? "There is hope for you after all." Bingo! Hope. That's it.

I needed a scripture about hope and I knew exactly which one to use. Isaiah 40:31 "…those who hope in the Lord will renew their strength. They will rise up on wings as eagles. They will run and not grow weary. They will walk and not grow faint." Perfect. Let me run through it again. "Those who hope in the Lord will renew their strength. They will rise up on wings as eagles. They will run and not grow weary. They will walk and not grow faint." And again.

I started to notice the trees around me. I was in one of the most beautiful parts of Washington. The sun was shining and throwing bright patches of light on the roadway. I would aim my front wheel for the next patch. I noticed birds singing. Lots of birds singing. I am sure they had been singing all along, I just hadn't noticed them since we started to climb. I repeated the verse again as I enjoyed the world around me. I made a few more cuts around the bends.

Finally, up ahead I saw John waving, "The top is around the next bend!"

With a fresh energy I pushed the cranks harder as I joined Darla and John and the three of us crested the mountain. We did it. All three of us had crossed the bridge and conquered the hard road ahead.

Chapter 5

May 17, 2008

Let us get back to Hope and Courage Across America. We left the Cushman Trail. Up ahead was the Narrows Bridge, a two-mile expanse across Puget Sound that connects Gig Harbor and Tacoma. The view was beautiful. There are actually two bridges, one for each direction. We were riding on the new eastbound bridge that was opened a year earlier. It has a much improved pedestrian/bike lane. We had meant to give it a trial ride before our start but never got around to it. We entered on the west end and began the uphill climb to the mid-span.

I started to notice the heat. May is typically not a hot month in western Washington. This year had been colder than normal. We were prepared for a chilly day. However, Darla prayed for sunny weather for our send off. God sure heard her prayer! The sky was clear and the sun brought the temperatures into the high 80s. It was the hottest May 17 ever recorded in Gig Harbor. Darla loves hot sunny days. I do not. I much prefer the usual mild overcast weather of the Pacific Northwest. The heat was wearing me down. I thought of stopping but all these people were following us. Or, more accurately, following Darla and the kids.

I was slowing down. I set my sights on the mid-span and knew I would get a downhill run when I reached there.

On the highway portion of the bridge the police had a patrol car guiding our RV, the motorcycles, and the film crew. They traveled at a slow pace with the bicyclists. We wanted to stop and soak in the moment but knew we needed to keep going and get across the bridge. The Narrows Bridge was symbolic of the start. It physically separated us from home and connected us to the wide expanse of America ahead. Behind us were our home, our families, our friends, our church, and our community. As I looked around I saw pieces of all those things riding with us. Hope and Courage Across America wasn't just ours, it was theirs also. They were truly sending us on this journey.

Crossing the mid-span gave me a break as the slope went downhill for awhile. I became more aware of the heat.

Why is it so hot today? I am not prepared for this.

I absorbed the wind as it blew into my face and body. I got to the bottom of the downhill and looked at the steep hill climbing up to the first crossroad. I had never noticed how steep this hill was before. Of course, I had always been driving a van, not pedaling a handcycle.

We really should have taken a practice run across here.

I started to shift to my easier gears. My handcycle was new and I had only put about fifty miles on it before today. It seemed heavier or stiffer than my original handcycle. All I knew was that it was harder to pedal than my old one. I kept shifting but it kept slipping out of the easiest gear. No time to think about that now. The riders following me soon moved on ahead. We were going to rendezvous at the park on the east end of the bridge. There were a few that stayed back for a while before my pace became too slow for them to maneuver their two wheeled bikes. I shook off my feeling of embarrassment. I had to get up this hill. My arm muscles began to weaken.

Oh, no! I had let myself get dehydrated. *C'mon, Bob, you know better. You are the one that pushes the water on everybody when we are riding in the heat.* I just did not expect this heat. I really should have made time to pedal more but there was so much other stuff to do to get ready to go. *Stop making excuses, Bob. The bottom line is that you didn't prepare physically and you didn't hydrate. Now you are paying the price and there is no one to blame but yourself. So dig in and push yourself up this hill.*

Darla and the kids rode off the bridge and into the park with the other cyclists. I brought up the rear. Finally, I rolled into the park. The cyclists were there, the Christian Motorcycle Association bikers were there, the support vehicles were there. I saw shade under the pavilion and rolled out of the sun. I looked drained and felt lethargic. I knew I needed water and rest. I quickly downed 16 ounces of water and opened another. I made feeble apologies for my performance and joked about my chances of making it to New York. I was in no hurry to leave the shade until I had recovered. Darla and the kids were visiting with everyone and excited to be on their way.

There was a bride and groom in the park getting pictures. They were drawn to our activity and asked what this was all about. Someone explained about Hope and Courage and our plan to ride across America. The bride asked if she could get her picture with some of the team. We gathered around her for the photo. We could see the eastern suspension towers of the Narrows Bridge. This wasn't the side that disconnected us from home. This was the side that connected us to the journey ahead. The unknown, the unexpected, and the unpredictable were all before us. And already we were attracting attention. That was the purpose of the ride. Attract attention to explain the message.

Our first stop gave us our first opportunity. We wished the bride well in her marriage and encouraged her to have a life full of hope and courage.

We bid farewell to our friends who crossed the bridge with us. They were going back to fulfill their own journeys for the summer. We were so appreciative of all they were doing to send us on our journey. Darla's brother Daryl and his boys rode the rest of the day with us. We wound our way through Tacoma and into Puyallup. The city riding was much different from the trails we had trained on. Darla was very aware of the safety of the children. Especially Chanel, she was our youngest and had the least experience on a bike and on the roads. We decided to limit her riding to the trails until she got more experience. It was good having Daryl's family with us. They helped us transition from the crowds of the send-off to being alone.

We pulled into the Fred Meyer parking lot in Puyallup for a break. Jeanne and her husband, Don, were waiting for us there with ice cream bars. They were our support team. Jeanne had taken a leave from her job at McCutcheon's Photography Studio to travel with us the whole summer. Jeanne was a perfect combination of encourager, nurturer and promoter. Don was starting out with us to help Jeanne get acclimated to the truck, RV and support role. The ice cream hit the spot and helped us recover from the heat. We discussed the route for the rest of the day. We would pedal through Sumner and hook up with the Interurban Trail on the other side.

Sumner was Darla's hometown growing up. Her family moved there in the early 70s while she was in elementary school. Darla is the youngest of seven children and all but three of her siblings had married and moved out of the house while they still lived in Petaluma, California. Darla would graduate from Sumner High School in 1978. She was Homecoming Queen that year. Quite an achievement for a shy girl who did not think anybody noticed her. The truth is Darla has a beauty that radiates from the inside out. You cannot help but notice her. She smiled inwardly at the stroll down memory lane she was taking today. Who would have ever thought back at Sumner High that the gentle, quiet girl sitting at her desk would someday be heading off across America on a bicycle? Certainly not Darla. Life is full of surprises.

We reached the Interurban Trail. What a relief to be off the roads and on a familiar paved trail. We pedaled ten more miles to Kent and reached our goal of forty miles. We were scheduled to speak at Riverview Community Church in Kent the next morning. Riverview's pastor is our nephew, Brett Hollis. The congregation has always been supportive of all our ministries. We were glad they were going to be our first stop.

We loaded our bikes into the vehicles and drove back to Gig Harbor. We parked the RV and truck in front of the house. We were so close to home it seemed right to go back and sleep in our own beds. Our heads hit the pillows. The events of the day swirled in our minds. Wow! We had started the journey. *Thank you, Lord.*

Crossing the Narrows Bridge May 17, 2008

Chapter 6

Darla thought it would be a good idea if we all kept a journal of our trip. I agreed that was a good idea. However, I did not give her much hope that everyone would do that. Nicole said she would write blogs for the website on a regular basis but was not keeping a journal. Grant uses even fewer words writing than he does talking. Chanel said she could add it to her other plans. Ten year olds are busier than you think. I let Darla know from the start that I would not be writing every day. I know myself well enough to accept the fact that I am undisciplined and would not follow through. I consider acceptance of my faults as a sign of maturity. I am not sure Darla looks at it the same way. Fortunately, Darla has strengths to cover my weaknesses. She would keep the journal. That is really best because Darla sees things from a different perspective than I do. You will get more details from her. I will include her journals as much as possible throughout the rest of this book.

DARLA'S JOURNAL ENTRY

May 18, 2008 – Sunday

It was an early start. Todd and Media Culver came over about 7:30 and we headed up to Brett's church for two services. Todd drove the fifth wheel. We wanted to have it in the church parking lot. The graphics on the vehicles were beautiful and a direct result of Tim Smith. Tim designed all of our graphics and oversaw their application from hats to RV. Tim and his family were members of Riverview Community Church. Bob did a great job ministering and at the close of each service, Brett had our family go up for prayer. Bob shared about how Tim Smith had been such a blessing for doing all of our graphics and for donating his time and talents to this project. Tim was very touched by what he said.

My sister Betty and her husband, Dave, their son Devin's family, my brother Frank & Char, Brett's family, my brother Daryl's family, and Bob's sister Jeanne & Don were the family members who were there. It was another great send-off. Today was a very emotional day saying goodbye to everyone. Through their tears, Betty told me she wanted me and my family to come back safely and Dave told me I was an amazing person for doing this. Those words meant a lot to me. There were lots of hugs and tears as we said goodbye. As I have mentioned before, this journey is not just about us pedaling, it is about all the people who have become a part of this trip by their prayers, encouragement, support, and love. We can't abandon this trip now because so many people are sending us. We are on a Mission.

At Brett's church, we saw one hand go up for salvation and several pray for courage. Little Gracie was one of

them who wanted prayer for courage.
Gracie is Devin's five-year-old daughter
who has ulcerative colitis just like
our daughter Nicole. In fact, Gracie's
middle name is Nicole in honor of our
daughter. She has been suffering from
a flare-up and had recently been in
the hospital for a week. She told Bob
at the altar she had raised her hand
for courage to face the mountains
ahead and so he prayed with her.

A man named Mike came up to Bob
after the service and said he liked what
Bob said about reading our Bibles and
memorizing Scripture. He wanted to
provide Bibles for us to hand out at
the churches. He wants everyone who
needs a Bible to have one. Nicole knew
of a Bible called "The Journey," and so
we chose to have that be the one to
hand out. Mike is going to send them
to the churches ahead of us so that
we can have them available when we
arrive in that community. He also said

he felt the Lord had told him to pay for
our gas all the way to NYC! Diesel gas
is around four dollars a gallon and our
Ford F-350 uses a lot of gas pulling
our 35-foot fifth wheel. He wanted
to donate enough money to cover the
gas and vehicle expenses and repairs.
What a HUGE blessing! God, we are
so humbled that You are providing for
us in this way. It is obvious You want
us to bring hope and courage across
America. We are just honored that You
have chosen us to be the messengers.
Thank You, Lord, is all I can say. What
a journey life is when following You!

Brett's church provided us with
sandwiches and then we were on our
way. Brett, Chuck, Jeff, Nick, Brian and
Jeff all road with us to Issaquah. It
was really great to have them with us
and they were such a help! Bob was
having problems with shifting and so they
helped push him up some of the tough
hills. Jeanne had ice cream sandwiches

waiting for us at the end of the ride!
It was a great day all around. Tough
hills, but uplifted spirits. It was
really special to have Brett with us.
He reminded me that other than Uncle
Daryl's boys, he was my only nephew
to ride with us on the bike trip. We
were talking of how we would have
never thought that we would be riding
our bikes together on a journey across
America. We both commented that
when following Jesus you never know
where He will lead. Chuck's wife told
me at the end of the ride that Chuck
(who is 62 years old) really wanted to
ride a part of this journey with us. He
did not want to miss this opportunity
and was going to do everything he
could do to make it happen. As we
went to say goodbye, Chuck told
me through tears that he would be
praying EVERY DAY for us. That was
music to my ears! Thank You, Lord,
for sending this saint to us. It was
truly a blessing to have that team join

us. Nick, who is from Holland, said
he wouldn't have missed this bike ride
for the world. He had hurried home
after church to grab his bike. I felt
really bad when he had a fall on the
ride, but he assured me he was fine.

Todd and Media had taken our fifth
wheel back home for us and had it
ready for us to load tomorrow.

Thank You, Lord.

Riverview Community Church
cycling and support team

May 19 - Monday

Today was set aside to get the fifth
wheel all packed and get on our way.
No riding planned. We finished packing,
cleaned the house and did all the last-
minute errands we could do before
pulling out. We had a couple of
neighbors check in to make sure that
we were okay. We stopped by to pick
Jeanne and Don up and then ... Hope and
Courage were on their way! A little
later departure than was planned but
it was the earliest we could get going.
Lots of extra things had come up, but
praise the Lord we finally left home.

We spent three nights at a
campground in Issaquah. They gave
us two nights free lodging. We had
to back in our spot and it was kind
of hard but Bob got it straight in the
end. It is a little tricky with needing
space on one side for the pullouts
and then space on the other side for

the wheelchair lift. It is a learning process. When we were getting set up, we found a surprise from Tom and Cindy in our kitchen sink. She had made us pumpkin bread and included a keychain with a prayer for safety. It was a perfect way to end a long day.

May 20 - Tuesday

Today we woke up to a drizzle. The RV had an electrical problem with the power supply. Bob tried to fix it but finally we had to call an RV repairman. While waiting for the repairman, Grant and I took Bob's bike down to a bike shop in Issaquah with the special part that Robby had picked up for us on Monday in Seattle. The bike guy told us the new part wouldn't work. To break up the day, I took Nicole, Grant, Chanel and Jeanne to Boehm's chocolate factory. We got to watch them dip chocolates and then one of the workers brought us samples. When we told them what we were doing they said, "Oh, take them all; you will need the extras for added energy!" Chanel and I saw a little bunny in the RV park and Bob met a guy who had walked across America and ministered along the way.

After we got the RV fixed and had something to eat we decided to start our ride from Issaquah. We had just gotten onto I-90 (which is definitely not my favorite place to ride) and I noticed a young guy walking toward us I thought maybe he had car trouble (even though I hadn't seen a car). When we got up to him he said he had heard about our ride on the radio and wanted to stop and encourage us. And encourage us he did! He was our first encounter with whom we refer to as our "angels along the highway." He said he would be praying for us and so Bob asked him if he would pray for us right now. So along the freeway we were huddled together praying. He

was such a nice kid. He had parked
his car and had walked about a half
mile. That spoke volumes to us. I
gave him a hug and thanked him for
being our angel. We wanted to give him
a Hope and Courage button but had
left them back at camp. We realized
that we needed to have our buttons
with us even on the freeway. Thank
You, Lord, for sending us our highway
angel. We never know, Lord, when You
may send an encourager our way.

Not long after that, Grant got a flat
tire. He felt really bad but it was surprising we didn't get lots more with all
the debris on the side of the highway.
Once we got it fixed, it was dark and
drizzling and so we called it a night.

*Not our first flat. Not our last flat.
Just another flat.*

Chapter 7

Whenever you set out on a huge project your biggest mountains come early. Whether you are making a life change, building a house, starting a marriage, or riding bicycles across America, you will face your toughest struggles in the beginning. We have a tendency to want to know who put this mountain here. Is it from the enemy of our souls? *Is this an attempt to throw us off our path and to keep us from success?* After all, we are weaker now than we will be later. We are untested and inexperienced. On the other hand, *is this mountain from God?* Maybe He is trying to condition us because He knows what is on the other side of that mountain. But honestly, when there is a mountain in front of us does it really matter how the mountain got there? We just know we are facing a mountain and we have to get over it.

May 21

Five days out we hit Snoqualmie Pass. Snoqualmie will prove to be the toughest pass we cross on our journey. Snoqualmie Pass is 3,022 feet above sea level. That may seem low compared to the passes in the Rockies, but you have to remember that the climb over Snoqualmie starts much closer to sea level than the Rocky passes. Our camp is at 108 feet. It was raining again, only this time it was a hard rain. The burning sun of the weekend vanished and it seemed like winter was trying to return. I was getting a little worried. You see – I had a schedule, I had a plan, and I was in charge. The RV repairs yesterday had already set me behind a day. It wasn't just the RV repairs. My handcycle had given me problems coming up the hills to Issaquah. My easiest gear didn't seem as easy as it did on my old bike. I had ordered the same gear rings but had increased my tire size from twenty-four inches up to twenty-six. I didn't do the math on that change. The bigger tires made my cranking harder. I had spent the last two days tracking down a smaller gear ring that would fit my bike. I really didn't want to pedal over the pass without the smaller ring. I finally had to order one from Invacare out of Florida. They sent it overnight and I found a shop to switch it out with my old one. All of this just added to the delay.

I got my bike out of the shop by noon but the rain didn't look good. It just didn't want to let up. It's not that we are against riding in the rain … after all, we are from Washington. But this wasn't just the usual drizzle. This was a hard, steady rain. Well, if I'm in charge I better take some leadership action.

"Get on your rain gear. We need to get over this mountain."

We bought the gear for days like this. We all had rain pants. Mine were cut short and hemmed shut at the legs to keep the rain from getting on my stumps. We had rain jackets with our logo on the back. We put the clear lenses on our eye protection and strapped on our helmets. We left Chanel back at camp with Aunt Jeanne and pedaled out to the interstate.

The good thing about riding bikes on the interstate is the twelve-foot shoulder on the side. The bad thing about riding bikes on the interstate is the traffic passing at seventy miles an hour. Oh, and a lot of that traffic is semi-trucks. And the problem with trucks is they have eighteen wheels and in the rain those eighteen wheels throw up a lot of water. And every time one would go past us it would spray us. Now, I admit, that is not their fault. The interstate was built for cars and trucks. I'm the idiot out here riding a bike with my family in the rain. We were getting drenched. Grant and Nicole pulled out ahead. Darla was concerned and I encouraged her to catch up and ride with them. I was not far behind. None of us was traveling very fast. My eye gear started to get muddy. I reached up with my hand to wipe them off and just ended up smearing the mud.

Maybe I can see better without them.

I took them off. Another truck passes by and when the water hits my face I remember why I wear eye protection. I put the glasses back on. More trucks passed by.

I can't believe how many trucks there are on this road today.

I squinted through the mess at Darla and the kids. Every time a truck passed I watched a wall of water hit my family and those two wheeled bikes would wobble. Thoughts of crossing the mountain are replaced by thoughts of my family's safety.

It is just a matter of time before someone gets hurt. I can't have my family out here. I'm supposed to be protecting them and I make them ride bikes on a freeway in a rainstorm. I give up.

I holler ahead, "Get off the freeway! Take the next exit!" I know we are not getting over this mountain today.

We pedaled off the freeway at the next exit. Just getting away from the trucks makes a difference. We pulled into a convenience store and found an overhang to park under. We are soaked but I am impressed how Darla, Grant, and Nicole are in good spirits. We call Jeanne and ask her to come pick us up in the truck. While waiting we start to peel off our rain gear.

We soon realize rain gear is designed to protect you from the water coming out of the sky. We had water hitting us from every direction. We were soaked to the skin. I had the ends of my pant legs sewn up to keep my stumps dry. I guess they were sewn pretty good. The water collected at the ends like a balloon. We all got a good laugh when I emptied a few quarts of water out of them. The others went inside to use the restrooms while I waited on my bike. People stared and pointed at us as they walked by. We looked like quite the team. Jeanne, Don, and Chanel arrived with the truck. We loaded the wet bikes in the back of the truck. We loaded the wet bodies in the front of the truck.

Driving back down the interstate we pulled into a restaurant to warm up and get a bite to eat. The waitress came to take our drink orders. Coffee, sodas, and water seem to be the usual order. The waitress is curious about our bright yellow jackets with "Hope and Courage" emblazoned on the back. Jeanne explains to her about our ride and the message.

But right now I don't feel the hope and courage. I am getting discouraged. I have a schedule, I have a plan, and I am in charge. My schedule has been delayed and my plan has been blocked by rainstorms. At least I am still in charge. But to be honest with you, that doesn't bring me much comfort. I look around our table to see the people that are depending on me to lead them. Jeanne and Don are sitting at the other end. What a great couple. Jeanne took a four-month leave from her job to help us on this journey. Her husband, Don, is a retired elementary school teacher. Having him with us is a great comfort to Jeanne as she acclimates herself to the rigors of living in an RV and providing support to the riders. Chanel sits between Jeanne and Darla. She feels real safe there. She does not ride with us all the time. Her goal is to ride when we think it is safest. Most of time she is with Jeanne back at the camp. When Darla gets off her bike, Chanel stays as close to her as possible. She sure loves her mommy. Across from Chanel is Grant. He doesn't say much and he doesn't get upset. We depend on him to do a lot of the tasks involved with the bikes and the RV. Darla and I knew from the start that we could not move forward with this journey if Grant was not for it. We need him. Next to Grant is Nicole. Nicole has just finished her junior year at Northwest University on her way to earn her bachelor of science in nursing. Not bad for a girl who has not yet had her twentieth birthday. On my left is Darla. What did I get her into with this crazy idea? What did I get us all into?

I keep up my brave façade. If they knew all of the doubts I am having right now they would all run back home.

I'm just trying to do something for the Kingdom. I am going to tell people about Jesus. I am doing this for You, God. Hope and Courage Across America. Yeah, right! I can't even get my family across the first mountain. Some leader I am.

Nicole interrupts my little pity party. She nudges me, points to the table on the other side of the restaurant, and calmly says, "Hey, Dad, that baby over there is choking."

She knew this before the mother knew it. The mother knew soon enough, though. The woman grabs her child and stands up shouting, "Something is wrong with my baby! Somebody do something! Help my baby!"

Nicole gets out of her seat, quickly moves across the café, takes the baby from the mother, turns the baby across her arm, and does something she learned in school called a 'pediatric Heimlich maneuver.' Food dislodges from the baby's throat and the child starts wailing. Nicole calmly hands the baby back to the mother. The mother is overcome with gratefulness. Nicole turns to return to our table and sees us staring with our mouths open. Ten minutes later, I look over at the baby and the child is happily eating apple sauce.

At that moment I realized something. I do not have a schedule, I do not have a plan, and I am definitely not in charge. God had to storm us off the side of a mountain. He sent semi-truck after semi-truck to soak us so we would get off the freeway. He stopped us in our tracks because He knew there was a baby who was going to need help at the base of the mountain and one of our riders was the one trained to give it.

What a relief. What a peace. I am not in charge. I do not have to worry about our schedule or route. That is all in God's hands. If this journey is for His Kingdom then it only makes sense to let Him be in total control.

Thank You, God. My hope is in You. Give me the courage to face the mountain ahead.

Snoqualmie Pass in the rain.

Chapter 8

We stayed off our bikes the next day. We needed to regroup. I decided we would break camp and move the RV over to Ellensburg on the other side of the mountain. We needed to get away from this rain. We could shuttle back in the truck to our start point. Driving into eastern Washington reminded us it was not raining everywhere. It was good for morale. I parked the truck and fifth wheel into the campsite. I was getting better at that. I would have to start training Jeanne how to do the driving soon. So far, I was the only one comfortable pulling that thirty-five foot trailer behind the truck. That evening we went into town to celebrate Jeanne's birthday. What a great sister. She cheerfully gave up her summer to come serve us on this journey. What a blessing.

May 23

It was the start of Memorial Day weekend. The temperature was in the fifties. The sky was cloudy. No rain. Now, if you intend to pedal anything over Snoqualmie Pass, fifty degrees, cloudy and no rain is a pretty good weather report.

I tell my family, "Get the bikes ready. Let's see if God is going to let us over this mountain today."

We loaded the truck and drove back to the place we stopped in the storm. We were twenty-two miles from the summit. The first fifteen miles are a slight, steady incline that lets you gain some altitude. The last seven miles get serious. Our plan was to take the Denny Creek Road exit and pedal the forest service road for that last seven. We had taken this road when we pedaled across Washington four years earlier. That road gained elevation through a long series of cutbacks to the summit. It was a little longer than the interstate but I figured the incline was less intense because of the cutbacks. I remembered from our 2004 ride that it was still going to be a challenge, though.

Darla, Nicole, Grant and I put on our riding gear. Chanel would stay with Aunt Jeanne and Uncle Don as the support team. This was definitely a day that we needed our support team nearby. We transported our bikes back to North Bend, the point we had stopped in the rainstorm. Memories of semi-trucks and sheets of water haunted us. However, this was a new day and there was a new hope. We checked our packs to make sure we had all our supplies. Water for hydration, energy bars and trail mix for nutrition, first aid kit for injuries, and spare tubes for all bikes. Everything seemed to be ready and if we needed anything, Jeanne, Don, and Chanel would only be minutes away in the truck. Enough getting ready. Time to get going.

We eased out of the gas station parking lot and pedaled onto the freeway access. The ramp inclined slightly toward the merging traffic. Get used to it. Today is all about inclines. Keeping to the broad shoulder we found our positions. I was in front, Nicole next, then Grant with Darla bringing up the tail. We liked this order for safety. It allows us to keep the kids between Darla and me. It is also the slowest formation we use because I am the pacesetter. But for now, slow was okay. We needed to get comfortable with this traffic. And there was a lot of traffic. It is the Friday before

Memorial Day and the freeway was already becoming crowded with people heading over the mountain for the weekend.

It was a relief to be out here and making progress. It took a few miles to get settled down. I watch my speedometer. I like having a speedometer. Watching the numbers and doing the math for upcoming stops has always been a fun distraction for me. I am averaging around six miles an hour climbing towards Denny Creek. The kids pedal past me. It is hard to hold them to my pace when they want to go faster. Darla follows the kids. Darla has a strong concern for their safety. She is especially worried on the freeway. It kills her to watch them go out of her sight. All kinds of possible dangers flood her mind. They could lose their balance on the bikes and fall into traffic. They could be hit by a drowsy driver in a truck or car. A hubcap could come off and strike them at seventy-five miles an hour. A bear, a mountain lion, a Sasquatch or who knows what could come running out of the trees and snatch them away. These are not my fears. I figure the kids are old enough to watch out for themselves. Besides, we couldn't stop most of those events from happening even if we were right next to them. I do not try to reason with Darla or understand. The bottom line is she is truly concerned for their safety.

She tries to find a place in the line that allows her to see the kids in front of her and hear me behind her. This only works until the kids get far enough ahead to be out of her sight. At the first stop, we discuss this with the kids and decide they will always wait at the next exit for us to catch up. This satisfies Nicole and Grant but really does not ease Darla's fears. I could tell that this internal struggle for Darla was going to be something she will deal with for the whole journey. Whether she stays back to help me or goes on ahead to protect the kids would be a question Darla would answer often.

The miles click away on my speedometer as morning slips into afternoon. The freeway is getting busier and busier. It really is not much fun anymore. The constant roar of traffic is the unwanted soundtrack to our day. The tranquility of NF-58 is going to be a relief. We stop at the last exit before Denny Creek and meet up with Jeanne, Don, and Chanel. We chat about the traffic and the noise. They encourage us about our progress and replenish our supplies. We have not used up much. We have not drank a lot of water because of the cool temperatures. It is in the high forties, low fifties. Quite a change from the eighty-degree weather we started in last weekend. We tell Jeanne to scout NF-58 and we will meet them at the turnoff.

The next few miles go rather quickly as we get to the Denny Creek exit. Nicole and Grant leave the freeway first, turn left onto the overpass and head toward the Hope and Courage truck pulled to the side of the road. Darla and I follow behind them, glad to be off the busy interstate. A short rest and then we can head up NF-58 and finally get over this mountain. We reach the truck and Darla dismounts her bike and removes her helmet. I come to a stop and set my parking brake. I stretch my fingers and straighten my arm. Chanel and Don come our way with a concerned look on their face.

"What's the problem?" I ask.

Chanel tells us, "The road up ahead is blocked with snow! We could only drive a short distance in the truck. Then it was totally blocked by snow!" Her voice is a mixture of concern and excitement.

Snow? I didn't factor snow into the equation. It is the end of May. There should not be snow. I wonder if the road is only blocked there and opens up further on. That doesn't make sense. We climb higher and the snow will increase, not decrease. I guess we have to go to Plan B ... pedal up the freeway to get over the pass. Even then, there are bound to be piles of plowed snow on the shoulder. Well, we have already learned not to question God's roadblocks and snow is definitely within God's toolbox. The freeway it will be then. The good news is it will be a mile shorter by freeway. We gear up and get ready to roll. There are no more turnoffs before the crest so we tell our support team we will see them at the top.

Back on to the freeway, I immediately can feel a greater incline than before. I start to shift my gears. My handcycle has the brake and shifter mounted to the hand crank I use to pedal the bike. I can do most things without taking my hand off the pedal. It is really quite convenient. Now, my bike has twenty-seven gears. The man who sold me my bike said I had something called an 'easy' gear. I never found his 'easy' gear. I shifted to my 'easiest' gear but it was not 'easy.' Even with the new gear ring I put on the other day, it was still an effort to move up the mountain. It is not long before I have lost all of my momentum. I have to exert force for every yard of progress. I watch my speedometer. No more six miles an hour. Now it is five miles, four miles, three miles ... two miles an hour. I begin to wonder how low this gadget will register.

The traffic has become heavier and slower. I feel as if I am cycling in city traffic. People honk and wave. All the local publicity before we left has made us celebrities. I shake off the feeling of embarrassment about my speed. I am going as fast as I can. My attention is on getting to the next mile marker. Not the green ones that count off the whole miles, I am talking about the obscure ones in between that register the tenths of a mile. I start to do the math. How many tenths to the top? I stop figuring. It is too many to think about right now.

Nicole and Grant have moved ahead. The mountain has slowed them down but not as much as me. They can pedal several miles an hour. They ride ahead and then wait. Ride ahead … wait. Darla could ride with the kids. In fact, Darla could ride ahead of the kids. But she doesn't. She stays back and rides with me.

This is a good time for me to step aside from my story and share a little marital advice with you. I know you did not pick this book up for marital counseling, so consider this a bonus. In marriage, there are going to be times you have to face mountains, things that loom ahead and cannot be avoided. I guarantee you that every time you reach a mountain, one of you is capable of getting over that mountain easier than the other. You do not have the same baggage, the same past experiences and scars. For whatever reason, you could ride on ahead and leave the other to struggle alone. Do not do that. Stay back and ride with your spouse. It will not do you any good to get to the top first. Besides, you may be able to help them get over it quicker if you stay next to them. Marriage is not a race … it is a journey. Darla knows this and she stays back and rides with me. She is stressed from the fear of the kids riding ahead, but she's not willing to leave me back. She pedals with me at two miles an hour on a two-wheeled bike. Two miles an hour. You know how when you are riding a bike slowly and you go so slow that it is a struggle to keep the bike upright? Well, that speed is around two miles an hour. And this is the speed Darla is pedaling up the side of Snoqualmie. For me.

In the meantime, I am wearing down. I start measuring progress in quarter mile increments. If I can make it a quarter mile I can stop and get a drink, let my heart rate get back to a safe range, and try to eat a snack. At every stop, I am gasping for oxygen and my heart feels as if it is going to burst. I turn my back to traffic. I do not want to see their faces and I do not want them to see mine. *Why does there have to be so many cars?* The holiday has made the pass look like Seattle rush hour. The kids are actually pedaling past the cars at times. But not me.

I square myself in my seat, unset my parking brake, and muster enough strength to start the bike moving uphill. That is when I start to notice the pain. My biceps and triceps muscles take turns aching with each revolution of the crank. They loosen up after a hundred yards and the ache subsides. Now the tendons in my elbow are burning. Tendonitis is what our team nurse, Nicole, calls it. It is commonly referred to as tennis elbow, or in my case, cranking-up-a-mountain-pass-on-a-handcycle-with-one-arm elbow. Freeways, like most roads, are designed with a slight down grade from the middle crown to each shoulder. This slope allows water and sleeping drivers to naturally drift to the side of the road. You don't notice this slope much when you are driving a car. I notice it on my handcycle. The slope, along with pedaling with the right crank, causes me to exert constant opposing side pressure to keep the bike going straight. This torque on my tendons causes more pain the further I go.

The only thing that distracted me from the pain in my elbow was the pain in my shoulder. It wasn't a muscle pain. It was radiating from the socket. Thirty-two years of depending on one limb for mobility, dressing and feeding myself, hugging my wife, and raising my children had caused some wear and tear. Add cycling over a mountain to the workload and you have to expect some pain. I don't want you to get the idea that I am complaining. In fact, if you have ever been around me, you know that I am not a whiner. I really don't mention these pains or inconveniences to people. I just think if you made the commitment to read this far in the book, you deserve some inside feelings.

As I push the cranks forward my shoulder flares with a deep ache. As I pull the cranks toward me my elbow burns with a sharp pain. There is no escape. Occasionally, my focus is distracted by a motorist. "Way to go! You're my hero!" I must admit their words are encouraging. Push – pull. Push – pull.

I am crawling up this mountain and there is no end in sight. I make the next quarter mile and stop next to a pile of plowed snow and set my brake. I take my hand off the crank, lean back in my seat, and stretch my body. I inhale deeply through my nose and exhale slowly through my mouth. Gaining control of my breathing gives me a sense of accomplishment. How pathetic is that? I'm really clinging to the small stuff now. I can't stay here any longer. There are more quarter mile increments ahead than I want to know. I start back up the freeway. Every part of my body shouts, "No!" but my mind says, *Shut up and pedal.*

God, I need a little hope and courage, here.

Behind every good man...

Chapter 9

Immediately I remember Isaiah 40:31, "but those who hope in the LORD will renew their strength. They will soar on wings like eagles; they will run and not grow weary, they will walk and not be faint." That verse had helped me over this mountain before, it could help me again. But this time my mind is drawn to the verse before that old, familiar one. Isaiah writes, "Even youths grow tired and weary …" Wow! That is exactly what I need to hear. Even youths grow tired and weary. That's right! Even a young person would be struggling up this mountain. In fact, there were two of them pedaling up ahead of me. Nicole and Grant were going faster than I was but they were still wearing down. They pedaled further between stops but they were still tired and aching. I needed to be reminded of that. I had started thinking this was about my age. *I am in my early fifties trying to get over this mountain. I should have done this in my thirties.* But no, it is not about my age. It never is about our age. God doesn't stop using us when we age. If we are still breathing, God is not finished with us.

The verse continues with "… and young men stumble and fall." Young men stumble and fall. That is an interesting passage of Scripture. It is a personal passage of Scripture for me. When I was a young man I stumbled and fell.

At twenty-one I stumbled out of a tavern and got into a car to make my way home with my brother Tom. Tom is three years older than me and one of my four brothers. I am the youngest of five boys. Survive that! No, that is not how I lost my limbs. The brothers were not bored with tearing wings off flies one day, looked around and said, "Where's Bob?"

Tom is my closest brother. Wait a minute ... I am trying to be too diplomatic here. Let me just say what I mean. Tom is my favorite brother. Now, before you start telling me I should not have favorites and I should treat them all the same, let me explain. First, if you feel that way, most likely you do not have multiple siblings. If you had multiple siblings you would admit that you have one you get along with better than the others. It may not even be the same one all your life. It changes as your life changes. Tom has been most consistently my favorite throughout my life. And second, it doesn't mean I don't love and appreciate my other brothers. Joe, Don, and Pat all understood this and at times may have had my favorite rating. I doubt they ever felt the need to compete for the extra attention from the youngest brother. All of you youngest brothers understand.

Back to the tavern in Olympia. Tom and I stumbled out and started our fifty-mile drive back home to Hoquiam, Washington. We had only been back in the state for five weeks. Two years earlier we had hitchhiked to Ohio with our brother Don. Can you picture three brothers hitchhiking across America? That journey was a bit heavy on courage and a little light on hope. After two years flipping burgers in Ohio, Tom and I returned to Hoquiam on the Greyhound bus. We were looking for good paying jobs and we knew where we could get them ... Grays Harbor County. Mom lived in Grays Harbor County – Hoquiam, to be exact. She, my little sister, Reenie, and I had settled there when we moved to Washington after my dad died in 1971. The rest of the siblings eventually followed.

For those of you not familiar with the Pacific Northwest, let me tell you a little about Washington. In Washington we grow trees like Iowa grows corn. It is our crop. It takes twenty-five years for our crop to come to harvest. We can plant a crop that our children will harvest. This was back in the mid-seventies when timber was king in our state. Microsoft had not been invented yet. Costco and Starbucks were dreams. Boeing had laid off so many people that someone put a billboard along I-5 reading, "Will the last person leaving Seattle please turn off the lights?" The only thing that kept our state going was those big, beautiful trees. Back then, if you could stand on your feet and talk in complete sentences you could get a job somewhere around timber. In fact, talking in complete sentences was optional. It was good, hard, sweating, spitting work. And Grays Harbor County was a hub of the industry. Tom and I got off the bus and walked into a sawmill. The man looked us over and said, "Both of you show up Monday morning. Oh, and be ready to work."

Bob, on left, and Tom

I could not believe it. I was working shoulder to shoulder with my favorite brother and we were getting paid union wages. What could be better? Our first paycheck we bought a '63 Plymouth Valiant. This was typical of the relationship I had with Tom. We pooled our money together. I don't even remember whose name was on the title of the car. It didn't matter. What's mine is yours and what's yours is mine. Remember when you used to say those kinds of things, too? We typically stop talking like that when we start to accumulate more stuff in our lives. But this was simpler times. What was mine was his and what was his was mine.

Our second paycheck we had something we had never experienced before ... money left over after payday. Not just a little money, either. Two full union paychecks. We took some of our hard-earned dollars and decided to go celebrate. At this point in my life, celebrate meant to go out and drink beer at a tavern or a friend's house. I had forgotten how to have fun sober, but that is a different story. We called some old friends in Olympia and said we were coming down to see them the next day. We planned to spend the night at their place. Driving fifty miles, meeting up with friends you had not seen in two years, drinking, and driving fifty miles back home is a very irresponsible (dumb) idea.

Saturday morning I got up, took a shower, came back to my room and put on my best 'Saturday go to Olympia' shirt. I slipped on my shoes and bent over to tie them up ... for the last time. We drove fifty miles to Olympia to see our friends. Evening came and blended into night as we drank and told stories of the last two years. Around midnight Tom and I left the last tavern. Tom got in the driver's seat.

Okay, I guess he's going to drive this time.

I went around to the other side, put my hand on the passenger door and climbed in. You know, I have learned over the years that you can make all the responsible drinking plans you want at twelve o'clock noon. Plan a designated driver, surrender your keys, or plan to spend the night. But once you get to drinking, come midnight you'll change those plans.

I looked at Tom and said, "Hey, Tom, this is no fun. Let's go home."

I suggested we take the back way home. Even after two years I was confident I knew the roads. We could go from Olympia to Tumwater, then to Little Rock, take the farm road to Oakville, and catch Highway 12 to Grays Harbor.

Tom said, "Okay."

Have you ever noticed how little it takes to make sense after spending the night drinking beer and telling tales?

We made it to Tumwater and on to Little Rock.

Maybe I really do know these roads. Ah, there's that farm road to Oakville. That was the one I was afraid we would miss.

The clouds blocked all moonlight and it was very dark. Very, very dark. I fell asleep in the passenger seat. Tom drove down the narrow road, paying as close attention as he could. The sign indicated curves ahead. He slowed as he started into a series of winding curves. Barely going thirty-five miles an hour, he successfully negotiated every curve until the last one. His right wheel went off the pavement onto the shoulder. He turned the steering wheel to bring the car back on the road but he over-corrected the wheel just a little. But a little was enough to take the car to the other side of the road. The car smashed into something that stopped our forward motion as it slid off the road, down an embankment and came to rest at the bottom of the hill.

I woke up and jumped out of the car. Tom got out of the car and we started to check each other.

"Are you hurt?"

"No, I'm not hurt. Are you hurt?"

"No, I don't think so. See if I'm bleeding anywhere."

By the interior lights of the car, we looked each other over.

"You're not bleeding."

"Neither are you!"

No cuts, no broken bones, nothing! I walked around to the front of the car and the headlights were looking at each other.

"Hey, Tom, what did we do? Did we hit a tree up there or something?"

"I don't know what we hit. I was coming around the curve and went off the road. Next thing I know we are at the bottom of this hill."

We started laughing and then joking about what a great story this will make Monday morning at the mill. I noticed the headlights shining on some knocked down brush on the hillside. If the car came down that way, the road must be up there. I took off up the hill. One thing I could do is climb the hill quicker than my brother. I may me younger but my legs were longer.

"Tom, I think I know where the road is. Follow me."

Once away from the headlights the darkness closed in. I kept climbing, reaching for shrubs and roots to pull me up. I got quite a distance ahead of Tom. I could not hear him but I was sure he would find his way. Finally, I reached level ground and stood up. I felt the gravel under my shoes and then pavement.

I cannot believe I just walked away from a crashed car unharmed.

Sometimes the most dangerous thing we do is walk away unharmed. Every time I did not get hurt, every time I was not caught, I became more confident and more bold. I began to think I could not get hurt and I could not be caught. After all, I was young. I was invincible. The trouble with walking away unharmed is that you never know about next time. In fact, you cannot even be sure about this time.

I walked away from a crashed car unharmed but I didn't know ... I did not know we had hit a power pole. I did not know the cross arms at the top of the pole snapped off. I did not know there were four power lines lying in the road. The lines were not broken. They were not arcing or making any noise. They swung down from the previous pole, across the road, and up to the next pole. The lowest wire was hardly touching the road and the highest one about waist high. I took a few steps forward and my left hand hit one of those wires.

I stumbled and fell on my knees. Electricity will enter your body where you make contact with it. It will leave your body where you make contact with something else. For me, that something else was my knees pressed against the road. Twelve and a half thousand volts came in through my arm, through my body and exploded my knees into the pavement as it exited. It was as if someone had taken a shotgun and blasted my knees from the inside out. They were gone.

If this was a lucky night, the next thing I would have done was fallen backwards away from the wires. However, this was a night when things kept going from bad to worse. Out of the frying pan and into the fire. I fell forward. When I fell forward, I ended up lying across the rest of the wires as they continued to burn the front of my body.

Tom came up the hill and his eyes began to adjust to the darkness. He made out the silhouetted wires against the grey clouds.

Power lines shouldn't angle that sharp toward the ground. Where do they go? Tom wondered.

He followed the lines to the road and saw my body lying still and silent on the wires. His heart sank to the pit of his stomach.

He's dead! What happened? How could this be? He was fine coming up the hill.

The grief weakened his knees as he sat on the road. A million questions raced through Tom's mind.

Why didn't I hear him hit the wires? Shouldn't I have seen a flash? Why didn't I come up the hill first? We should have stayed in Olympia. How am I going to tell Mom? What am I going to tell Mom, "Bob is dead"?

The silence of the night wrapped around him like a blanket and time stood still.

"Dear God, help us."

Tom's thoughts went to all those roads he and I walked together in the past few years.

We hitchhiked through the South, slept in barns, worked those cheap jobs in Ohio, came back home, got these great jobs. Walking, always walking. We never had a car until this one. Stupid cars. And Bob whistling all the time. I don't remember which one of us brothers taught him how to whistle but that was a mistake. He smiles at everyone. He doesn't have enemies. As soon as he sees you, he starts smiling. If he were a dog, he would be wagging his tail off. Who couldn't like him? Man, this is going to be a lonely road without him.

Tom looked over at my body draped across the wires, "Oh, Bob, what have we got ourselves in to tonight?"

I moaned. Tom jumped to his feet, "You're still alive!"

Running over to me, he strained to hear what I was saying. My voice weakly uttered, "Pull."

"Pull? How can I pull you off these wires without being electrocuted? I need to find something rubber. Your shoes! The soles of your shoes are rubber."

Tom nervously grabbed a hold of my shoes anticipating the jolt. No jolt. Great! He pulled on both shoes to drag me off the lines but I was stuck.

"Come on! What are you caught on Bob?"

Tom let go of my shoes and looked closer at my body lying face down on the wires. My stomach and chest were free. My hands and arms were free.

Whoa, that arm looks bad.

Looking at my head, he saw the last wire running under my chin and across my right ear. It had seared to the skin on my neck. That was the problem. He had to get my neck off that power line. Shoes were not going to protect him. Tom felt time was ticking away.

How much longer could Bob stay on that wire and live?

Then he did what only a favorite brother could do. He forgot about himself, took a deep breath, and placed his hand on my forehead. Again, no jolt. There was no more electricity going through the lines. A transformer down the road had blown up and blacked out the area. Tom did not get shocked when he touched me but when he freed my neck from the wire and rolled me on my back he got the shock of his life.

My left arm was burned and curled from fingertip to elbow. He looked at my legs, and where my knees used to be, there were holes in my pants. He tore the holes open to see what damage had been done. Burned flesh and blood surrounded exposed bones. He looked at my chest. My shirt was gone. It had either burned off me or burned into me. Tom lowered his ear to my chest to see if he could hear a heartbeat. The smell of burnt flesh filled his nose. His face felt a mixture of moist blood and dry, burned skin. My chest was so hot from the heat of the wires, my chest burned a scar on to Tom's cheek. He beat on my chest to get my heart pumping stronger. He leaned over and blew air into my lungs.

"Bob, come on! You are not dead! Inhale!" I was in such bad shape I had forgotten how to breathe.

"Inhale!" Tom shouted louder.

Somewhere in my unconscious mind, I heard a familiar and trusted voice.

Inhale? That's a strange thing to ask me to do. Well, if Tom wants me to inhale there must be a reason.

I took a deep breath. Tom watched intently as my chest filled with air. Seconds ticked by slowly.

"Bob, exhale!" I let the air out of my lungs, "Inhale!" Pause. "Exhale!" Pause. "Inhale!"

As oxygen revitalized my bloodstream, I slipped in and out of consciousness. Tom looked around and noticed for the first time exactly where we were. The road was dark and empty. Trees surrounded us and the lights from the car glowed eerily through the underbrush. Between the power lines crossing the highway, me lying on the pavement, and Tom kneeling next to me the road was totally blocked. That probably did not matter. Who else would be out here on this road after midnight? Tom peered up and down the road to see if he could spot any lights from a nearby house or farm. Nothing but darkness peered back at him. God only knows where we could get help.

He went back to tending to me. "Keep breathing, Bob. You've made it this far and I'm not going to let you die. Inhale ... exhale."

A faint rumble could be heard from the direction of Oakville. It sounded as if it were getting closer. *Could it be a car? Wait, are those lights? Yes, those are lights coming this way. Someone's coming!*

"Bob, someone's coming! We're going to get you out of here!"

The car entered into the curve and came around the bend. The car's headlights caught the wires crossing the road and the driver immediately hit the brakes. As the car stopped, the head-lights fully illuminated the scene in front of them. The driver gasped seeing two men in the road, one kneeling next to the other. The other was so badly injured it was hard to tell if he was dead or alive. He turned to see his passengers staring out the windshield. It looked like a picture from a war zone but this was not a war zone and it was not a picture. This was way too real for a Saturday night. The road was blocked ahead. He could not turn around and leave these men in need. Climbing out of the car, he stood behind the headlights. Tom got to his feet and tried to make out the face of the man. The glare of the lights obscured his features.

Tom hoped he was a man of compassion, "Help us, please. We've had an accident. My brother is electrocuted. We need help. Please help us."

The driver didn't know what to do. He probably thought, *Help? What can we do in a situation like this? We're not medics. We're just trying to get home.* He walked in front of the lights and said to Tom, "Get in the car! We'll take you to a phone."

"I can't get in the car. I cannot leave my brother here alone. If I leave him here he will be dead when I get back." Tom knelt down next to me and pleaded, "Won't you please help us?"

The driver realized this man was not going to leave his brother's side. "Pick him up and get in the car. We'll take you both to a phone."

Tom scooped me into his arms and climbed into the back of the car. The other passengers sat silent in the front seat as the car turned around and headed to Oakville. Tom cradled me, thankful to be off the road and getting me closer to medical care. The driver pulled into a parking lot with a payphone. Tom laid me on the seat and jumped out to the phone. He dialed 9-1-1.

A calm voice on the other end said, "Hello, 9-1-1, what is your emergency?"

"We have been in a crash and my brother is hurt really bad!"

"Can you give me your location?" the operator replied.

Looking around, Tom saw the neon sign of the business we were at and told the operator.

"Help is on the way."

Tom returned to the car and held my right hand in his. "Help is on the way, Bro. Help is on the way."

There seems to be no longer time span than between 'help is on the way' and the sight of flashing lights. Sirens could be heard in the distance minutes before the EMT vehicle pulled into the parking lot. The Washington state patrol car followed closely behind.

Tom took the EMTs to the car and pointed to me, "He's my brother, and he walked into power lines. His name is Bob."

"We've got him from here." The medics immediately began to assess my injuries. They talked quietly amongst themselves, "This man is in really serious condition. How did he keep him alive?"

They looked over at Tom, "You're a good brother. You saved his life."

Tom did not feel like a good brother. He was feeling the guilt of hitting that pole.

As the medics loaded me into their vehicle Tom asked, "Is he going to be okay? Where are you taking him?"

"We'll do our best. He's going to Saint Peter's Hospital in Olympia." they said, not wanting to tell Tom what they were really thinking. *We hope he's alive when we get there.*

Tom took my hand again and said, "They're taking you to the hospital, Bob. I'll be there as soon as I can." He didn't want to tell me what was in the back of his mind. *I hope you're still alive when I get there.*

With the ambulance lights disappearing down the road, the patrol officer came over to Tom and began to ask questions. Tom told him of the crash and downed power lines and the waiting for help. The officer drove Tom back to the site. Seeing the wires in the road, he called the power company to get a crew out there. He walked with Tom down the hill to the car. He noticed some beer cans on the floor and confirmed what he had suspected.

"Mr. Mortimer, have you been drinking tonight?"

Tom was not hiding anything. He said, "Yes, sir, we we're drinking with friends in Olympia."

"Mr. Mortimer, I am placing you under arrest for driving under the influence of an intoxicant – DUI."

Tom held his hands behind his back as the officer put handcuffs on him and placed him in the backseat of the patrol car. Tom did not resist.

On the way to Thurston County Jail he thought, *What can they do to me? Take away a few of my paychecks; make me spend weekends in jail; revoke my driver's license; go to some meetings? Is this all they can do to me? I feel like I've just killed my brother and what they can do to me is no punishment all."*

The ambulance pulled up to the emergency entrance at Saint Peter's Hospital. The EMTs unloaded the gurney from the back and rolled me quickly through the doors.

"We've got a bad one here!"

The doctors on duty looked at me and quickly said, "He is too badly burned. We cannot treat him here. We are not that kind of hospital. He has to get up to Harborview Burn Center in Seattle."

"Seattle? We barely kept him alive the twenty minutes it took to get him here. He'll never survive the fifty mile drive to Seattle."

"He's not going by ambulance. We've called a helicopter to airlift him up there."

Within minutes, the helicopter settled on the landing pad and they moved me into the passenger bay. The whine of the engines increased, building power for lift-off.

As the helicopter rose from the pad and headed north to Seattle, two truths were seared into my life: Sometimes you do not walk away. And Isaiah was right – young men stumble and fall.

Chapter 10

"Give up! You'll never make it!"

I turned in the direction of the voice to see a young man leaning out of the passenger window of a car moving slowly over the pass in the holiday traffic. In my reminiscing about the crash, I had forgotten I was pedaling over Snoqualmie. The heckler's words brought me back to reality.

"Give up! You'll never make it!"

Is that his best shot? He would have to do better than that to discourage me. Pedaling over this mountain with one arm is not the hardest challenge I have ever faced. In fact, it may not even be in the top ten. I flash him a big grin and push-pull my hand crank with renewed vigor. I have learned that there are times you need to give young men a little extra grace.

Darla is pedaling a short distance ahead of me. Nicole and Grant are still in sight heading toward the curve ahead. It isn't long before they disappear around the bend. Darla immediately begins to worry about them. The traffic is not moving as fast as the other day in the rainstorm but there are still dangers on the freeway when you are riding bikes. Darla and I get around the corner to see what would be a common sight. Grant is fixing a flat on Nicole's bike. We pedal up next to them and stop. She had run over some unknown debris. We have spare tubes so we don't try to repair the old one.

Nicole holds up her palm and shows us a scrape with torn skin and minor bleeding.

"What happened?" I ask.

"Her front tire skidded out from underneath her a short ways back and she went down on the pavement," Grant calmly said.

"I told you they could get hurt," Darla quickly added. "Let me see. How bad is it?"

We cleaned her palm with antiseptic wipes from our packs and put a small bandage on the wound. Nicole directed the procedure. Being a student nurse earned her the status of team medic.

I look over our team. I can tell everyone is wearing out. Between the physical energy to climb, the stress of the constant traffic, and the emotional drain of a looming mountain our Hope and Courage team was being pushed to the limit. It has been a long day. It has been a long week.

"How's everyone doing?" I ask.

"We're doing fine, Daddy. But more important, how are you doing?" Nicole replies.

You have got to love these kids. They are teenagers crossing the pass on bicycles. They have crashed, had flats, been hot and cold, tired and thirsty, watched by thousands of people in cars, SUVs, and trucks and they want to know how I am doing.

Darla brings us back on focus, "Everyone is doing well but we are all getting tired. I worry about you two kids. I don't like it when I can't see you. There are no more freeway exits between here and the top. Stay together and wait for us at the half-mile markers. Everybody get a little snack. I hope Chanel is doing okay with Aunt Jeanne and Uncle Don."

You have got to love Darla, also. She just can't let go of those God-given mothering instincts. She is tired and walking stiffer every time we stop. Her palms and wrists are numb from gripping on the handlebars and her neck aches from leaning forward. Not to mention, she has been sitting on that very uncomfortable bike seat for hours. Looking at her makes me smile with admiration.

"Are you doing alright, Hon?" I ask. "Anything I can adjust to make your bike more comfortable?"

"I'm stiffening up a bit. This seems harder than it was back in 2004. I may have you and Grant look at my bike tomorrow and adjust a few things but not now. It can't be much further to the top and we all need to get off these bikes," she replies getting back on her bike.

"Hang in there, Babe. You're doing great."

"You are too. And I'm sure proud of those kids. They never complain."

We start pedaling again with a new strength. I am not sure how far it is to the top but I can keep knocking off those quarter-mile increments. I think again about the Scripture in Isaiah, *"but those who hope in the Lord will renew their strength. They will soar on wings like eagles; they will run and not grow weary, they will walk and not be faint."*

I used those words to help me get over Snoqualmie Pass four years ago. Today I am just happy to be able to go through them in my head as I work my way up Snoqualmie again. The rhythm of the words synchronize with the pedaling of my cranks. Over and over again.

A few more quarter miles pass by and I am looking in my rearview mirror. The mirror helps me see drivers before they pass me. To be honest, I don't look at it as often as I should. I especially ignore it while going uphill. I am too busy climbing to look in a mirror. I do glance every once in a while, though. As I look, I see the bottom of the sun break below the clouds in the western sky behind us. The gap between it and the horizon isn't much.

Lord, I know it is Your schedule, Your plan and You're in charge. I have learned that lesson. However, I would sure like to wake up tomorrow and not have to send my family back up this mountain. Could we please get over it today?

I see a sign ahead that reads, "West Summit 1 Mile."

One mile! Darla and I stop below the sign. The kids are up around the bend somewhere. Darla gets her camera out of her pack and walks back down the road to get a picture. One mile. We can make one mile. Darla gets back on her bike and we push off. Rounding the next curve we see Nicole and Grant standing at their bikes.

Getting closer we see their smiles, "Did you see the sign?"

"Yeah. Less than a mile now. YooHoo!"

"Okay, on this next stretch, stop before you actually reach the summit and wait for us," I tell them between gulps of water.

Grant says, "We'll ride with you guys from here on up. We started together. We finish together."

"That's a great idea!" Darla exclaims, almost too enthusiastically.

"Hey, Family, I have been reciting that verse from Isaiah. You know, 'those who hope in the Lord will ...'"

"'Renew their strength!' We know! We know! Let's get going!"

Forget the quarter miles. My strength is renewed. My biggest obstacle is the sun setting now. Occasionally, it flashes off my mirror when there are no obstructions blocking its rays. I look at the reflection as it races into the hilltops behind me. I take a deep breath and push harder. West Summit ½ Mile. Darla is riding with Grant and Nicole about fifty feet ahead of me. At this slow speed it is safer to ride ahead of me than behind me. I can wear out and stop at any moment, becoming a huge object to plow into. But I don't want to stop. *West Summit ¼ Mile.*

Darla slows and waits for me to catch up, "Do you want to take a break?"

Between breaths I gasp, "No. Let's keep going." Darla gives me a look that indicates she thinks differently and pedals back to the kids.

"West Summit Exit – Next Right."

What a beautiful sign to see. We begin to pull away from the traffic as we enter the turn off.

Darla shouts back, "We're stopping!"

It takes me an embarrassing length of time to close the short distance between us, "What's the problem?" I say in a voice that is so breathless it is barely heard.

"The kids are tired and want to stop. They want to get something to drink and freshen up before anyone sees them at the top. Isn't that right kids?"

"Yeah. We're beat," they both chime.

I see right through their little charade and if I had any oxygen in my lungs I would have called them on it. "Okay (wheeze), we better let them (wheeze) get rested up."

Drinking our water, everyone is in good spirits. We relive a few of the spectacular moments of the past few days. We know that once we come off the exit there will be other people around us and we won't have this privacy. This is a moment 'for the riders.'

As my three companions climb on their bikes for the last time today, Darla says, "You go first, Sweetheart. We want to follow you." I don't think she knew the impact those words had after these last few days.

Up ahead, the rest of our team waits in the parking lot of the businesses at the west end of the summit. They are as important to this day as the riders. They have supplied us, encouraged us, and cheerfully waited for us all day long. The Hope and Courage truck is prominently parked toward the road. The exit is a popular stop on this Memorial Day weekend. Jeanne has been answering a lot of queries about this Hope and Courage Across America team. People are curious.

Jeanne says, "They're not far away. If you stick around you can see them reach the top." Chanel stays by her side to assist her, "Aunt Jeanne, your cell phone is ringing!"

Jeanne takes the phone, listens, responds and breaks into a big smile, "They're coming up the exit right now!" Chanel grabs the video camera, Aunt Jeanne grabs her camera, Uncle Don grabs a few bottles of water and they move down on the road for a better view. Tourists and travelers follow close behind. At first they see a clump of fluorescent green in the fading sunlight. It must have seemed like slow motion to them as we came closer and closer. Before long they could see the distinct shapes of four separate riders. I was in front with Grant, Nicole and Darla fanned out behind me. We couldn't help but smile seeing the rest of our team up ahead filming and cheering. Then we noticed the others clapping and cheering. Cars passed us getting off the freeway and honked. It was hard to interact with the people around us and control the emotions inside us at the same time.

The Hope and Courage logo emblazoned on the truck beckoned to us. That logo had already become our favorite rally point. Darla got off her bike and went straight to Chanel. They both needed a hug. Nicole and Grant dismounted and were met with handshakes and back slaps. They deserved at least that. I set my brake and took my helmet off and hung it from the hand-crank. Jeanne and Don congratulated me as I took my glasses off and set them in my helmet. I gripped my glove in my teeth and peeled it off my fingers. I clenched my fist a few times to limber my knuckles. Darla came over, bent low, kissed me and said, "We did it."

"I couldn't have done it without you, Babe." I wouldn't have done it without her.

People asked questions as we posed for pictures in the parking lot. Travelers in the restaurant and shops stared out the windows at the show. I wished we could have stepped aside and watched it ourselves. I silently wished one of those lookers was the young man who had leaned out his window shouting, "Give up! You'll never make it!" But this wasn't about what I could do. This was about hope in Christ and having the courage to use that hope to face mountains.

Sitting on my bike, with my family standing next to me, I said with a strong voice, "We made it, Team! We crested Snoqualmie Pass ... together!"

We all cheered. I looked to the west to see the sun wink its last gleam.

Thank you, Lord. Now we only have 2,900 more miles to go.

An encouraging sign.

The Hope and Courage team at the
summit.

Chapter 11

When said of life, being "over the hill" is typically not some-thing to look forward to because it means you're "getting up there" in age. Or, when one person advises another, "It's all downhill from here," it may solicit a groan. But when you live life on wheels, these sayings can never be more uplifting. They are a breath of fresh air, or a tall drink of cold water on a hot day. In other words, one of the best rewards for reaching the top of the mountain is the long free ride down the other side. So, if you don't mind, I'll let you read Darla's journal while I sit back with my hand gently gripping the brake and enjoy fifteen miles of "Wheee!"

May 24 ~ Saturday

We rode in the truck back to the summit and unloaded our bikes. The first part of the day was all downhill. I was nervous the whole way. I don't like going fast downhill. I squeezed my brake most of the way. We got off I-90 at Cle Elum and took a county road into Ellensburg. We could actually hear ourselves think. Those fast cars and trucks are sure loud on the freeway. It is scary watching from behind as they quickly pass by my family. Thank You, Lord, for keeping us safe. Chanel got to ride with us part way on the county road. She did really well going up the hills. Today was our longest day so far, about fifty-five miles.

We have had several encouraging encounters with people the last few days. While climbing the mountain yesterday, a young dad with two little

boys from Gig Harbor waited for us
on the side of the freeway. They were
actually at our send-off party. The
dad told Bob he was hoping to catch
us because he wanted his boys to
see us. The dad prayed for us along
the side of the road. We gave them
Hope and Courage buttons and were
back on our way with a new strength.
We had lots of truckers and cars
honk and wave to us. Today started
with free drinks at an espresso shop
in Ellensburg. The owner remembered
Bob telling her about our bike ride last
year when we passed through. She
treated us to lattes. Later we saw a
couple waving at us from the overpass
on the freeway. That was fun, having
people cheering us on like that.

We stopped for a break and Jeanne
had ice cream sandwiches for us.
We talked to a guy who said he and
his wife had ridden their bikes across
America a few years ago. We began

pedaling and a man was stopped on the side of the road. He said that he had ridden with us at the Gig Harbor bike trail. He gave Nicole a $20 bill and said this was for our trip. What a huge blessing it was to us. He brought encouragement with him. It was so nice of him to reach out to us in this way.

Today had its share of struggles, too. The clamshell cargo box on top of the truck flew open and Jeanne and Don got out looking for stuff along the freeway. Nothing major was lost. Not like yesterday morning when Bob's bike cushions flew out of the back of the truck. We had to call Jeanne's son, Robby, to go to our house and get Bob's old cushions and bring them out to us. Bob started up the mountain with his wheelchair cushion to sit on and a shirt wrapped around the back of his bike seat.

He was glad when Robby showed up with the cushions from home.

This morning Jeanne thought she had seen Bob's bike cushions on the freeway and so I ran back on the freeway looking for them. It was just a log. Then we were told to go the wrong way and rode one mile to a dead-end and had to turn around ... not so bad in a car but not a great thing when you are on a bike and already pedaling a long distance. When we were going back to Ellensburg, the clamshell flew open again, we stopped, and we went running alongside the freeway looking for stuff. Luckily, we don't think that anything flew out. Bob is going to go to the hardware store and get something to hold it shut.

After our ride, we went back to the RV park and packed up to leave. We headed to Moses Lake and parked the RV at the Shilo Inn. The church we are preaching at tomorrow had provided rooms for us here. It is a large room with a shower right in the same room! It is a nice convenience after several days in campgrounds where I walk to my showers. We ate dinner at Bob's Café at the motel. We walked back to the RV and started getting it unhitched and carrying things into the motel room. Bob went to park the truck and drove under the motel's covered parkway. He forgot that we had put Chanel's bike on the rack on top. All of a sudden, he heard a crash and realized that he had knocked the bike and the clamshell off the truck roof. Our day was going from bad to worse and we felt like it was time to call it a night.

Poor Bob, his lips have cold sores and his muscles ache ... and he is the one speaking early in the morning for three services with a message of Hope and Courage. We are going to need to ask the Lord to help us bring

some encouragement ... and maybe we
are going to find some for ourselves
as well. It has been quite a day. It
just seemed that if anything could go
wrong it would. We really feel that
Satan is trying his best to discourage
us. We know that we are supposed
to do this ride and many times we
totally feel God's hand upon the
journey. Whether it is from our
highway angels or the tears I see in
people's eyes, I just know we are to
do this journey. Jesus, please keep
confirming that to us. Thank You.

May 25 ~ Sunday

After a short night we woke up to a
beautiful sunny day ... that is always a
great way to start a new day. We had
to get up early because I needed to
drop Bob off at the church at 7:00
a.m. for the first of three services.
We spoke at the Moses Lake CMA
church. It was a great day. I really

prayed that You, Lord, would give Bob the extra energy, strength and stamina to get through all three services and to bring a message of encouragement. We had had quite a week of frustrations. It seemed as though each day created a set of new problems that we had to face. But, Lord, You helped with each trial and gave us a fresh start. We are feeling that this journey must be pretty big because of all the unforeseen problems that have occurred so far. Satan is trying his best but we will not be defeated.

When we arrived at the church, there was a table in the entry for us to put our buttons and prayer cards on. And there was a big box of Journey Bibles. Mike had them shipped to us from Kent. They were a perfect addition to our table.

When I looked through the bulletin, I saw that the pastor had a rough week also. He had written about several trials their family had experienced. It was a hard week for a lot of families. The pastor told me he really needed to hear Bob's message of Hope today. I had a man tell me this was a perfect message for him because his company was really going up a mountain and he needed to hear about Hope.

There was a little eight-year-old boy in a wheelchair crying when he saw Bob after the first service because he thought he had missed him speaking. He was so happy when he realized that Bob had another service to do.

The church was so nice and friendly to us and blessed us in many ways. It was really fun to learn that one of the ministers was from North Lima, Ohio! North Lima is the little town where Bob grew up. Small world! Jeanne knew his aunt and this guy graduated with Don's nephew.

I had a trucker tell me he would be looking for us and if he saw us on the highway, he would stop and pray with us. I also talked with a couple who plan to come find us on our ride and encourage us along the way. One man asked me when we planned to finish the ride and when I told him that it was September 11, he broke down in tears. It was a great day for us to encourage the church and for the church to encourage us. We felt the day was a blessing all around.

Bob told the story of knocking the clamshell off the truck. At the end of the second service he asked if anyone would want to bless us by putting the rack back on top of our truck. And sure enough four angels appeared to help Grant and Don put on the clamshell. What a blessing they were!

We had ten salvations! Great day of ministry. This is what it is all about.

May 26 ~ Monday, Memorial Day

I started working on the laundry
first thing this morning. I had left
the motel laundry room with a load
of clothes to put away in the fifth
wheel and I noticed a young woman
sitting at a picnic table. It was
early in the morning and she seemed
out of place. I greeted her with a
smile and 'Good morning' on my way
to the RV. The next thing I knew
she was following me. When I got
to the steps of the RV I turned
around and she was right behind me.

Timeout. Sorry for the interruption. It's me, Bob. This story is too good to be told in a journal. So, I'm going to take over for a bit. (Oh, and in case you were wondering, the ride down Snoqualmie was more fun than Disneyland.) Okay, here's what happened.

Darla took the first of many loads of laundry out of the dryer. It was not as convenient as home but it was good to get clean clothes for her family. Taking an armload of folded clothes, she started across the parking lot to the RV. Living out of an RV was better than living out of suitcases. There were drawers and closets in the RV to put clothes. Not far from the RV, she noticed a young woman sitting on a picnic table. A girl, really, she was in her late teens, maybe twenty. She seemed out of place. Her eyes followed Darla as she walked past.

Darla, noticing her attention, smiled politely, "Good morning." No response.

Oh well, she's probably not a morning person.

Climbing onto the first step of the RV, Darla sensed something. Turning, she faced the young woman right behind her.

"Can I help you?" Darla quickly asked.

"I'm ready to go," the girl said matter-of-factly.

"What do you mean 'you're ready to go'? Go where?"

"In the motor home. I'm ready to go."

This did not make any sense to Darla. "Why do you want to go in the motor home?"

"My boyfriend is in the motor home. I'm ready to go."

A chill ran down Darla's back. The woman reached her hands into the pockets of her sweatshirt and gripped something. Darla wondered if she had a gun.

Darla's mind raced to grasp the situation. *I am on a step facing a woman who is possibly armed and wanting to follow me into the RV. She claims her boyfriend is waiting in the RV. If she has a weapon, the boyfriend will most likely have a weapon, too.*

Darla became frightfully aware of how alone she was right now. Nobody else was in sight.

I wish Bob was here. Lord, You have to help me.

"I'm ready to go now," the woman repeated.

Darla decided she was safer outside the RV than inside the RV. With one hand clutching the folded clothes and the other firmly on the handrail, she prayed and stood her ground.

Having finished my free continental breakfast, I rolled out of the motel to see how Darla was doing with the laundry. I could see her at the RV with a young woman.

She must have met another of her 'angels,' I thought, rolling toward her.

Getting closer I saw a look on Darla's face that alerted me something was not right.

"What's going on, Hon?" I asked while studying the girl.

"She says her boyfriend is in the RV and she wants to go with us."

My conversation goes directly to the girl, "What do you mean your boyfriend is in the RV? What makes you think he is in our RV?"

"He is in the RV and I'm supposed to go with you."

"That doesn't make sense." I start walking her away from the RV as I continue the conversation, "He shouldn't be in our RV. If he is in there I need to call the police."

Darla relaxed a bit and stepped away from the RV.

"No, you don't need to call the police. Let's just go in and he'll be there," the girl stated.

"I do need to call the police. Put yourself in my place. I have a wife and children and I am being told there is a man in my RV who does not belong there. You would call the police if you were me. Come on, let's go to the motel office and use the phone."

She followed me out of the parking lot and into the lobby. I explained the best I could to the desk clerk and let them dial the police. I told the dispatcher the situation and she said they would have officers there right away.

I guided the girl back to into the parking lot. I was surprised how easily she went along with what I said without objecting. Once outside, her cell phone rang. She answered it and walked a few steps away from me. I could easily hear her side of the conversation.

"I'm here. (pause) I'm doing the 'thing' you told me to do. (pause) No, I'm doing it."

Maybe her boyfriend was in the RV. Maybe she was supposed to get Darla into the RV for who knows what purpose. Whatever the plan was, we needed the police. The patrol cars pulled into the parking lot. I brought the girl over to them and told them all I knew and about the phone call from her boyfriend. They took her aside and began to ask her questions. I went back to Darla and gave her a tight hug. We both needed one. The officers came over shortly and said the girl had been drinking all night and had some sort of disagreement with her boyfriend. He was pretty sure there wasn't anyone in the RV but to be certain they should go in and check it out. I said that would make us all feel better. They cautiously went in and did a search of the likely hiding places. Then I went in and pointed out the nooks and crannies they may not have noticed. After a very thorough inspection we all felt assured there was nobody in the RV who wasn't supposed to be there. They said the girl hadn't committed a crime but they would take her with them and see to it she got home. We were glad to get her away from the RV. We could never be sure what God had protected us from that morning. Just like we will never know all the other things He protects us from. We did learn a valuable lesson, though. And that is that not all strangers we meet on this journey will be angels.

Alright, I'll let you get back to Darla's journal.

Dorlin Gaenz, my sister's brother-in-law, had called yesterday and said that while we were in Moses Lake he had some good friends, Paul and Judy Jones, who would be a great help to us if we needed anything. We gave them a call and they drove over to the motel. They were so nice and wanted to help us fix a couple of mechanical problems. Before they left, they invited us to come and park our RV at their place. We decided to accept their generous offer and dropped off the RV at their ranch before heading out for our bike ride. They were so gracious and said we could use the shop bathroom, including a shower and washing machine and dryer. What a huge blessing! They were so kind and giving we were reluctant to impose on them. Judy said this is their ministry and that we shouldn't deny them the blessing of helping us.

As we were leaving, Paul said, "Do you like hamburgers? Why don't you plan to come back tonight and we will have a barbeque."

We were overwhelmed with their generosity. They were so genuine and really made us feel so welcomed. So, guess what?! We took them up on it and tonight we are going to have a Memorial Day barbeque. How much more Americana can you get?! The kids are really excited. Judy said she hoped they could be an angel to us ... and they definitely are. Thank You, Lord, for the many angels you keep providing. They come in all shapes, sizes, and personalities at just the perfect times.

We rode our bikes today from Ellensburg to the Vantage bridge across the Columbia River. It was about 28 miles of upward and downward hills and LOTS of wind. I was hoping that we wouldn't get blown over. Thank You, Lord, for not letting us crash and for keeping us safe. Especially on those fast downhill runs. We stopped for ice cream treats at the end of the ride. Reenie and Fred were with us today. (Reenie is Bob's little sister.) It made our riding really special to have Fred join us on bikes. He brought an old bike he hadn't ridden in years. And of course it was fun to have Reenie in the support vehicle. Chanel loved spending extra time with her Aunt Reenie.

After our ride we went back to the Jones' home for our barbequed hamburgers along with homemade ice cream! We even had a bonfire. It was a great way to end the day. They are such nice people with a gift of hospitality. Last year I read "A Walk Across America" about a man named Peter Jenkins who crossed America on foot. I was amazed at how many times total strangers would just open their homes and hearts to him. And now I am finding that this is happening to us. So many people are reaching out to us in a variety of ways. Some reach with words of encouragement, others with financial giving, some with practical help and most with prayer. Thank You, Lord, for sending Your angels to us.

Also, this morning at the Shilo Inn, Bob was talking to a young man who had been at the church yesterday. He told Bob he really never believed in God but was going to give Him a try. Bob asked him if he had raised his hand to accept Christ and he said he was the first person. Bob gave him one of the Journey Bibles. Those Bibles are really going to be a blessing on this journey.

We talked with another man who had been at the church and he said that so many people had been talking about the service and how they needed to hear that message. He said a friend of his who is a 6'4" big burley guy cried through the whole service. Thank You, Lord, for giving Bob such a great message of Hope and Courage. And thank You for allowing us to share this message with so many people in so many ways.

It was a good day, Lord. Thank You for all things. I love You.

May 27 ~ Tuesday

This day began normal and ended not so normal. But then again ... I'm not so sure what normal really means anymore. It seems that if something could go wrong it usually does. I'm sorry, Lord, if I am sounding a little negative. It's just that we have had so many mishaps that I'm almost afraid to see what else is going to happen. I have to keep reminding myself that we are supposed to do this ride. When others encourage me it helps me to

stay focused and be reassured that
this is what we are being called to do.

We felt we were making really good
time and doing a good job on our riding.
We made it up the Vantage Hill! (The
Vantage Hill is where the highway drops
down from the flat eastern Washington
farmland to the Columbia River. The
ancient gorge created eight steep miles
of hill on both sides of the river. ~
Bob)We stopped at George, Washington,
and ate lunch at the Subway. I bought
Jeanne and Don an anniversary card in
the little market. We planned to all go
out for dinner to help them celebrate
their anniversary that night. We saddled
up and resumed our journey. The
ride was long and hot but it was
a great day of riding. As we neared
Moses Lake, Don and Jeanne were in
the truck and had to turn around on
a narrow road. They got stuck in ash
from Mt. St. Helens. The deep, fine
ash from the volcano lined the side of

the road. The locals know it is too soft to drive on. We are not locals. So needless to say, they had to call a tow truck to come and pull the truck out. That took much longer than we had anticipated. Fred went on ahead and as he rode into Moses Lake some families from the CMA church were at an overpass bridge cheering him on. They knew he was a part of our team and thought we would be soon following. They waited for over an hour (with small children) to see us ride through. Unfortunately, we never went that way. We had to deal with the stuck truck.

The truck was so dirty and full of dust inside and out that we had to go to a car wash before going back to the RV. While washing it, I got a call from a couple from the Moses Lake CMA church. They said they had something for us and wanted to meet up with us. I told them we were at a car wash and five minutes

later, they arrived ... with gifts in
hand. But more importantly were their
smiles, encouragement and love.

When they called me, I said we would
love to see them but they would have
to excuse the way we looked. I told
them we were hot and sticky but we
would have weary smiles on. When they
got there, she kept saying she could
not believe that after such a long day
we were still smiling. They were the
inspiration that I needed. They said
that the Bible verse that Bob shared
on Sunday, Isaiah 40:31, is one of
their favorites of all time. They are
farmers and they gave us three bags of
wonderful dried cherries. They are so
yummy! They told us that they have
had a bad crop of cherries this year,
so we know what a precious gift they
gave to us, and let me tell you we are
going to enjoy and savor each cherry!
They were our angels for the day!

Thank You, Lord, for providing us with angels along our route. You know just when we need them. It had been a long day for everyone.

Bob and Fred climbing the Vantage Hill.

May 28 ~ Wednesday

It was wonderful to stay at Paul and Judy's. They just opened their home and hearts to us. Judy told me that I could do as many loads of laundry as I needed. That was music to my ears! Chanel helped Judy pick weeds in her garden. Bob and Nicole were at two schools about three hours away doing school assemblies. When they came back, we went to a little park and the Moses Lake newspaper journalist came out and did an interview with us. Then we went back to Paul and Judy's and Chanel got to ride a horse! This was something that she was hoping to do on this trip ... she didn't think it would happen this soon. Paul called his neighbor and they brought over their horses. They were real cowboys with hats, boots and spurs. It was a dad, Hurk, and his son, Wakeen. The name of Chanel's horse was Spirit.

She was gone for almost two hours and was having such a great time! It made such a fun memory for her. She gave Spirit an apple when she was done. After all that, we went to dinner to celebrate Jeanne and Don's anniversary.

Chanel and Spirit

May 29 ~ Thursday

The next morning we had coffee and
toast with Paul, Judy and a friend of
theirs, Bud. The sun was shining so
we ate on their patio. As I was visiting
with Bud I told him it was nice to meet
him, he said it was really an honor for
him to meet us. I knew he was sincere
because he had tears in his eyes.

The secretary from the Moses Lake CMA church stopped by Paul and Judy's to drop off an offering from their church. We were amazed and so blessed. Thank You, Lord, for providing for us. We appreciate all that You are doing to encourage us on this trip.

An interesting little story happened this morning. When I was in Judy's kitchen helping with the toast I told her and Paul about the book, "A Walk Across America" and that I had felt like Peter Jenkins, the author. I told them I was amazed at how people we didn't even know were reaching out to us in so many ways. We had just finished that conversation when the church secretary stopped by and we were telling her about all the nice things people were doing for us. She said, "This may sound kind of random but have you ever read 'A Walk Across America'?" I said, "YES! I had just mentioned that book to Paul and Judy."

When we left, we gathered around in a circle and held hands while Paul prayed. It was a great send-off. They were wonderful people to meet and become friends with. What a blessing they have been.

We unhitched in Ritzville for the night. There was a little restaurant/gift shop that we could walk to from our campsite. It was called Cow Creek. It was such a cute place with nice gifts and great food. But it was the people who made it so special. It was run by a mother, Karen, and her daughter, Janelle. We told them what we were doing and they were so overwhelmed with our story. It was obvious they were Christians. It was a really fun stop in a little tiny place.

After setting camp, Bob, Grant and I began pedaling. Nicole was not feeling well so she decided not to ride. It was probably a very good choice because we had strong head and side winds on I-90. It was very hard riding. Bob almost blew off the side of the road and Grant and I nearly fell over when the semis would pass us. We rode about eighteen miles and turned around and pedaled back to Ritzville. Thanks, Lord, for protecting us.

May 30 ~ Friday

The next morning we riders got up early to get a full day of riding in. We went back up to the Cow Creek restaurant for cinnamon rolls and coffee. We were the only ones in the store and had a great time visiting with Karen and Janelle. Karen was all teary eyed and said, "You have touched my heart." She said she had only ever heard of people like us but had never met any. I'm not sure how we are so different but anyway we felt like we were able to bring a little Hope and Courage their way. Karen insisted on giving us all the cash she had in her pocket ... which was $11. She also gave us two bags of jerky and a 'Dan the Sausage Man' summer sausage. When we went to pay, they would not take our money. And when Don, Jeanne and Chanel came up for breakfast later they didn't charge them either. Another angel on our journey.

We had a good long day of riding, fifty-six miles. We went from Ritzville to Spokane. We had two flat tires. Bob and Grant are really getting good at changing them. We stopped at a rest area for a break. There was a guy who was moving to Denver who used to attend Christ Memorial Church in Poulsbo and heard Bob speak when we were there in November. It was fun to have him come over and say, "Hi, Bob." Someone else asked me where our final destination was and when I told her it was the Statue of Liberty she was so surprised.

It was a great question to be asked, and it was a great answer to give!

We made our destination to the edge Spokane and were feeling really good with our progress. We called Jeanne to be picked up at a little gas station with a little market. I went in and got ice cream bars for a well-deserved treat. Jeanne and Chanel showed up soon after with some disappointing news. On the way, Jeanne clipped a guard rail and broke the right mirror off of the truck. She felt really bad. Poor gal.

We headed back to Ritzville, hitched up the RV, grabbed a quick bite to eat at a hamburger place, and headed to Coeur d'Alene. It was a long ride and we were all tired. We arrived after dark in the RV park (which is never a good idea) but Bob did a great job and got us parked in a tight spot. The bed felt good. We all needed a good night's sleep.

Chapter 12

As you can tell from Darla's journal, the day-to-day events were a mixture of struggles and blessings. Before we left home, I told the team not to judge the whole ride by the first few weeks. I fully expected a learning period. This is part of a lesson I have tried to teach my children. Whenever you try something new, don't get discouraged because it didn't go well the first time. Whether it is a job, a musical instrument, a sport or any other new thing, you get better by doing it over and over. The same is true for moving a team across America on bicycles, living in an RV, and presenting a message of hope and courage.

I scheduled us to have a few days in Coeur d'Alene to evaluate and adjust. Coeur d'Alene, Idaho, and its nearby sister city, Spokane, Washington, were the last large populated areas we would see for quite a while. If we needed supplies and repairs, this would be the best place to find them. We pulled into the camp after dark and I backed the trailer into our spot. I much prefer pull-through sites but one was not available. I was still trying to get comfortable maneuvering fifty feet of truck and fifth wheel trailer. Everyone started going through the routine of setting camp. Grant hooked up the water and electric. Darla went inside the RV to extend the slide-outs and prepare the living quarters.

Nicole and Chanel started getting ready for the night. Jeanne and Don went to the garage portion of the RV and moved the bikes out so they could lower their bed and prepare their room. The garage was separated from the rest of the RV by a wall and door. It allowed the room to be converted into a private living space for Jeanne and Don. Privacy was a precious commodity in a 400 square foot home shared by seven people. I was pleased to see how everyone was doing his or her tasks smoothly. We were all more confident and effective than we were two weeks ago.

I went inside the RV and hooked up the laptop computer. After fifty-six miles of pedaling and 100 miles driving, I just wanted to check the emails and get to bed. We had been getting frequent emails from people all along the way. They would find the website on the RV graphics and send us encouraging notes. Sitting at the kitchen table, I read this one aloud to Darla and the kids.

> Dear Bob - On Friday, May 23, my husband, son and I were driving to Spokane to go wish our oldest daughter a happy twentieth birthday. It was a marathon weekend for us as we left late afternoon from Port Angeles and arrived in Spokane by 9:00 p.m. On our way up Snoqualmie pass, my husband said, "Jen, look - I think that man has only one arm and he's riding a bike up the pass." We were in disbelief. We had already passed, so we didn't think what we saw was for sure. We thought surely he has two arms. But we are people of faith and we believe that anything can happen. So then we were driving back to Port Angeles from Spokane the very next morning (we had to be back for our church commitments) and we passed you

again, this time you were coming down the pass. It was real. Our eyes did not deceive us. I can't wait to tell my husband I found your website. We are so proud of you. Go all the way! You are an inspiration. God is so good.

We had our 11-year-old son in the car with us and we have been talking to him about you since we saw you. We tell him he has no excuse to complain about any little thing that we ask of him (which he always thinks is too hard. We have been working so hard to help grow his character). We tell him, "If that man can ride a bike with one hand over Snoqualmie pass, then you can use the two hands that you have to put away dishes and the two legs that you have to do any other chores that we ask of you." He then says to us, "I know." He is probably going to wish that we hadn't seen what we did on Friday and Saturday, but we are glad we did.

Thank you for your courage to face this mountain pass and many more … our prayers will be with you all the way. Especially in Montana. Don't give up! Greater is the one who is in you than the one who is in the world! What a blessing for us to witness your courage. Silly us, how tired can we be after an 800 mile drive in 24 hours when you covered how many one-handed???!!! Thank you. Jen & Craig.

I replied and thanked them for their encouraging words. I apologized to their son for making his life harder. Poor kid.

We all got ready for bed, hollered, "Good night" to the Oesches through the closed door, and settled into our beds. I lay in bed but could not sleep. It was time for me to make an honest assessment of how Hope and Courage Across America was going. Along with the logistics, methods and mechanics of the trip, I had been paying close attention to everyone's comments and attitude. I could see their joy when we were spreading the message of Hope and Courage, getting encouraging emails, and meeting daily 'angels,' as Darla liked to call them. I could also sense the frustration at the struggles and delays that had nothing to do with pedaling a bike.

I closed my eyes but my mind saw right through my eyelids. A myriad of thoughts overpowered the weariness of my body.

Lord, help me to sort all this out.

As soon as the words left my heart I knew what I had been missing. I missed my dialog with God. I had been praying. I had been praying a lot. But it had become monologue prayers uttered in the face of need or a quick, "Thank You." I needed quiet time with Him. I used to get it on the long bike rides at home. My bike riding the last two weeks never gave me much quiet time. I was always pushing for miles and thinking about my next decision. I guess lying in my bed is as quiet as I can get right now.

Lord, You are in charge. What do I do?

I began to throw anything out of my thoughts that was not of God. I had learned decades ago to use this method to defeat worry. I mentally picture myself tossing subjects out of my head and locking the door behind them. I know it sounds hokey but it works. Before long, my mind was at peace. There were very few obstructions to crowd God's voice. My body relaxed and my breathing was slow and deep.

What did you expect to happen on this journey I am leading you on?

It's a non-audible voice that reassures me it is safe to talk here. I can speak openly and honestly without fear of judgment. Ironic, since I am speaking to the Judge of Judges.

What did I expect? Where do You want me to begin?
Begin wherever you want. I am in no hurry.

I start giving Him my list:

- We would pedal our bikes across America to draw
  attention to our message of hope in Christ and having
  the courage to do something with that hope.
- We would pedal about fifty miles a day. Darla, Grant
  and I would be the primary riders. Nicole would
  ride when she was with us. Chanel would ride
  when it was a good place to ride and Jeanne would
  take care of her when she wasn't riding with us.
- We would schedule churches to speak at each
  week along the route and take the time to interact
  with people we would meet along the way.
- We would give Bibles to people at
  churches and along the route.
- We would be examples of Hope and
  Courage while meeting others who were
  also examples of Hope and Courage.
- Jeanne would drive the truck and RV ahead of
  us and be waiting in the towns for us when we
  arrived. She could stir interest in the ride with
  the RV logos and her natural 'people skills.'
- We would do interviews with reporters
  about our journey and the message.

Oh, Lord, I wanted so much for this journey. This has been
on my heart for years. I can't even think of it all. Please help me
sort it out.

After a moment of silence, my mind is empty again. God does not use His non-audible voice this time. Instead, He guides me back through the list, letting me do the evaluation.

- We were pedaling our bikes across America and drawing attention to our message of hope in Christ and having the courage to do something with that hope. The interest and reaction people were giving to our ride and message was overwhelming at times. So, that is on track. Nothing major to adjust.
- Darla, Grant and I were the primary riders. Nicole has ridden nearly each mile, also. I know she is scheduled to go back home a few times. Chanel has ridden a little but she has been a great helper to Aunt Jeanne at camp. Jeanne was taking great care of her. Everything pretty much as expected.
- The two Sundays we had ministered in churches have gone amazingly well. We have had great interaction along the way.
- We have given Bibles to people at churches and along the route that really appreciated getting the Word.
- Hopefully we were being examples of Hope and Courage and we were meeting a few other examples of Hope and Courage. I would like to meet even more.
- Jeanne hadn't quite caught on to driving the truck with the RV yet. It was an intimidating rig to maneuver. I had let her try it on the freeway without any turns with me coaching her. She did well but not well enough to drive alone. She could drive the truck without the RV okay. At this point I was the only one driving the RV and that required a lot of

back tracking. Jeanne was great at stirring interest in the ride with the RV logos and her natural 'people skills.'

- And we were getting interviews with reporters about our journey and the message.

You know what, God? Things are actually going pretty good. We are accomplishing most of our goals and expectations. We are encountering mechanical, logistic, and equipment problems on a daily basis. We can deal with that stuff. The biggest issue is the lack of a designated driver. I have to accept the fact that with the team we have out here on the road, I am going to be the driver. How is all of that going to work?

You're no stranger to adapting, He reassures. *You will figure something out. Oh, and I think things are going pretty good, too. Now get some sleep.* The weariness of my body easily conquers my mind and I drift into slumber.

We awoke to a sunny day. Sunny days are nice. We would not be pedaling today. Everyone had tasks they had been putting off until Spokane and today was the day to start doing those tasks. Before we all headed in different directions I called a team meeting. I wanted to go over the last two weeks and make plans for the journey forward. I thanked them all and let them know everyone was doing a great job. And they were doing a great job.

Darla juggled her myriad of roles like a circus performer. She was a mother, wife, missionary, and cyclist rolled into one. I knew she was way out of her comfort zone most of the time. Darla likes things orderly, predictable and constant. I do not remember using any of those adjectives in the last two weeks. Or even in the last two months, really. I was proud of her.

Nicole was a vital part of the team. Being a week away from turning twenty, she didn't even have to come on this trip with us. She had a life, you know. She was in between her junior and senior years of college and engaged to Justin Jurgens, a young soldier from the town next to ours. Justin was currently in Iraq and they planned to marry a year after he got back. We appreciated her being with us. Nicole's nursing skills had already been used and she was writing much of our blogs.

Grant was becoming our team anchor. He rode alongside us every foot of the way. He was the bike tech on the road. He loaded and unloaded bikes into the truck and the RV. He was hooking up and unhooking the RV in camp. He would do his tasks in all kinds of weather and without grumbling. Not bad for a fifteen year old.

Chanel was truly our Ambassador of Happy. She would help us get started on our bikes, making sure we had drinks and snacks in our bags. She would be the first one to greet us at our stops. Sometimes she would have a bottle of water other times she would have ice cream bars. She would wait patiently in the truck for us to reach the pick-up points. She would fuss over us in the evening with special treats. Always with a smile. Chanel is truly a gifted ten year old.

Jeanne and Don were amazing. They both had the heart of a true servant. They always did what they were asked to do. And they never complained. And we were asking Jeanne to do quite a lot. Her primary job was to watch over Chanel while we were riding. We also needed her to be on call with the support truck, making calls to stops up ahead, monitoring things at camp and running errands. On top of that, she had to get used to living in an RV and camping all summer long. It wasn't easy taking care of this family of bike riders. We had already started calling her Aunt Bea in reference to "The Andy Griffith Show." She had a constant smile and a 'can do' attitude. I felt guilty asking so much of her but we truly needed her. I was glad Don had volunteered to start out with us. I could tell he helped Jeanne get accustomed to all these changes. I am sure there had to be times Jeanne needed his encouragement during some of these past weeks' trials.

Don also was a great help around camp. He had recently retired from thirty-plus years teaching elementary school. I watched him help Grant with the bikes and the RV. He would let Grant show him how to do things all day long. You see, Don is a great teacher. He knows students learn better when they think they are the teacher. I was reminded when I was Grant's age I worked summers for Don painting barns in Ohio. Don would set the scaffolding and ladders up for me to paint the peaks. I will confess that I was slightly apprehensive about heights. No, I was afraid of heights. All right, I was knee-knocking, body trembling scared of high places. And the peak of a barn is definitely a high place.

Don would comfort me by saying, "I don't know what you are worried about; that plank up there is twelve inches wide."

"Twelve inches wide? That is twelve inches thin. I can't walk on twelve inches," I replied.

Noticing the panic in my voice he calmly said, "When you are walking on the ground you don't use more than a twelve inch path."

Looking at my feet, I realized he was right. Twelve inches are plenty of room. I climbed onto the scaffolding and painted the peaks. For the record, I was still scared. It was good to see my son get some time working and learning with Don, also.

I thanked Don for all he had helped us with so far and told him I thought this was a good time to start making plans for him to head home. He and Jeanne were already scheduled to fly home at the end of the week. Their son, Robby, was getting married in August and there was a bridal shower for their future daughter-in-law, Marlo. We figured Don could stay home and Jeanne could fly back out to us. I wish I could have allowed Jeanne to stay home also but we could not get along without her.

I addressed the group, "After these first two weeks I realize we have to make some adjustments. First, I cannot expect Jeanne to drive the RV. It's a very big rig."

"If I had more time I might be able to get the hang of it," Jeanne volunteered. It killed her to think she could not do something we wanted her to do.

"You have other things we need you to spend your time doing," I reassured her.

Grant asks, "Can we get someone else to come drive?"

"Your mom and I went through the list before we left home. There is no one that would fit into our group. Besides, we have been crowding seven people into a six-passenger truck for two weeks and none of us wants to do that all summer. I will drive the truck when the RV is attached."

"How are you going to move the RV and ride your bike, too?" I recognized Darla's voice of logic and reason again.

"We'll just keep doing what we've been doing. We will move the RV, set camp, and then use the truck to shuttle back to where we left off. We then pedal toward the camp. After we reach the camp we spend a couple of days pedaling away from the camp before we have to move again."

"That is a lot of backtracking in the truck."

Grant brings up an idea. "Could we ride twenty miles away from camp, turn around and ride twenty miles back to camp and count it as forty miles? Or would that be cheating?"

"No, I don't think that would be cheating. We don't have a set of rules here. It is not what we intended to do but I think it would keep us true to our intent of riding across America. That is not a bad plan. We wouldn't have to drive the truck back and forth as much." Grant's suggestion was a good one and I was glad to have the input.

At the end of the meeting I wanted to make sure that regardless of which of us was leading this team we all knew who we were following. "Let's take a minute and pray."

"Lord, this is Your journey and we want to follow You. Help us to make the right decisions and guide us where You want us to be. Protect us all on the road ahead and thank You for bringing us safe this far. Amen."

I took Darla and the kids into Spokane for the day. We went to a bike shop. We had to get Chanel a new bike. I had destroyed her old one when I drove under the parkway in Moses Lake. It really was Grant's old bike that he outgrew. She got to pick out a white one with pretty butterfly decals. This one was truly hers. We also bought a bunch of tubes for the bike tires. I figured as long as Nicole was with us we would be getting flat tires. We went to the mall for haircuts.

Grant told the man, "Cut it short."

The man listened. Grant came out with his hair cut close and neat to his head. He looked like a real cyclist now.

Darla picked up household supplies. She spent the next few days organizing the RV. She had not had a chance to get us moved in yet. Getting things in their proper place made her feel more at ease. I took the truck into Spokane to replace the mirror that got knocked off on the freeway. While there, Nicole and I were able to share our message with the people waiting in the dealership. The mirror was fixed better than new and when the man handed me the bill I could not complain. I could not complain about the price of diesel going over four dollars a gallon, either. God had provided the money for fuel and repairs for our equipment on the first Sunday of our ride. *Thank You, God.* And thank you, Mike. Nicole and I had lunch with Nicole's college classmate's brother and his mother. He had been in an accident and needed a little hope and courage. We gave him a Journey Bible. All the hope and courage he needed was in those pages. The mom gave me homemade oatmeal cookies. Now we are talking blessings.

Pedaling out of Coeur d'Alene, we realized it would be a while before we saw Washington again. Interstate 90 was behind us and we headed north to connect with US Highway 2. US2 was going to be our friend for at least a month. By midweek, we were out of Idaho and setting up camp in Montana. Now we were not only out of our home state but we had a state between us and our home state. It really feels like were going across America. Thoughts of Gig Harbor are few and far between.

Our friend, John Diezsi, met up with us in Kalispell. John rode with us across Washington a few years ago. He had a break in his summer schedule and was able to ride with us for a few weeks. It was great to see him again. His cycling experience was helpful, and having the extra vehicle in camp came in handy, too. John arrived in time to help celebrate Nicole's twentieth birthday, spend some time with Don and Jeanne before they flew back for Marlo's bridal shower, and witness our next little bike spill.

John, Grant, Nicole, Darla and I were pedaling between Kalispell and Columbia Falls. About ten miles from reaching camp, it started to rain. We were too close to call the support truck and too far not to get wet. The road was great for cycling. It had a good smooth shoulder and the speed limit kept the traffic from throwing water on us. As we came through town we approached a railroad crossing. John pedaled ahead and waited at the tracks for the rest of us. John had more experience and knew those steel tracks could get very slippery when wet. The best way to approach them is to get your tires ninety degrees with the track. In other words, go straight across and not at an angle. As Nicole approached, John told her to go straight across, motioning the direction with his arm. Nicole straightened her wheels but did not get them straight enough. Her back wheel hit the slippery tracks and slid out from under her. She braced herself to cushion the fall as bike and rider hit the road. Grant saw what happened, straightened his wheels, and crossed easily. He stopped to assist Nicole off the ground. I crossed without a problem. That is another advantage of a three-wheel bike.

As Darla came to the tracks, her motherly instincts drew her attention to Nicole and she did not get her wheels straight. Her bike slid out from under her and she hit the road. Both girls were up right away and we checked them for injuries. They had scrapes on their hands and some extra mud on their pants but nothing that required bandages. We mounted our bikes and left with a greater respect for railroad tracks. I could not help but wonder if that was how John learned his lesson with tracks. When we got back to camp, Jeanne, Don and Chanel came out to greet us. When they saw me, they started laughing. I did not see what was so amusing.

"You should see the back of your jacket, neck and helmet. You're covered with mud!"

My two back wheels slant inward for stability. When I went through the muddy water, they both threw mud on my back. I was a mess. I had to hose off my bike, jacket, helmet, and head before getting off my bike. So much for the advantages of three wheels.

Support Team – Don and Jeanne Oesch

Chapter 13

Our next camp was in Columbia Falls, Montana. Columbia Falls is a small town near Glacier National Park. We were scheduled to speak at a community youth service at the Assembly of God Church on Friday night and then speak to their regular congregation on Sunday morning. Friday was also Darla's and my anniversary. We would have never imagined celebrating our twenty-seventh year of marriage in Montana while riding bikes across America. It is natural to reminisce on anniversaries. Darla's thoughts went back to our wedding day. She pictured the beautiful platform at the church with the flower-draped arch framing a white park bench. Darla wanted to sit down at my level during the ceremony. She recalled all the attendants and guests who shared the day with us. All I can remember is the beautiful young lady in that amazing white dress sitting next to me. However, my anniversary thoughts drifted a little further back than the wedding. My mind went to the first day I met Darla.

It was four years after I lost my limbs. And yes, I know, I haven't quite finished that story yet. Being our wedding anniversary, this is a good time to tell you a love story, a story about true love. A story about Darla, a young lady who was able to meet me and not even notice what most people can't take their eyes off of. As I said, it was four years after I lost my legs and arm. I was sitting at home minding my own business when the phone rang.

"Hello."

"Bob," it was my sister, Jeanne. "I've got a favor to ask you. Darla, our babysitter, is watching Jenny and Robby tonight and we didn't make plans for their dinner. Could you pick up some chicken and bring it over to the house?"

This was a setup by my older sister. It had to be a setup. I lived over an hour away from Puyallup, where Jeanne lived. She wanted me to meet this babysitter. I had seen this babysitter from a distance and frankly, driving an hour to meet the babysitter was not a bad idea. Now, before anyone gets any funny ideas here, let me explain something. This babysitter was a nineteen-year-old college student. I was a twenty-five-year-old young man. This was not a thirteen-year-old neighbor girl from down the street. This is well within the parameters of social decency. This babysitter used to be a teacher's assistant for Jeanne's husband, Don. They always said she was the only non-family member they would consider to watch their kids.

I said, "Sure, I can run some chicken over there."

I got in my van and headed for the fried chicken drive-thru closest to Jeanne's house. I pulled into my sister's driveway and parked the van. I got out of the driver's seat onto the floor of the van, opened the sliding side door, lowered my wheelchair out of the van, climbed into the wheelchair, balanced the bucket of chicken on my chair, and rolled toward the front door. If I told you I was not nervous I would be lying. I straightened myself up and rang the doorbell, ding-dong, and waited. The door opened and there she stood, five foot ten and three quarters, blonde hair, and hazel eyes. I was head-over-wheels in love.

I knew from the first time I saw Darla that she was going to be my wife. If you have a hard time believing that I would stand a chance with a girl as wonderful as Darla, you are not alone. Darla, even to this day, doubts me when I say I knew from the start that she would be my wife. However, I need to remind you of a few character flaws I confessed to you earlier in this book. I have a tendency to be overly optimistic, impulsive, and I have a difficult time identifying the impossible. And in my own defense I can't help but point out ... Darla did become my wife.

Let's get back to this introduction. I bent my neck backwards to look into those beautiful hazel eyes. This was a critical moment. This was 'first impression' time.

I opened my mouth and said, "Hello. I'm Jeanne's brother. I brought chicken."

'Hello, I'm Jeanne's brother. I brought chicken' is the best I can do? Why didn't I at least say my name? So much for being cool. Before I could embarrass myself further, my niece, Jenny, came to the door.

"Darla, this is Uncle Bob. Uncle Bob this is Darla. Come in and have chicken with us."

I cannot believe I was just rescued by a two year old. I found myself sitting at the table across from Darla eating chicken. I was trying to remember all of my social graces: chew with my mouth closed, use my napkin, and do not stare. But I can't help but stare. She is beautiful. The meal ended way too soon. Jeanne had left a project to do while the kids were asleep. Their annual Christmas letter needed to be folded and inserted into envelopes.

Looking for a reason to stay, I pointed to the stack of letters, "I can help you fold and stuff those."

Not wanting to question my ability to fold with only one hand, Darla politely accepted the offer. We sat at the table and folded paper. I quickly found my technique to do a neat tri-fold on the paper then slide it into the envelope and reach for the next. I am not going to take the time to describe how I did it. If you have two hands, you do not need to know. If you have only one hand, I am sure you have already figured out how to fold paper. We made small talk as I watched the stack of papers get smaller. I began to get worried.

When this job ends, I will need to leave and I may not get a chance to sit across the table from Darla again. I need to do something. I need courage. And I need it quick.

I looked into those hazel eyes and I was lost. I took a deep breath and said, "Would you like to go to dinner with me?"

Darla said, "Yes."

Yes? She said 'Yes!' Now I am going to tell you young ladies something about us guys that the young guys around you won't tell you. When we ask you that question, "Will you go out with me?" we don't expect you to say 'Yes.' We expect you to say 'No.' We are ready for 'No.' We've rehearsed at least three scripts in our minds on how to respond to you after you have rejected us so we can leave the room with a little bit of our dignity intact. We are not ready for 'Yes.' 'Yes' throws us off.

Darla said, "Yes."

"Yes? Oh, I mean of course, 'Yes.' Dinner, uh, how about Thursday? Thursday good for you? Thursday is great for me. Do you eat dinner?" *Of course, she eats dinner.* "I can pick you up at seven. If that is good for you. Any time is good for me. Seven is good for you? Great! We have a date."

I could not believe it. I had a date with Darla Hollis, Thursday night, at seven for dinner.

Thursday night arrived. Darla lived with her mother in the town next to Puyallup. I pulled my van into her driveway and immediately noticed the steps going up to her front door. Not good. It is not impossible for me to negotiate steps unassisted.

It is just a little messy for my clothes. I would need to roll to the steps, get out of my chair onto the ground, climb the steps on my stumps, pull my chair up behind me, and climb back into my chair. As I said, not impossible, it is just a little messy. I was dressed to take Darla out to dinner and did not want to scoot around on the ground. I looked once more at the steps and made a decision. I did something that I do not recommend any young man ever do on a date. I honked the horn. Fortunately, Darla (and her mother) were aware of the extenuating circumstances. Darla came out of the house and I leaned across the van and opened the van door for her. She looked just as beautiful as she did the day I met her.

We went to a nice restaurant to enjoy dinner and talk. I chose the Quarterdeck, a nice steak/seafood place with a good reputation. Entering the restaurant Darla had her first encounter with something she would deal with for the rest of her life. People stared at me. Not the discreet glance-when-you-think-you-won't-get-caught kind of staring. The uninhibited 'look at that man with no legs and one arm' kind of staring. This was new to Darla and it bothered her. It wasn't that it made her embarrassed to be seen with me. No, it was not that it all. It bothered her that people would be so rude. Now I had already come to terms with this staring and did not consider it rude. It was just people reacting to something they did not see every day. There are not a great number of people in America with both legs and one arm amputated. Honestly, when I see a person like that I look pretty closely, too. However, this was Darla's first encounter with staring and it offended her. I counted that as a good thing.

We browsed through the menu. I knew I wanted a steak. I am a meat and potatoes kind of guy and at this stage of my life I wasn't really that interested in the potatoes. I suggested the salmon for Darla. She likes salmon but she was more excited about the baked potato and salad bar that accompanied the fish. Our waitress came and I gave her our order. She was a good waitress. She treated me as if she would treat any other young man on a date with the most beautiful girl in the world. She spoke to me directly. (We have had occasions when the waitperson looks at Darla and says, "And what would he like?" That does not cultivate generous tipping.) Our waitress said we could help ourselves to the salad bar.

Darla looked over toward the delicious array of lettuce, vegetables, cheese, and toppings. "Would you like to go to the salad bar?" she asked politely.

"No, I don't think I would like any salad."

"I guess I won't have any either."

I was so clueless. There was no way Darla was going to go over to the salad bar if I did not go. I should have escorted her. Then, to make matters worse, when our meals came I did not eat my baked potato. Darla did not want to seem as if she ate more than I did so she barely touched her potato. Don't even ask about dessert. I didn't want dessert. I know now it is her favorite part of the meal. Poor girl, I knew nothing about going out to dinner. I am so glad that was the last first date of my life.

Well, fortunately, we did not just come to eat, we also came to talk. Conversation with Darla was easy. She has a gift of being a compassionate listener. She can sit with a person and let them talk while being truly interested in what they have to say. That is a gift. Our conversation was mostly around topics that helped us to get to know each other. We had a few things in common. She was the youngest of seven children. I was next to the youngest of seven. Darla's dad passed away from a heart attack when she was just turning fifteen. My dad died when I was sixteen. We both had moved to Washington when we were young. And we both still lived with our mothers. That last one actually sounded better when she said it than when I said it. We continued our chit-chat through the meal and lingered awhile at the table.

We left the restaurant and drove back toward her house. I looked at her in the passenger seat next to me. It was apparent to me that her beauty did not come solely from her appearance. Not that she was not physically beautiful. No, she was all of that. But there was more. Her beauty radiated from deep inside. Darla was a Christian. I knew she was a Christian when I asked her out. I don't know how I knew, I just knew. Moreover, I did not want her to talk about it. This was not about that 'God' stuff. This was about dinner and conversation. We were on our way home and I had made it through the evening without having to talk about Jesus. That is why what happened next is still baffling to me today.

I turned to Darla and said, "So, you go to church don't you?"

As soon as I said it I thought to myself, *What am I doing? I was almost home free. She didn't mention Jesus. Why am I bringing up this God stuff?*

"Yes, I go to church. I've been going to church all my life."

"So, what religion are you?"

"I go to an Assembly of God church but I don't really think of it as a religion. It is more like a relationship with Jesus. If you're interested you can go to church with me sometime."

I had better stop this conversation before it gets out of hand. "Thank you for the invitation. I'll have to do that someday."

I pulled the van into the driveway. We both acknowledged it was a fun evening and said our goodbyes. Darla went into the house and I drove back to Hoquiam. I called her six weeks later. What? Too soon? Should I have waited longer? Before you answer let me give a little more background. At this point in my life, I was not a model citizen. I had slipped into a pattern of drinking and drugging for my social life. I did not have any constructive plans for my future. I was spiritually lost and adrift.

Darla, on the other hand, was top-drawer. I had never met a girl like Darla. I did not have the right to go out with her the first time, let alone go out with her again. It took me six weeks to get enough nerve to call her. It took me two days of sobriety to be ready to actually go out with her again. But we did go out. This time we went to a boat show. Next time it only took me five weeks and we went to the zoo. Then three weeks. We soon became comfortable seeing each other occasionally and talking on the phone.

Summer came and Darla took a trip to Kansas to see her dad's siblings. Family heritage is very important to her. She had finished a year at Northwest Christian College and was beginning to wonder what to do next year. A trip back to the roots of her family tree might help her decide which direction to spread her branch. Her aunts and uncles were so glad to have Ralph's youngest child visit them. She was a sweet reminder of their brother who had passed away five years earlier. In the meantime, I moved to Cottage Grove, Oregon, with my brothers and younger sister. I thought it would be nice to get out from under the clouds of Hoquiam. Driving south on I-5 to my new home I knew it was not the rain I would miss most. It was that girl visiting her relatives in Kansas. I was hoping she was missing me, too.

Darla came home and began working at her church's daycare and Christian school. I began to schedule trips north to coordinate with her free time. I really enjoyed talking to her. Darla is a person in my life, and I hope all of you can find a person like this, who has a mirror-like effect on me. When I look at Darla, it makes me look at myself. When I look at myself, I don't always like everything I see. Especially during the fall of 1980, I knew there were things I needed to change. I would ask Darla about her summer, her work and her Jesus. The conversation would often end with an invitation to go to church.

Finally, there came the time I said, "Yes. I would like to go to church. What time do I pick you up?"

I followed Darla into the church and followed Jesus out. But I don't want to tell the details of that part of my journey yet. I will save that for later.

After I started following Jesus, my life began to change. One of the changes was that I quit drinking and drugs. Another change was in my relationship with Darla. I told you I knew Darla was going to be my wife the first time I met her. Darla did not really feel that way. And even though we were spending time together on dates and talking, she kept me at arm's length. At five foot ten and three quarters, Darla had long arms. She was not going to allow herself to be emotionally tangled with a non-Christian. She knew the Bible taught it was not good to be unequally yoked.

Unequally yoked is one of those illustrations used in the Bible that usually needs explaining in our modern world. But in Bible times everyone knew if you put two oxen that were not equally matched in the same yoke they could not plow a straight line. They would waste their time going in circles. Modern counselors will tell you couples that are not equally matched in their beliefs waste a lot of time going in circles, too. After I had become a Christian, I sensed Darla's arms were getting shorter. I was sure she was loosening the strings of her heart. This brings me to the saddest day of my life. Would you like to hear about it? No, the day I touched the power line was not the saddest day of my life. There are more painful things in life than being electrocuted.

I had been visiting Darla and was getting ready to make the five-hour drive back home to Cottage Grove. We had gone out to the driveway and I transferred onto the floor of the van. Darla sat down next to me. In a minute, we would say 'goodbye' and

I would head home. I looked toward her face and was immediately drawn to her hazel eyes. I was hopelessly captured.

I took a deep breath and said, "I love you."

And I waited.

And I waited.

The silence hung in the air. Seconds ticked away but they seemed like full minutes.

And I waited.

It became awkward. Very, very awkward.

"Oh, my! Look at the time. I have a long drive ahead and it's getting late. I really should be going. I'll call you. Bye!"

She got up, did not say a word, and went into the house.

I pulled my wheelchair into the van, swung myself into the driver's seat, drove out to the interstate, and took the longest five-hour drive of my life. Five hours! Five hours gives you a lot of time to think about things, doesn't it guys? What happened back there? And ladies, stay out of this. Don't try to tell me what happened. I was there, I know exactly what happened. I took my tender young heart, put it in my hand, and extended it to her. And she slapped it out of my hand and stomped it in the dirt! C'mon! I said 'I love you' and she's supposed to say it back to me. "I love you … you love me." We all know that song. Why didn't she say it to me?

Five-hour drive.

Oh, I know why she didn't say it. It's the alcohol and drug thing. I had only been clean for several weeks. Several weeks seems like nothing to a person who has never been trapped by that kind of stuff. Who wants to tie their heart to someone who allows alcohol and drugs to control their life? I could go back on drugs any time. Who can blame Darla for not wanting to risk that? Yeah, that makes sense.

Five-hour drive.

I bet it's not the drugs. She thinks that my following Christ was just a dating trick. Some guys will do that kind of thing, you know. They will find out who you want them to be and then they will pretend to be that as long as it gets them closer to you. When they are not with you, they will go back to being who they want to be. Don't worry, young ladies, not the guys you're dating. Other guys. Maybe Darla thinks this whole 'Christian' thing is just a trick so she'll let me get closer to her. Yeah, that's got to be it.

Five-hour drive.

No, no, wait a minute, Bob. Wake up and smell the latte. It's the amputations. It's the missing legs and the missing arm. I'll be honest with you, folks. At this time in my life, I don't know if I could have dated a person missing three limbs. And I am one. Here I am asking the most beautiful person I have ever met to not just date me but to love me. Who could blame her for not saying 'I love you'? Yeah, that is definitely it.

The five-hour drive ended.

I parked my van and went into the house satisfied I had it all figured out. The only problem was that I was wrong. Not just a little wrong. I was completely wrong on all three counts. It was not the drugs. I had been clean for several weeks. I have now been clean for a few decades. I am getting the hang of this drug-free life. It was not that she doubted the sincerity of my relationship with Christ. She was there that morning and saw the change that came over my life. And whether Darla was going to be a part of my life or not would have no effect on my relationship with Jesus. It was, is, and will be forever real.

It was not the missing limbs, either. If you have read this far, you have already figured out something I was about to learn. Darla is smarter than I am. Darla knows that you do not fall in love with looks. You do not fall in love with bodies, abs and curves. I know that is hard concept for you teenagers to grasp when you are standing in the lunchroom and 'you know who' walks by. All of a sudden your heart beats faster and all you can think is 'I'm in love.' Well, that has more to do with biology than love. Darla knows you do not fall in love with looks, money, cars or fame. Those are temporary things. Looks fade, money is spent, cars rust and fame passes. You don't believe me? Have you seen your oldest living relative lately? The only thing that is keeping you from looking very much like them is time. If you are the oldest living relative, please accept my apologies. But let's be honest, we don't look like we did when we were nineteen.

If you fall in love with temporary things, what do you think is going to happen to your love when those things begin to fade? Your love is going to fade. I roll past couples every day whose love is fading because the thing they based their love on is showing its age. Darla is smarter than that. Darla knows that you fall in love with a person's essence … that part of them that is eternal. You fall in love with their soul. Your soul will last an eternity. If you base your love on that part of a person that lasts an eternity, how long do you think your love can last? An eternity. Darla knows this.

Darla knows something else, too, girls. Darla knows you do not have to say 'I love you' to every young man that says 'I love you' to you. It is not like 'Have a nice day.' It is 'I – love – you.' Only you. Always you. Those words, when shared between a man and a woman, do not become more precious by sharing them with more people. They are sweetest when saved for that one person God has already selected for you. Darla had made that decision long before she met a young man named Bob.

The next day I finally got up the nerve to call her. I nervously waited for her to answer the phone.

The first thing she said was, "I love you, too."

And do you know what? I have never doubted those words from Darla. You see, she did not say it when I was leaving and would not see her for 'I don't know how long.' She did not say it when everything was warm and fuzzy and I pipe up and say 'I love you.' She walked right out of that situation. She needed to think about her response. She knew the power of those words. She knew the promise of those words. As I said, Darla is smarter than I am. I have never been so happy to be so wrong in all my life.

It was not long before I was asking Myrtle Hollis if I could marry her youngest daughter, Darla. On Valentine's Day, I took Darla to dinner. I ordered steak, she ordered salmon. I escorted her to the salad bar and ate all of my baked potato. I had come a long way since that first date. After dessert, I opened a small box and removed a ring. Taking her hand, I looked into those hazel eyes. I was hopelessly captured again. I took a deep breath.

"Darla Yvonne Hollis, will you be my wife forever?"

And I waited.

But Darla didn't.

"Yes," she replied.

I wonder if she would have answered so quickly if she knew twenty-seven years later she would be riding a bicycle across America ...

Bob and Darla
June 6, 1981

Chapter 14

Montana is a very big state. A very, very big state. No offense, Alaska and Texas, but you are not on our route across America (this time). We had two scheduled stops in Montana. The first was the weekend in Columbia Falls. The other stop was for Sunday services at the Assembly of God church in Havre. (Pronounced hav 'er.) One week, 300 miles, and a very large mountain range separated the two stops. Did I mention that Montana means 'land of mountains'?

I am going to let our daughter, Nicole, tell you about some of our adventures in Montana. At the start of the journey, we asked Nicole to write our blog. If you are not familiar with the term 'blog,' that is okay. I did not know what it meant until we started planning Hope and Courage Across America. 'Blog' is a shortened version of the two words 'Web' and 'log.' If you cannot imagine the words 'web' and 'log' together you probably do not have a computer. We had set up a website, www.hcjourney.org, to let people track our ride. The web log is a journal of our ride published on our website. A blog. Nicole wrote much of our blog. She is a great writer and you will enjoy reading her reports.

▶ **Surprising Sisters and Snowstorms**

June 10

Hello from the snow. As always, much has happened since my last posting. Our week got off to a great start on Sunday with Dad preaching at the Assembly of God church in Columbia Falls, Montana. In addition to the message garnering several salvations, we had some special people show up in the congregation. First were Pastor Dave and Bev Tonn, who live two hours away and preach frequently at the church. Their history is deep-rooted in our family – he was the pastor at the church Mom attended in middle and high school, preached the message under which Dad accepted Christ, performed my parents' wedding, and dedicated me as a baby. Then, as a super extra surprise, they walked into the sanctuary followed by my Aunt Betty and Uncle Dave (Mom's sister and brother-in-law). They live in Washington but drove all the way to Montana to visit the Tonns (the two couples are long-time close friends) and to check in on us. You should have seen Mom's face when she saw her sister! We were able to go out to lunch with both couples and Aunt Betty presented us with a box of delish homemade goodies (which are gone by now, of course). Also on Sunday, we met Christina Quick, a reporter from the Pentecostal Evangel who interviewed and photographed us for a September issue of the magazine. The interview went well and we all enjoyed fellowshipping with Christina.

Since Sunday things have gone, well, less lovely than we had hoped. In an unusual twist of nature, we found

ourselves stuck in a rain/hail/snow/thunder/lightning/
wind storm. We were set to cross Marias Pass, but after
careful weather monitoring and decision-making, we
opted to drive across the pass before the worst of the
storm arrived. The risk of getting stuck or injured was
just too great; there is a big difference between being
courageous and being stupid. We had hoped that once
we got over the pass the weather would clear up and
we could continue with our ride. Unfortunately, that
was not the case. The bad weather continued and has
prevented us from doing any riding thus far. And even
though we have not been riding, we were not without
injury – several team members got hit with marble-
sized pieces of hail (I was not one of the victims, but
from their shrieks and reports I can conclude that they
hurt a lot). And just to add a little more adventure to
the situation, Grant passed out yesterday. He had been
out working on unhooking the fifth-wheel in the snow
and without proper clothing (we did not plan for snow
in June!). He has poor circulation so his heart was so
focused on keeping his body warm that it could not
pump enough blood to his head. He went bradycardic
(which for you non-healthcare professionals means a
slow heart rate), passed out gracefully against a wall in
the fifth-wheel, slid to the floor, and was unresponsive
for fifteen to thirty seconds. He then awoke and got
warmed up. And in his true hard-working spirit, was
back outside finishing his job within a few minutes. He
is a huge asset to our team and I know we could not be
out here without him. Oh, and I've been keeping my
eye on him and he's doing just fine now.

And so now we are in Shelby, Montana, sitting in our fifth-wheel watching the weather rear its ugly head and wondering if we will be able to cycle at all today. I will be honest here – we are all starting to feel very discouraged and tense. In many ways, we feel as though we should just "power through" and ride despite the elements, but our common sense is telling us to hold back. Still, it is hard to not be doing what we set out to accomplish. We feel beaten, defeated. And though we know the storm will pass, it's hard to just sit in it. Please pray for us as we are all starting to get a bit upset and on edge from all the waiting. Thank you.

Hopefully my next entry will be from a warmer climate and we will have put some cycling miles behind us. Until then, we will sit here in the snow. In June. Sigh. God must have a sense of humor. Or He is trying to teach us patience …

Cheers, Nicole

Grant trying to stay ahead of the snow.

Did you like her blog? We'll get back to it in a minute. Grant's fainting was a scary moment for all of us, especially for Darla. I will not pretend to know the feelings and concerns a mother has for her children. I am a father not a mother. I can tell you that Darla, as a mother, constantly has the safety of her children at the top of her awareness. And for the sake of this discussion, the definition of 'children' has nothing to do with age. You are your mother's child forever. We thanked God for Grant's quick recovery but realized the severity of the weather we faced. I sent this note to everyone on our email list:

"It is snowing today. We are in Columbia Falls, Montana, with a mountain between us and our next scheduled ministry. I am fighting discouragement as we fold camp and get ready to drive over the pass before we get stuck on this side. Montana was the one state I struggled with the most while planning the route. It is a very beautiful state but the unusual June weather is daunting.

"I feel bad that we are driving through what we wanted to pedal through. I am trying to come to terms with that decision. I feel as though we are letting all of you down.

"On the positive side, all of the ministry along the journey has been better than expected. We have seen a dozen salvations and many, many people blessed by the message of Hope and Courage. Our daily encounters with individuals are equally powerful. We have been blessed as well as being a blessing. I have said from the start, 'It's not about the miles, it's about the message.' I guess this is where I need to face that statement.

"Please pray for us today. I am watching road conditions carefully. It is a fifty-mile drive to the summit. I will be cautious and prudent in my decisions but could sure use a lot of God today. – Bob."

We were immediately flooded with emails of encouragement. The common theme was "You're right, it's not about the miles;

it's about the message. Keep moving forward any way you can." I needed to hear that. Now back to Nicole.

▶ Welcome to America, Part 1

June 20

Greetings, faithful blog-readers. I am very excited about this blog because it is the last time I will write from Montana. Yea! (Montanans: Please do not take offense; Montana is a beautiful state but is very long. Especially when you are pedaling.) Anyway, much has happened since the last blog. For one, we are not facing snow anymore! Instead, we are beginning to experience the heat of summer. And with the heat come the bugs. So we are all now sporting some pretty attractive tan/burn lines and bug bite welts. Especially Grant who has so many bug bites on his legs he slightly resembles a leper.

The past week has brought forth a multitude of enjoyable and interesting encounters with people all throughout Montana. On Sunday, we did two great services at the Assembly of God church in Havre. There were three salvations and many people pledged to pray for us. After the service, we were treated to a palate-pleasing meal graciously provided by the women of the church. We spent the afternoon celebrating Father's Day and joined the pastor and his wife for ice cream in the evening. A few spoonfuls into our sundaes, two women pulled into the parking lot and quickly made their way over to us. One of the women, Carol, introduced herself to us as the "one-legged woman with the three-legged dog." The other woman was her support person. They both proclaimed over and over again how happy they were to have found us. They then informed us that Carol is on an extensive prayer walk around the perimeter of the United States and is currently heading west along our route. Turns out, they were staying in Havre, heard we would be at the Assembly of God church, and really wanted to come listen to Dad. Unfortunately, though, there was a miscommunication and they thought we would be doing an evening service at the church. After arriving to an empty church, they unsuccessfully drove around the town in hopes of finding us. Finally, in their discouragement, they decided to just go get some ice cream instead, to lift their spirits. And there we were right in front of the ice cream shop! We were all able to share our stories and encouragement in a more private, friendlier setting. Once again proving that God's timing is always best.

On Monday, we pedaled out of Havre and headed toward Harlem. On route, we noticed a car pull over and a man step out. As we got closer, we realized it was none other than Daryl – a man we met while at the Columbia Falls Assembly of God church. The funny thing, though, is that we ran into him multiple times while staying in Columbia Falls (he was the one who led Grant, Chanel, and I in singing "Happy Birthday" to a grocery store clerk), so it didn't seem that surprising to bump into him once more. He said he had been hoping he would "find those turkeys sooner or later," and he prayed for us on the side of the road.

A few hours later, we stopped for lunch in Chinook. We were trying to find a sandwich shop so Aunt Jeanne asked a local if there was a Subway in town. He said no, but they had a train. She further explained that we were looking for the sandwich place to which he replied, "No, ma'am, we don't have none of that fast-food type stuff here in Chinook." So instead we grabbed hamburger hotdogs (hamburger meat in the shape of sausages and served in hot dog buns) from a small ice cream shop, The Creamery. We were served by a very friendly woman and her eleven-year-old daughter. They brought our food out to the fifth-wheel (which they graciously permitted us to park on their property) and even came inside to chat with us awhile. As we were enjoying our unique hamburger hotdogs, John noticed a police officer approaching the door. At first, we thought perhaps we were violating something by where we were parking our fifth-wheel, but the woman then informed us that the police officer was her husband. He, too, came in the fifth-wheel to hear about our journey. He told us about life as chief of police for such a small town. He said he rounds up a lot of cattle and that when he gets a call about something, nine times out of ten he already knows who was involved, he just has to find a way to prove it. He also confessed that his deputy looks a bit like Barney Fife (for those of you too deprived to recognize who that is, he's a character from the old "Andy Griffith Show").

The chief of police then asked where we were hoping to spend the night. We said we were planning to make it to Harlem. He told us there weren't any RV parks that he knew of, but he was sure we could park our fifth-wheel outside of the Harlem Police Station. We thanked him for the tip and he went on his way – probably to round up more cattle. Ten minutes later, though, he was back. He told us he called the deputy in Harlem and everything had been okayed for us to park our fifth-wheel outside the police station. The deputy even said he'd leave the station unlocked so we could have access to the restrooms and showers!

When we arrived in Harlem, we began to set the fifth-wheel up for our night at the police station. We were not alone, though. First we were approached by a clearly inebriated man who told us he was so inspired by us, gave us a bottle of bug spray, and invited us to come to his home for a shower or a warm meal. We gladly accepted the bug spray and politely declined the shower and meal. He then proceeded to tell us all about how he was an ex-monk and an ex-Navy Seal, how his mother holds the record for killing the most mosquitoes in one swat (twenty-seven), and something about buffalo suicide that I really could not follow. He proved to be harmless and entertaining (a modern day "Otis" for all of you "Andy Griffith Show" fans out there).

After "Otis" left, we were greeted by two incredible women, Carol and Jean, who were going to spend the night on benches within the police station. They, too, were cycling across America on a route similar to ours (they were doing it without a support vehicle or crew, though). We were all really happy to see them because when we were driving over Marias Pass, we actually saw them pedaling over the pass and were hoping to run into them somewhere along our route. Any ladies that could pedal over that pass in the snow had earned our respect. We invited them into our fifth-wheel for some fellowship and snacks and to get away from the heat and bugs. They were both Christians and very interested in our ride. We had such a great time swapping stories from the road and it was a real encouragement for all of us to see that we are not alone out here. If you remember, please pray for Carol and Jean and the walking Carol as they, too, continue their journeys.

What a wonderful past couple of days it has been! We have all really been blessed by the people we have run into along the way. Ultimately, we are out here to encourage and be encouraged by people and to be able to define our country on our own terms from our own perspective. I would definitely say we have accomplished this in the past few days. There are more encounters I want to share, but will save them for the next blog as this one is already quite lengthy. In fact, I applaud you if you actually read it thus far!

Cheers, Nicole

► **Welcome to America, Part 2**

June 20

Hi again. Well, I just finished writing the last blog so I'm going to make an attempt to get this one pumped out before my writing inspiration leaves me. So let's see, I left you with us at the police station. We packed up that morning and ate breakfast at a local diner with Carol and Jean. While chatting, we discovered that the waitress was an Assemblies of God minister. Later in the conversation, she mentioned she homeschools her children. Mom said we did, too. To that the waitress replied that she could tell … that there was just something different about Grant, Chanel and me. I'm not entirely sure if that was a good thing, but I like to go with the belief that there is nothing worse than normalcy so we took it as a compliment.

We rode as long and as hard as the heat and bugs would allow us that day. Along the way, we encountered a zoo-full of animals. Some of the interesting ones include a live turtle (that I was extremely tempted to pick up), a dead owl, frolicking ponies, three dogs that started to chase Mom and me but luckily turned back after a bit, two dead and one live rattlesnake (they were big – at least a yard in length and an inch and half in diameter), and another hundred or so dead prairie dogs/gophers (we aren't exactly sure what they are, but the locals tell us they are shipped to Japan as pets). Seeing those huge rattlesnakes was a real wake-up call for all of us (especially Grant who accidentally pedaled over both dead ones), so we are using more caution on the road and I read up on how to use our rattlesnake venom-extractor kit. But I'm praying I never have to use it because, frankly, slicing open and suctioning a family member's skin is not high on my list of fun things to do.

Yesterday was a really good day of riding. We were able to get sixty miles in before it got too hot. And we had more fun encounters with people along those miles than any other sixty-mile stretch. First, during a short water break, a Native American man (we were on a reservation) stopped his truck to see if we were okay and if we needed any water. As he drove away, the three beautiful little Native American girls in the back of the old pickup waved like princesses and shouted "good luck." Dad described it as resembling a shot out of Life magazine. I agree.

The second encounter was one that even the most skilled writer could not fully describe, but I will make a feeble attempt and try my best. We had stopped for a water break along Highway 2 when a minivan pulled up beside us. The driver leaned over a bundled up passenger and asked if we were okay. We said we were and that we were cycling across America. This excited her as she began to ask us more questions and revealed an accent (she was from Germany). After a few minutes chatting in the middle of the road, she parked her van and came out to talk to us. Her name was Helga and she was on a road trip from New York (where she serves as a nanny/surrogate grandmother to two children) to Washington and back. We asked about her travels and she pulled out a large scarf with a printed map of the United States. On it she had stitched the routes of all her many road trips. This woman got around! We joked that she should join us on our ride. She replied, "Oh no! I'm seventy-six! I don't know how much more time I have left and I have so much to do and see. I do not have time to ride a bike. I must hurry!" What's more is that she makes all of these trips while living out of her minivan. If that's not an example of courage, I don't know what is! Oh, and the passenger? It was a bust of Mark Twain attached to the headrest and covered with blankets. She said they have shared many engaging conversations along the way. She told us life is what you make it. And I'd say she makes hers fun, something we should all do a little more frequently.

Helga and her hand-stitched map of her journeys.

We took our last stop at a gas station in Wolf Point. And somehow the whole town (where we had never been before nor did we have any contacts in) seemed to be expecting us and know of our journey. People came out of the gas station and nearby shops to ask us how we were doing and to confirm that we had left that morning from Glasgow (which we had). Someone asked us how much longer until we reached New York. A woman from the gas station brought us out a handful of pens with the town's name on them, because she wanted us to remember our stop in Wolf Point. A little girl rode into the gas station on a bike with her mother and pointed to us, yelling

"Look, Mama! The cyclists have made it! The riders are here!" Soon another half dozen or so Native American children approached us on bikes to meet us and ask questions. One even convinced Dad to flex his bicep, which produced a great round of "oohs" and "ahhs." We gave Hope and Courage buttons to them all and they proudly posed for pictures. We rode out of Wolf Point shaking our heads with perplexity, but filled with encouragement.

Today was relatively uneventful. We ran into Jean and Carol again and chatted for a few minutes. We also made it into North Dakota, which we all felt was a long time coming. I will be leaving tomorrow to Wisconsin for a wedding of a dear friend of mine. Even better is that my fiancé (Justin) will meet me there to begin his two-week leave from Iraq. To say I am happy and anxious would be the understatement of the year. If anything major (whether good or bad) happens while I'm gone, Dad will blog about it. Otherwise, I will write up their reports on Wednesday when Justin and I meet up with my family to spend a few days on the road. Oh, and please pray they don't have any medical emergencies while I'm gone!

Cheers, Nicole

Chapter 15

I won't miss the June snowstorms of Montana, Marias Pass or the mosquitoes and gnats of Montana. I will miss the beauty of Montana, the people of Montana and the wide open roads of Montana. I will even miss the rattlesnakes ... a little. Of course, I didn't really have to worry about rattlesnakes. I had an Early Snake Warning System with me at all times. Her name is Darla. As long as Darla was riding in front of me, I knew where the rattlesnakes were. I would hear a loud, high-pitched scream, "SNA-A-A-AKE!" and figure there was a snake up ahead somewhere. I also knew that rattlesnakes are not an aggressive creature toward humans, they are defensive. And that means a rattlesnake is not going to stalk a person. They will strike at a person if they feel the person is a threat to them. And they will usually give you a warning that you are making them feel threatened.

This was a lesson learned pedaling on the eastern slopes of Montana. We stopped our bikes for water and snacks along Highway 2. It was our practice to stop every ten miles and get refreshed. We pulled off the road into the grass to catch our breath. I could give my hand and arm a break from the constant cranking. It gave the other riders a chance to stretch their legs and get off the bike seat. I sat on my bike as Darla and the kids milled around. I was admiring the beauty of where God had brought us. Eastern Montana is truly one of the beautiful places on our planet. The rivers and streams meander through the rangeland in a way that brings to life every Zane Grey novel I ever read. Sitting off the highway my dreams of the wild west were interrupted by a strange sound. Ch-ch-ch-cht. Ch-ch-ch-cht.

What is that? I thought, *a raspy buzz. No that's not the way to describe it.* Ch-ch-ch-cht. Ch-ch-ch-cht. *There it is again. Like a large grasshopper flying. No, that's not it, either.* Ch-ch-ch-cht. Ch-ch-ch-cht. *More like a rattle. Yeah, that's it. It sounds like a rattle. A rattle? Wait a minute! That's a rattlesnake and we are close enough to make it nervous ...*

"Everybody out of the grass and get your bikes on the road!" Hustling out of the grass and onto the road they all stared at me.

"New rule," I explained. "This is just for eastern Montana. When you stop for a break do not stand in the grass. Stand in the road. We have less of a chance getting hit by a car in the road than we do getting bit by a rattler in the grass in eastern Montana."

After Montana we entered North Dakota. North Dakota is one of the flattest states in the union. I love it. We had two scheduled stops here, Minot and Williston. I had been to Minot before. I had spoken in their schools and churches a few times. The local Youth for Christ director had worked with me in the past and was very helpful in arranging churches to host us on our journey. The first stop we had, though, was Williston, a new town for us.

Williston was an interesting community. While the rest of the nation was heading full speed into an economic recession, Williston was experiencing an 'oil boom.' New drilling regulations and/or techniques allowed them to drill sideways as opposed to straight down. Somehow this opened up large deposits of oil. Everyone who wanted a job could work. People came from all over to work the oil fields of western North Dakota. In fact, so many people were working in oil it was hard to get people to work in town. We went into a popular restaurant to eat dinner and were greeted by a handwritten sign stating, "Due to the lack of workers, we will be closed on Tuesdays."

Kyle Anderson, the pastor of the Assembly of God church, had read a short article on our ride in the spring. He contacted me and invited us to bring Hope and Courage to Williston. Kyle was an avid cyclist and had ridden quite a bit of North Dakota. He was excited to have a cycling ministry team visit his church. Kyle joined us on thirty miles of our ride while his wife, Cheryl, followed in her car as support. We ate a picnic lunch at a country store. Darla and I really felt an instant friendship with the Andersons.

The services at their church went great. After the morning service, John Dieszi packed up and headed back home to Redding, California. It was great having him with us and we all knew we would miss him. Before the evening meeting a man named Joel wanted to take us for a ride in his classic cars. He had a 1923 Studebaker and a 1931 Ford Model T. We all climbed into the cars and he drove around Williston. The cars definitely attracted attention and we felt like we were in a parade waving to people along the way. We had so much fun we almost forgot about the church service. We rushed back to the church as fast as an eighty-year-old car could go and entered the building just as they were finishing the music time. After the service we apologized to Kyle for being late. He laughed and said he was glad we got to have such a good ride in Joel's cars.

Monday morning greeted us with blue skies and warm temperatures. It was time to leave Williston. These past four days were some of the best we have had. The church put us up in motel rooms. The extra privacy was a welcome treat. We had also been able to get our laundry done and replenish our supplies.

Nicole had left a few days before to go to a wedding in Wisconsin. Justin, her fiancé, was taking his mid-deployment leave from Iraq to attend the wedding. They both would meet up with us at our next stop in Minot. The camp in Minot was a two-hour drive from Williston. This allowed us time to get a good bike ride in before leaving town.

"Why *don't* we ride on some of these country roads?" Darla asked. "We've been on Highway 2 for weeks. These farms look so pleasant and I bet they wouldn't have much traffic."

Good question. Why don't we ride on some of these country roads? They had beautiful farms. We noticed as soon as we crossed the border from Montana to North Dakota the geographic spirit changed. Montana was ranches and western … real western. North Dakota was farms and north central. You wouldn't think an arbitrary, nonexistent line drawn on a map could make a difference, but it does. We were becoming very aware of the unique attributes of each region we pedaled through. We should get a closer look at these NoDak farms and getting away from the traffic would be a nice break. Kyle stopped in to say goodbye and I asked him to suggest a good country ride. He mapped out a forty mile route that would return us to where we started. Twenty miles out … twenty miles back.

Darla, Grant and I put some supplies in our packs and started out on our day in the country. It didn't take long to get out of town. The roads were flat and the temperatures were reaching eighty. What a beautiful day for riding. I love flat roads. My handcycle performed best on flat roads. Downhill was great, also. But downhill was too easy. I know to reach a downhill I usually have to pedal uphill and therefore earn the free ride. However, I still feel like those downhill miles are a gift. With flat roads, I have to exert enough constant effort to keep the momentum going but not so much as to wear myself out. On flat roads, I can ride in front without holding the others up. We were dealing with a strong side wind, though. That is the tradeoff for being in flat country. The wind is always a factor. A tail wind can make a flat road seem like you're cruising downhill. A head wind turns the same road into a mountain climb. It's the side winds that are most annoying. They are constantly nudging you and forcing you to correct your direction. Darla and Grant had the disadvantage of riding on two wheels as opposed to my more stable three wheels. I had the disadvantage of trying to keep an even keel with just one limb. All in all, I would say we were all equally bothered. Regardless, it was still a beautiful day to ride.

Our turnaround point was a little town. Rumor had it there was a good restaurant there to get a sandwich and piece of pie. There was no restaurant in town. Which meant there was no sandwich or pie, either. I think people started that rumor to get hapless out-of-staters to pedal their bikes twenty miles in the side winds. Luckily we always carry some snacks in our packs. We brought our bikes to rest in front of and old abandoned gas station. We chewed on nutrition bars and surveyed the village. The little town looked as if it were out of a movie.

Grant

They had a tiny post office and about four storefronts. The sidewalks were wood planks and the roads in town were dirt roads. There didn't appear to be any businesses open. This wouldn't matter much except we were kind of counting on the pie shop to have an available restroom.

About this time we were greeted by a voice, "How're you folks doin' this fine day?" Startled, we turned to see a man in a heavy work apron. His friendly smile immediately put us at ease.

I returned the smile. "We're doing great! Quiet little town you have here."

"Most of the time. Looks like you three are on some kind of journey."

"We're riding across America."

"Really? On those bikes? And you with only one arm. Where'd you begin?"

"We started from Gig Harbor, Washington, five weeks ago. We call our ride Hope and Courage Across America. Our message is to have hope in Christ and the courage to do something with that hope."

"Amen to that. How far you goin'?"

"Well today we are heading back to Williston but our goal is to reach the Statue of Liberty on September 11." I was curious about his clothes. "What kind of work do you do in that heavy apron?"

"I'm a blacksmith."

"A blacksmith? You can make a living as a blacksmith in this town?" I hope that didn't sound rude to him.

"My father before me was the blacksmith in this town, and his father before him was the blacksmith in this town. I am the third generation to work hot metal on that anvil over there." He pointed to the weather beaten building next door. "I never much thought about it as making a living. It's my life." His wife came around the corner. "Hey Honey, these folks are riding these bikes to the Statue of Liberty. Pretty amazing, huh?"

"My goodness! How long do you think it will take you?"

"We figure about four months."

Darla, glad to see a woman, interrupted and asked the question that was really on her mind. "Do you have a public restroom somewhere in this town?"

"The park has restrooms that they used to leave open but a family moved into town with some rowdy kids and so they had to start locking the bathrooms. They are one block that way and then to the left. I can go get the keys and meet you there."

Relieved, Darla said, "Each day God blesses us with an angel and you are our angel today." The blacksmith's wife just smiled. I am sure she thought being called an angel by a lady crazy enough to pedal a bike across America has to be taken with a grain of salt.

We started back toward Williston. The wind came from the other side now. In a way it made the road different than when we rode on it earlier. Again I was out in front, Darla next and then Grant. Aside from the wind, this day really was all we had hoped. The quiet roads, quaint towns and open roads were soothing to us.

"Car back!" Grant shouted. John Diezsi had taught us to do that when a car was coming from behind. Darla and I instinctively edged our bikes close to the shoulder. I watched the SUV come around me and drive on. I noticed the passengers pointing and talking excitedly as they passed. I stopped my crank at the top of a turn and gave them a 'thumbs up' and a big smile. They waved back. There was a large farm on the right and several smaller houses on the left straight ahead. As the SUV approached the farm, two very large and aggressive dogs charged after the vehicle. The driver sped up as the dogs barked loudly and gave up the chase. They turned and began to walk back onto the farm. We had to ride past that farm and those dogs. Turning around or going another way was not an option.

This is not good, I thought, watching the dogs intently as they trotted further onto the farm. *Maybe we can sneak past these dogs and they won't even see us.* I slowed my pedaling to quiet my bike. Darla and Grant behind me were aware of the dogs. Especially Darla. Two things were constantly on Darla's mind when she rode. First, the safety of her children as discussed numerous times already and second, dogs. She was more concerned (polite term for frightened) about dogs than she was about snakes. And she was really 'concerned' about snakes.

I kept my eye on the dogs. *Keep going back. Keep going back. Good doggies. I think we can make it.*

Just as I got even with them I heard a 'yip, yip, yip' from the other side of the road. I turned my head to see a little lap dog barking up a storm.

Oh, great. I looked back at the farm to see the big dogs reel around and lock in on me. I have never seen a more excited look on a dog's face. They saw me as something catchable and took off at full gallop toward me. I immediately started pedaling faster.

Two things raced through my mind, *Don't let these dogs bite me,* and *keep them chasing me instead of Darla and Grant. If a big dog makes contact with those two wheel bikes they are going to be on the ground and very vulnerable.* I am not going to say which of those two items were more important to me for fear of exposing another one of my character flaws. It doesn't matter. Both required me to increase my speed as quick as I could.

I heard Darla shouting behind me, "Pedal faster, Grant! Pedal faster!" Keeping pace with a man pedaling across America with one arm doesn't require a teenage boy to pedal fast very often. This was definitely an exception to that rule.

Out of the corner of my left eye I could see other dogs running onto the road after me. I didn't care about them. It was those two big, ugly ones I was worried about. Within seconds both of them were next to me. My bike rides very low to the ground. Where I sit puts me eye-to-eye with big dogs. They came right up to me barking and showing their teeth. I barked and yelled back at them.

Now, we had planned for this type of encounter before we started this journey. We had gotten little canisters of pepper spray and mounted them on the frames of our bikes. The idea was if anything aggressive came at us (four legged, two legged, no legged, whatever) we could grab the pepper spray and use it to stop the aggression. Pretty good plan, don't you think? Yeah, great plan. Unless you pedal with your only hand! It was at this moment the weakness in this plan became apparent to me. I looked at the pepper spray, looked at my hand on the pedal, and looked at those gnashing white teeth attached to the dogs.

I thought, *Forget the pepper spray. If you dogs want to bite me, you are going to have to earn it.*

I pedaled faster as the first dog came toward my wrist. I cranked those RPMs so quick there was no way he was going to get his teeth on me. The other one pulled in close to my right leg stump. He would lunge for it while keeping his distance from the back wheel. I have to admit, this dog was good. He maintained his speed and focus enough to make repeated attempts at my flesh. I could hear his fangs clacking together at each miss and feel his hot breath and saliva through my riding shorts. Finally I looked down and he had this puzzled expression on his face like, *What am I supposed to bite on this man? Where's his leg? There's nothing there!*

I kept up my pace and the two dogs started panting hard, then stopped chasing, and went over into the grass and lay down.

They'd had enough! I glanced back to see Darla and Grant pass by them without any problem.

We rode a ways and pulled off to catch our breaths. Darla said, "You had ten dogs chasing you!"

"Ten dogs? Doesn't anybody control their pets around here? Grant, you really pushed some speed back there."

"Yeah, my adrenaline kicked in. But you did great, Dad. Weren't you scared?"

"Scared? No, I wasn't scared. I just wanted to lead them away from you and Mom."

"Wow, thanks Dad."

"Yeah, thanks Hon. We didn't know how we were going to get through that."

"It's what any man would do to protect his family." Hey, they don't need to know whether I was pedaling fast for me or pedaling fast for them. The important thing is I was pedaling fast and nobody got bit.

Darla took a long drink of water, "I learned one thing today. Stay off country roads. There are too many uncontrolled dogs out here."

"I learned something, too," I replied. "If I had dogs chasing me the whole way we would be in New York by now."

We returned to town and told Jeanne and Chanel our adventures over lunch. They had finished the laundry and loaded the RV while we were gone. Bidding a fond farewell to Williston, we drove past the oil rigs toward our next stop, Minot. Glancing at the country roads leading to the farms, a satisfying thought came to mind, *I guess I can run with the big dogs.*

Chapter 16

I know we are not supposed to wish we are somebody else. That is a common theme of the talks I give to teenagers. *The biggest cause of low self-esteem is wishing we were somebody else. I wish I had their talent; I wish I had their grades; I wish my parents would buy me some clothes with brand names on them so I could fit in around here; I wish I was as big as him; I wish I was as skinny as her. When we wish we are someone else we always end up not feeling good about who we are.* I try to practice what I preach but I am only human. There are a few times I wish I was someone else. At home, I often wish I were the cat. We have an orange tabby cat named Bailey. And as far as I can tell he has no functional purpose on this planet whatsoever. He sleeps anytime he wants, up to twenty hours a day. When he is awake, he wants me to open the back door so he can go out or come in; open the door to the garage so he can come in or go out; fill his feed dish and make sure he has water to drink. Before I am allowed the privilege of doing these tasks for him, I must scratch his neck and ears to his satisfaction. There are days I wish I could be the cat. While we are on this journey, he is being cared for by our nephew's family, Devin and Tammy and their four children. I can only imagine what Bailey is doing to their happy home.

While pedaling across America there are days I wish I could be Chanel. She has the best role on the team. She rides when she wants; she stays in the RV when she doesn't want to go outside; she goes outside when she doesn't want to be in the RV; she goes swimming, shopping and exploring while we ride; and she has Aunt Jeanne as her personal companion. On top of that, she makes a new BFF (Best Friend Forever) everywhere we stop. Pulling the RV into the camp at Minot, Chanel immediately becomes friends with the camp hosts. A Fred and Ethyl-type couple are giving her rides in the golf cart, introducing her to their multiple cats, and showing her off to all the other Freds and Ethyls in camp. All of this under the protective watch of Darla and Aunt Jeanne.

To be fair, Chanel earns a lot of these perks. As our official Ambassador of Happy she shoulders a great responsibility. She has to lift us when we are down and make the tearful cheerful. She is continually thinking of ways to keep our spirits up. Last night she had a cookie party for us in the RV. This included invitations and printed menus. We chose our personal favorites from a grand selection of cookies and sweets. She then served them to us along with our beverage choice. For a moment, instead of being halfway across America eating cookies in an RV, we feel we are halfway around the world and having tea at Harrods in London. The imagination of a ten year old is more than big enough to capture everyone in the room. Forgive me for my envy but there are days I wish I could be Chanel.

Nicole rejoined us with Justin. It was great to have Justin out of Iraq and with us for a few days. We hadn't had the chance to spend much time with him. Being in the Army stationed in Texas, Tennessee or Iraq didn't allow us to be in the same state or country with him, let alone the same room. Several days in an RV made up for much of that. We are so proud of his service to

America and are glad God kept him safe. This time together also allowed me to see how he got along with my daughter. That is important to a father (and mother). I noticed he treated Nicole with respect at every level and truly cared for her. They had a date set for their marriage in the spring of 2010. He had asked for a transfer to Fort Lewis, Washington, after his tour of duty in Iraq. Fort Lewis is ten miles from our house. The 2010 wedding date would give them over a year of being in the same area to really be sure before they pledged their 'forevers' together. That is important to a father (and mother), too.

We had a Wednesday evening service at the Minot Assembly of God church. We realized earlier on this journey we needed these church services more than they needed us. Being in the local churches recharged us. They always reminded us of why we were doing this ride. The cycling kept our bodies fit; the encounters with Christians kept our spirits fit. During the service I introduced Justin to the audience and mentioned he was on his mid-tour leave from Iraq. The whole church stood and applauded him. What an honor!

The next day while Darla, Grant and I were pedaling, Justin and Nicole were Chanel's BFF-du jour and took her to the zoo. We had found a good road to ride. US 52 headed southeast out of Minot. Nice bike-friendly shoulder and beautiful scenery.

"This is the best road we have been on since we left home," Darla says while unwrapping a Clif Bar.

"I agree." Grant adds between gulps of Zipp-Fizz. Grant will never be accused of wasting the world's word resources.

"It is a joy and a relief from the 'dog road' yesterday," I added. Conversation had become so easy between us. Several weeks and a thousand miles of pedaling together had made us something more than mother, father and son. "I've been thinking about our

route across North Dakota. If we stay on this road it cuts diago-
nally down to Jamestown."

"Haven't you been to Jamestown before?"

"Yeah, Troy Gunderson brought me in to do stuff for Youth
for Christ."

"Maybe you should call him and see if he can find us a church
to speak at on Sunday." Darla's request was a bit unrealistic. To
call someone on Thursday to arrange a church service for Sunday
took a little courage and a lot of hope. Fortunately our journey so
far had strengthened both of those character traits in us.

"I'll call him when we get back to camp."

Back at camp I looked Troy's number up in my files and
called. I awkwardly explained to him why I was calling on such
short notice. We had planned on pedaling Hwy 2 from Minot to
Grand Forks but today found a great road that took us through
Jamestown. I asked if he knew any church that would like me to
speak on Sunday.

"This Sunday?" he said. "I'll see what I can do."

It was a few hours later when Troy called back. "You've got a
church Sunday morning."

"Really? How'd that happen so quick?"

"I called Pastor Steve at the Lutheran church. He remembers
you from when I brought you in for YFC. He cleared his schedule and said he didn't want to miss this opportunity."

"That's amazing," I said.

"Wait, there's more," Troy replied.

"What could be more?"

"Jamestown is celebrating their 125th anniversary. The
church is sponsoring a Blue Grass Festival in the park and they
want you to be the speaker at the festival."

"Wow! When God makes a way, He makes a big way."

We had some more days of good riding and moved camp to Jamestown. The church service went really well but the Blue Grass service was unique. The bands played old-timey music and everyone was having a grand time. Sitting on stage, I could not believe where we were. This was a true Americana experience.

After our meetings, we bid farewell to Justin. He had bought a car while on leave and was driving it back to his family home in Washington. We prayed for him and sent him on his way. We pulled up stakes and drove the RV to Fargo. We went directly to the airport and put Nicole on a plane. She was flying home to be there when Justin arrived and get prepared for her fall semester at college. I drove the truck and RV right up to the unloading zone at the airport. Nicole got her bags out of the RV and came out of the front door just like she was leaving home for college. Darla walked her into the terminal while I waited with the rig. I took a picture. It was just another surreal image on a surreal day.

In Fargo we did something for the first time that would be repeated several more times in the coming weeks. We camped at Wal-Mart. We couldn't find a suitable campground and Wal-Mart encourages travelers to park overnight in their parking lots. I think they realize travelers will come into the store and spend money if they are conveniently located in the parking lot already. And they are right. We always needed some sort of supplies and Wal-Mart had what we needed. Our bike riding now moved back to Interstate 90, our old friend from the start of our journey. There are two states out west that will allow you to ride bicycles on the freeway, Washington and North Dakota. The nice thing about I-90 in North Dakota is that you do not have any mountain passes to cross.

Aunt Jeanne had done some PR work and contacted the local TV and newspapers. They came out and met us on the freeway for interviews. Getting local coverage of Hope and Courage

Across America always helped spread the message. It also made it easier for us to meet people. It had become common for people to approach us because of a news feature on TV or in the paper. Sometimes they wanted to congratulate us. Sometimes they needed personal encouragement. And sometimes they just wanted to buy us ice cream. We appreciated all encounters but the ice cream was really sweet. While contacting the media in Moorhead (Moorhead, Minnesota and Fargo, North Dakota are separated by the Red River), Jeanne learned there was going to be a big Fourth of July parade. The City of Moorhead and Minnesota State University Moorhead co-hosted the biggest parade in the area. When Jeanne explained what we were doing, they invited us to be in the parade. We considered it an honor to be a part of their celebration.

Roadside interview

Chanel, Darla and Jeanne went right into decoration mode. They headed to the craft stores and came back with ribbons, flags and tassels. All in red, white and blue, of course. We moved out of Wal-Mart and into a campground in Moorhead. The girls spent the rest of the evening turning our ordinary bikes into something worthy of a nation's birthday parade. Red, white and blue ribbon wrapped our frames. Grant and I had two flags mounted behind us and Darla wove ribbons through her spokes. Chanel put a white basket on her handlebars filled with red, white and blue flowers and her teddy bear. The finished product was patriotically beautiful.

The next morning we brought our bikes down to the parade staging area. The organizers moved us up close toward the front of the line. This was definitely more than we expected or deserved but, thanks to Jeanne, we had been covered well in the local media and they were treating us like celebrities. We maneuvered our bikes into position behind the Classic Car Club. About this time it hit us that this was going to require some coordinated bike riding skill. We had to move at parade speed, stay together as a group, and interact with the crowd all through the route. All of this had to be done without crashing into each other. Parade speed was not a problem for me. The stability of a three-wheeled bike is not affected by speed. Darla, Grant and Chanel, on the other hand, had to maintain forward motion at a pace that made their bikes wobbly. They quickly learned to zigzag across the street to keep their speed up. At times, they had to straddle their bikes and walk them along the route. We all did a good job of not bumping each other or the 1963 Cadillac in front of us.

Interacting with the crowd took a little creativity. You need to remember, not everyone on our team is comfortable in the spotlight. I am fine with it, Chanel is okay with it as long as she has a little time to prepare, Grant can ignore it, and Darla would rather face rattlesnakes and dogs than be in front of a crowd. We would weave along the street in between the curbs, smiling and waving at the spectators. Actually, Darla, Grant and Chanel did the waving. I would give a 'thumbs up' as I pedaled. The trickier part for me was letting the crowd know who we were and what we were doing. I am used to being stationary and speaking to the whole crowd in front of me with a microphone for fifty minutes. This was pedaling past small portions of the crowd and only being within voice range for ten seconds at best. I needed to condense my message.

"Happy birthday, America! We are a family riding bikes across America. We left our home in Gig Harbor, Washington, on May 17 and want to reach the Statue of Liberty on September 11! Our ride is called 'Hope and Courage Across America'! Our hope is in Christ and the courage is in all of us to do something with that hope!"

Pedal a little ways and say it again. I was reminded of the simplicity of this journey's message. Hope and courage.

Thank you, Lord, for keeping hope simple to receive and simple to share.

Fourth of July Parade

We continued down the route waving, smiling and shouting like were in a … well, a parade. We learned to stay back from the classic cars. Classic cars emit a lot of carbon monoxide. They are, after all, old cars with old emission standards. I know, I own a 1954 Cadillac and the slower it goes the more it fumes. Pedaling slowly behind a whole pack of classics can get a little noxious after a while. We finished the parade and joined in on the other festivities. We met up with Dennis Jensen and his family. Dennis is the Youth for Christ leader in the Red River Valley. In fact, Dennis was the first one to bring me to North Dakota back in 2000. The evangelist, Luis Palau, invited me to join him on a campaign to the cities of Fargo, Bismarck, and Grand Forks. My job was to speak in the schools in those cities prior to the evening events. My contact for the Fargo/Moorhead area was Dennis Jensen, Red River Valley YFC Director. My first conversation on the phone with Dennis went something like this:

"Hello, is Bob Mortimer available?"

"You're speaking to Bob."

"Good. Bob, my name is Dennis Jensen and I was given your name as a possible school speaker during the upcoming Luis Palau events here in the Fargo area. Do you have a tape of your program you can send me?"

"Yeah, I can send you a tape. I can also send you some brochures and outlines for the schools. They can help you convince the school administrators my program is good."

"Just send the tape. You don't have to convince the administrators you're good, you just have to convince me."

This could be an interesting man to work with, I thought as I hung up the phone. I quickly sent the tape to him. A few weeks later Dennis called me back.

"All right, I watched your tape and you're okay."

"I'm glad. Do you want me to send you that material for the schools now?"

"I don't need it. I have you scheduled for twenty schools while you're here."

"Twenty schools? How'd you get twenty schools so quickly?"

"I've been working with these schools for over two decades. If I say I have a good speaker they trust me. Like I said, you don't need to convince them, you need to convince me."

That was the beginning of an ongoing ministry and friend relationship. Dennis connected me to the other YFC guys in Minot and Jamestown. He is a good man.

That evening we watched the fireworks at the university's stadium. What a spectacular finish to a spectacular day.

The next day we got back on our bikes for some real riding. Darla and Grant were having a hard time moving forward. It was not the topography. Remember, the Red River Valley is officially the flattest part of the U.S. Earlier in the week we were able to do our longest ride yet, eighty-five miles. It was a mood thing, kind of like the day after Christmas. The Fourth of July was a hard day to follow. We plodded along trying to ignore the feeling. But the mood was pervasive.

"There's a town up the road. If we make it that far we will have forty miles. If you guys want, we can call Jeanne to pick us up and call it a day," I offered.

"That sounds like a good idea. I don't know what's wrong with me today. Usually the riding is the easy part," Darla replied. "What do you think, Grant?"

"Sounds good to me, too."

We pushed ourselves the forty miles and pulled into a convenience store. As Darla and Grant got off their bikes, a woman from Canada got out of her car and started asking questions.

When we explained our ride, she reached back into her car and brought out a camera.

"I've got to get a picture of this," she said.

Darla and Grant went inside to get us ice cream bars. The clerk asked Darla, "How far are you guys going today?"

While I was outside waiting a man came up to me and handed me twenty dollars, "Use this for ice cream. What you guys are doing is great."

Two women came over asking, "Do you take donations?" handing me eleven dollars.

When Darla and Grant came out with the ice cream bars we sat and told each other our encounter stories. We started laughing at how so much had happened in such a short time. We forgot all about calling Jeanne for a ride and decided to keep pedaling. It is amazing how a few encouraging words and ice cream bars can change your mood.

We took the advice of a local person and headed toward a lightly traveled road that ran parallel to the freeway. It was a wonderful road. It was flat, smooth, corn fields, and very few cars. Oh, and no dogs. The kind of road you can cruise along and get lost in your thoughts. Darla led the way, I followed behind, and Grant brought up the rear. The miles clicked by and our speed created a breeze that made the summer heat and humidity bearable.

Grant took advantage of the quiet road to call Nicole. He guided his bike with one hand while holding his cell phone with the other. The wonders of technology. I heard my phone ring from inside my pack behind me. I was expecting Jeanne to call about a pick-up location for us. Now, I cannot talk and pedal at the same time. I am not that coordinated. I hollered 'phone' and applied the brakes to my bike. Grant did not hear the warning and was not watching his bike. I felt a solid jolt hit the back of my bike and saw Grant tumble off his bike to my right. The jolt launched me right out of my seat and into the air. I landed on my back and felt my helmet hit the road hard. I briefly saw the twinkle of little stars.

Darla heard the commotion and turned around. Seeing me and Grant on the ground sent her into a panic. We knew the only way to calm her down was to get off the road and back on our bikes. I quickly climbed onto my seat assuring her I was okay. Grant stood up and showed his mom he was all right. After everyone (Darla) was settled, we looked closer at our wounds. There was no significant damage. A few scrapes and no blood dripping. I looked at my helmet and saw the dent put in it by the contact with the road. Better the helmet than my head. What did we learn? One, there is a reason we always wear our helmets. And two, we shouldn't talk on the phone while riding our bikes. We finished our day with sixty-five miles pedaled. Not bad for the fifth of July.

The week before we started Hope and Courage Across America I was getting calls from Seattle radio stations. One day a Christian station called for an interview then a conservative talk station called right after them. It was only minutes later when the phone rang again. This time it was KMPS-FM, a Seattle country music station. Ichabod Caine and the Morning Crew wanted me to come on the air and talk about my ride. Glad to get the media coverage, I took the call. I realized immediately this was my kind of radio station. Not necessarily the music style. I am okay with country but it is not number one on my pre-set stations. It was the DJs. Ichabod and his cohorts were quick witted and funny. They wanted to know about my bike. They wanted to know about the ride. How'd I lose my limbs? When I told about hitting the power lines and said it was a 'shocking experience,' they roared with laughter and added to the pun. I talked about meeting Darla and how she helped me turn my life around through Christ. Oh, they loved that!

"So, you were saved by Jesus and a good woman! Thank God for Darla!"

Getting off the phone I thought, *That was fun!*

I was telling Darla about the interview and the phone rang ... again.

"Hello, Bob speaking."

"Hi, Bob, my name is Nicole and I work here at KMPS."

"Yeah, I was just on the air with Ichabod and had a great time."

"That's why I'm calling. The Crew really liked talking to you, too. Ichabod was wondering if you would like to make it a weekly segment during your journey across America."

"How would that work?"

"We would call you every Thursday at 8:00 a.m. Pacific Time. You could give us an update on the air."

"I would love it. What a huge blessing. Thank you for letting us do this."

"No. Thank you. We want our listeners to be a part of your journey."

So, every Thursday morning I stop what I am doing and talk to the listeners back in Seattle. They were with us going over Snoqualmie Pass and through the snow of Marias Pass. They heard about the rattlesnakes of Montana and the dogs of North Dakota. And they loved hearing about the people we met along the way.

I met a little ten-year-old girl named Cassandra at our last camp. She was born premature with spinal bifida. She is blind and mute as well as limited in her independent movement. Her parents do a great job of helping her have a wonderful quality of life. Cassandra loves to play her keyboard and played the background music while I did my interview on KMPS.

Ichabod said, "What's that music in the background, Bob?"

I told them about my new friend, Cassandra. What a joy! We had more people tune in and follow our ride through those weekly updates than anything else we did. Friends and family would set their schedule to be next to the radio on Thursday mornings. They told us later that after I got off the phone Ichabod would often say, "Thank God for Darla!" Amen to that.

At the same camp we met Cassandra, I also met a man who had lost his leg at fourteen months old in a lawnmower accident. He is and has been a farmer all his life. But what I liked most about him was that he is a father to four children and a husband to one wife.

I asked him, "Didn't anyone tell you that you can't be doing this stuff when you're missing a limb?" He just smiled.

We are making our way through Minnesota now. We spent a few days in Minneapolis to ride the bike trails and meet people. They have the best trails we have seen. They wind around lakes, through parks and over streams throughout the metro area. The people are equally great.

It is hard to visit the Twin Cities without stopping at the Mall of America. I believe it is the largest shopping mall in the United States. It could quite possibly make Minnesota the Land of 10,000 shoe stores. Grant and I agreed to tolerate a mall day with the girls. There we met Claire. Claire is a young Vietnamese mom working at a store to provide for her daughter. I mentioned we were cycling across America and her eyes welled with tears.

She said, "I saw you all on TV last night and I can't believe I am getting to meet you. My four-year-old daughter was born with problems in her legs. One is much shorter than the other and she has a struggle walking. I told her if that man can do all those things with no legs, you can do a lot of things, too."

She kept wiping her tears as she spoke. We encouraged her and told her about our message of hope in Christ and the courage to face whatever life brings. The puzzling thing is we did not know we were on TV in Minneapolis. No one had come out to film us. They must have picked the story up from another city. Or from God. Doesn't matter.

Sunday we preached at the church of a friend. Mike and Crystal Hilger pastor a small church in a small town. The building was erected in 1870 and had incremental upgrades throughout the last 138 years. One of the things that wasn't upgraded was the wheelchair access. There were twenty steps separating the entrance from the sanctuary. Typically, when in this situation I can find a few strong men to lift me and my chair up the stairs. This was a small church, though, and there were only thirty-five people in the congregation, including the five of us. I did not see two men that I felt were capable of getting me to the top of the steps.

Well, if I pedaled here from Gig Harbor, I cannot very well let a flight of steps stop me.

I got out of my wheelchair and climbed up the stairs while Grant brought my chair up behind me. God has a way of making sure I stay humble.

In that tiny congregation, five people gave their lives to Christ. We have seen dozens of people make the initial decision to follow Jesus at our services the last few weeks. And many more dozens chose to put their hope in Christ and apply their courage to use that hope to face their own mountains. That is the message God has put on our hearts and we continue to share it daily.

We were able to ride on bike paths for quite a few miles. Pedaling on a path in Rochester, we saw the tiniest frogs I have ever seen. Hundreds of them hopped across the path. It was hard to miss them all. I looked at them closely. They were not even an inch long. They were not tadpoles. They had completely formed bodies. They confused me.

I asked another cycler, "What kind of frogs are these?"

"They're not frogs. They're toads," he said.

Toads? I had never seen a baby toad. If they are this size fully formed they must be really small tadpoles. We caught a couple and put them in a bottle to show Chanel. As soon as Chanel saw them, she wanted to keep them as pets. So, we got an empty gallon water jug and turned it into a toad aquarium. She named them Frankie and George. She pasted their names on the jug and carried them with her everywhere. They stayed in the RV, rode in the truck, and went in more stores than we want to admit. She caught ants and put them in the jug with Frankie and George. The ants either escaped or were eaten. I never actually saw what happened to them. I just know she had to replace her ants often. I envied how well my youngest child adapted to being away from her home and how such little things made her so happy. As I said, some days I wish I could be Chanel.

Chapter 17

The next few days would take us through the corner of Iowa, across Illinois, under the tip of Lake Michigan and into Indiana. Nicole had flown in to join us again. Our next stop was in Northern Indiana. Our RV was built in Shipshewana, Indiana, and we wanted to take it in for a few minor repairs. In addition, we were scheduled to speak at College Mennonite Church in Goshen, Indiana. We had connections to Goshen. Vic and Marie Stoltzfus lived in Goshen. My first encounter with the Stoltzfuses was back in the early '60s when Vic took the pastor position at North Lima Mennonite Church in Ohio. North Lima was the little town where I was raised.

Vic was fresh out of seminary and ready to help the world. He followed a practical form of Christianity that figured if you want to help the world, start by helping your neighbor. I am glad because one of the first neighbors he chose to help was my father. Dad worked in the steel mills of Youngstown. By the time he was thirty he had a wife and seven children. He also had a drinking problem. Dad struggled with his use of alcohol. Some of you might think that having seven children by the time you are thirty would drive any man to drink. But drinking had dominated and interfered with my father's life since his teens.

It made raising, supporting and leading a family very difficult for everyone. To be completely open with you, he was clinically diagnosed and personally admitted to being an alcoholic. When I was six years old, my dad discovered AA, Alcoholics Anonymous. He was encouraged to attend a meeting by his father. Grandpa Mortimer had a similar problem with drinking and had joined AA to gain his sobriety. This ultimately led to Dad finding a sponsor and quitting alcohol. He would not have another drink until the day he died.

Vic was teaching a class at Youngstown State University to supplement his pastor's income. Vic Stoltzfus was the first paid pastor the church had ever hired. Being a small church in a small community, they offered him what they could. They offered a parsonage to live in (not the utilities, just the house), a vegetable garden to grow what he could, and $25 a week. Being a young pastor with a young family, he accepted what they offered. The teaching job at YSU gave him extra income and allowed him to feed his academic hunger, also. He became interested in the effect of alcoholism on our society. Meeting with the other North Lima pastors, Vic mentioned his desire to learn more about problem drinking. One of the pastors mentioned there was an AA group holding meetings at his church. He suggested Vic contact a local man who was very active in the meetings. The local man was my father, Harold Mortimer.

Vic met Dad and asked if he could sit in on some AA meetings and observe. Dad trusted Vic and brought him as a guest to the meetings. Before long, Dad revealed to Vic that while he was staying sober from alcohol, prescription drugs were becoming a problem. So much of a problem that Vic ended up counseling Dad and helping to get him into a Christian treatment program in Canada. During this time Dad started taking us all to the Mennonite church. Sunday mornings the girls would put on Sunday dresses and the boys would wear black slacks and long-sleeved white shirts. It was at North Lima Mennonite that I learned about Jesus. Sitting in Sunday school classes in the church basement led by teachers with the last names of Yoder, Blosser and Steiner I listened to the Bible stories and memorized the verses. I loved the stories about Jesus.

Upstairs in the sanctuary the Mortimer family would take up a whole pew. Dad, Mom, Joe, Jeanne, Don, Tom, Pat, Bob and Reenie all sitting quietly. It was difficult at times for us boys to control our squirming but we always had Dad to remind us of our church manners. At home, a snap of his fingers brought us all in line; in church all he needed was a glance in our direction.

Vic would preach about that practical Christianity. Following Jesus in your day-to-day life. His message would often carry the themes from the Sermon on the Mount. (Matthew 5 through 7, if you are wondering where to find it.) I have appreciated the Sermon on the Mount ever since those days of my youth. It is Jesus' sermon. The one He spoke to the multitude on the hill-side. It has the beatitudes: blessed are the meek, the merciful and the peacemakers. The encouragement: you are the salt of the earth, the light of the world. The instructions: turn the other cheek, love your neighbor and your enemies, don't judge others. It also has the Lord's Prayer right smack in the middle of it: Our Father, which art in heaven... It is an amazing portion of Scripture. But it wasn't just the way the young preacher presented the Scripture that left a lasting impression on this ten year old. It was the way he lived it.

One Sunday morning in the spring of 1965 I sat and listened to Vic explain to the church why he was going to Selma, Alabama, to march with some people led by a man named Martin Luther King. A week earlier, I had never heard of Selma or Martin Luther King. A lot of people hadn't. That all changed on

March 7 when several hundred people marched in Selma for black voter registration rights. The march was stopped by state troopers with nightsticks and teargas. The images of the confrontation and injured marchers were in the media all across the nation. We viewed them on our black-and-white TV screens. In 1965, a lot of America was viewed in black and white. Vic saw the images and could not ignore them.

Reverend King planned another march and had a simple three-word plea to all who would listen, "We need you."

Vic felt he was talking directly to him. I don't know what other people in the church thought of his decision to join the march. All I know is that I saw a man practice what he preached. Vic packed his bag and joined thousands of others in Selma. He did what was right because that is what Jesus would have done. That message has lasted a whole lot longer in my life than any Christian bumper sticker I have ever seen.

The next year Vic and Marie would leave North Lima Mennonite. Eventually Vic became president of the Mennonite college in Goshen and retired there. My family would move from North Lima in 1970 and head west.

I called Vic while planning Hope and Courage Across America to see if he would like us to include them on our route. Jeanne was excited about Goshen, too. She went to Goshen College back in 1965. She also had a great relationship with Vic and Marie and their girls. She lived with them for a brief period before getting married. To make it even better, there were other people from North Lima Mennonite who had settled in Goshen. It would almost be like a homecoming for her.

The past occupied our minds as we pedaled along Highway 30 through Indiana. However, Northern Indiana had more in store for us than old memories. I think this is a good time to visit Darla's journal again.

July 18 ~ Friday

There are those times in life when you
just know that you are in the right
place at the right time. Well, today was
one of those times. We were riding
on Hwy 30 in Indiana when both Bob
and Nicole got flat tires in the town
of Bourbon. It was hot and humid so
we stopped along the shady side of
the street. I noticed we were in front
of a newspaper office. I wondered if
I should go in and tell them about
our journey across America. I looked
at the door and they were only open
a couple of days a week and one of
those days was Friday, today. I went
in and told the editor about our ride
and she was very interested and felt
this was a really big story for their
little town. She said we had a flat
tire in her town for a reason. Her
name was Angel. Every day on the
journey God had blessed us with an
angel and today she was, literally, our

Angel. We fixed the flats and did a newspaper interview at the same time.

As we headed off, Angel told us of a road to take that would be a nice scenic route for biking. She was right. Our path took us through a beautiful Amish community with well kept farms. We shared the road with horse drawn buggies and Amish bike riders.

We can't pedal past this!

We saw a little sign along the road that read 'Bake Sale.' We followed the sign ... and a dream of mine came true. We

arrived at an Amish farm. We got off
of our bikes. I felt self-conscious in
our bright neon yellow clothes and it
made me nervous as I rang the doorbell.
The man of the house opened the door
and invited us in to take a look at their
baked goods. He disappeared into the
next room and his wife soon came and
introduced herself. I was in heaven! I
have always admired the Amish simple
lifestyle and their dedication to keeping
it that way. And to think I had just
been invited into their home was truly
an amazing gift to me. A banquet table
was covered with a wide variety of
delicious looking baked goods. She
was a young mother of three (2, 4 &
5 years old) and this was her second
weekend of offering baked goods out
of her home. We wished we had bigger
bike bags. We chose buttermilk cookies
and a loaf of fresh bread. They were
both baked without electricity.

She came outside and we had a nice long visit with her. We told her of our journey and our message of hope in Christ and the courage to use that hope to face our challenges. Bob told her how he lost his limbs. Then she told us that she and her family had been in a car/buggy accident when she was 14 and her 12-year-old sister was killed in the crash. She said for a long time they wished her sister back but now accept it as God's will. We were so sorry to hear of the tragedy but I was touched by the way her family accepted it. I am always amazed at how the Lord is encouraging and inspiring us each day of this journey with such a wide variety of people with a wide variety of experiences.

I will always cherish this memory of pedaling away from an Amish farm with a warm loaf of bread in my bike bag and my heart filled with joy knowing how blessed we are to see America in this way. And a lesson in God's perfect will.

We continued riding out among the beautiful country roads. Nicole had another blow out on one of her tires and we didn't have everything we needed to fix it so we had to call Jeanne and Chanel to come and pick us up. While we were waiting we found a really nice tourist area to wait. It was called Amish Acres. It had gift shops including a cheese store, a candy store and an Amish style restaurant. When Jeanne and Chanel came we had dinner at the restaurant. It was served family-style complete with fried chicken, roast beef, dressing, mashed potatoes, noodles, green beans, coleslaw, relish, fresh baked bread with apple butter, and your choice of pie. We went into the gift shop and Chanel found a little Amish porcelain doll to add to her collection. It was

a lot of fun and a great way to end
our day before heading back to camp.

The Yogi Bear Campground that we are
staying at is having their Christmas
in July celebration. They had an
outside movie night. We watched
a little as we went to the snack
shack. The lady working there wished
us a Merry Christmas. They were
going to have a contest to see who
decorated their trailer up the most
for Christmas. We didn't decorate the
RV but we did wash it before going
to bed. It was a family project.

July 19 ~ Saturday

We woke up to rain. It was still
warm but just wet and muggy. We
realized that Frankie and George, the
two little toads that Chanel had been
keeping, died. She was sad but we were
glad she had been able to have them for
a whole week. After we got packed up

we left camp. Just before we pulled
out of our campsite someone came over
to us and said be sure to stop at the
front desk. As we left we pulled up
and one of the workers came out and
said, "We just wanted to let you know
that we deducted one of your nights
lodging because we really believe in what
you are doing." She had tears in her
eyes as she was telling us this. What
a wonderful 'out of the blue' blessing!
Thank You, Lord, for taking such good
care of us in so many ways ... from
spiritual to practical. You constantly
amaze us by being such a part of our
everyday lives by allowing angels to
come our way. Nicole says we can now
say Yogi Bear is a proud sponsor of
Hope and Courage Across America!

We were heading to Goshen for the
weekend of ministry and seeing old
friends, the Stoltzfuses. Jeanne called
them to see where our motel was and
they said, "Why don't you just come

to our house and we will guide you?"
It was lightly raining and so when
we came up to their home both Vic
and Marie were outside waving us
down with their big smiles and a big
umbrella! It was a warm welcome
to Goshen. Vic directed us to the
motel where Bob and I would be
staying. Nicole, Grant and Chanel would
be staying with Vic and Marie (they
wanted to be Grandma and Grandpa
to them for the weekend) and Jeanne
was staying with Cal and Betty Graber
(old friends from North Lima). Bob
has often told the story of when he
was a young boy and Cal took him and
his brothers, Pat and Tom, camping
for their first time. They were in
a little scouting group that was a
part of the Mennonite church. It
was nice to actually meet him.

Vic and Marie paid for our two nights
of lodging at the Travel Lodge. They
invited us back to their home for

grilled hamburgers and a nice time of just visiting in their home. They had just built a cement ramp into their front door for Bob to use. There were two care packages at their home when we arrived. One was cookies and banana bread from Tom and Cindy, including jam and smoked salmon from Cindy's parents. And the other was from John Diezsi who sent Grant packets of hot chocolate and Dream Whip. He had always gotten a kick out of watching Grant enjoy his cocoa with lots of whipped cream! And he sent Chanel a little brown teddy bear. It is really special to receive love packages from home. What a wonderful way to cheer us on.

Vic picked Chanel up and asked, "What is one thing you would like to do while you are in Goshen?" "I want to go to an Amish farm," Chanel replied quickly. We told Vic and Marie of our wonderful day visiting with the Amish

lady, Brenda, and buying baked goods
from her home. We also told them
how sad Chanel had been that she was
not with us. He said they had some
Amish friends that maybe he could
take her to while the rest of us went
bike riding. Now I was sad. I wanted
to go to an Amish farm, too, but Bob
planned on us riding bikes today. I
reluctantly told Vic that I would love
to go but I better go ride instead.

Just as we were preparing to leave
their home and head back to the
motel to get ready to ride it began
pouring. Bob said, " Well, I think
we will spend the afternoon visiting
instead of riding." I was excited
because I REALLY wanted to meet
this Amish family. Thank You, Lord,
for sending the rain when you did.

We followed Vic and Marie (with
Jeanne) in their car out to the Nisley
farm. It was only about five miles

from their home. It was a little after 5:00 p.m. and Vic knew they would be home because it was chore time. I felt kind of bad that we were showing up with no warning but he said it would be okay. They do have a phone but it is only voicemail. It is in a little shed away from the house so that it doesn't interfere with their family time. When we pulled into their driveway Alma, the wife, came out of the barn and warmly greeted us. We began visiting right away and I could tell that we would have no problem becoming friends. When we arrived their ten-year-old son, Kenneth, was out driving their Bobcat (small tractor) and their twelve-year-old daughter, Rosemary, was helping Perry, the dad, with the milking. Alma took us into the barn to meet Perry and to watch the milking. My favorite part of observing the milking was seeing the farm cats happily lapping up the fresh milk put in a bowl for them. It was so cute watching them. Perry

197

told Bob he hoped we would stay
until he finished with the milking.
Alma really encouraged us to pull up
a chair and have a visit. So we did.

We sat on lawn chairs in their yard
under a big tree and began a nice long
visit. I asked Alma what it was like
to host the Sunday church services.
She explained to us the meal they
prepare for that day and also said
that she hosts it only about once a
year because there are so many host
families. She told us of a peanut
butter marshmallow cream that they
make for their Sunday sandwiches.
I learned how important family is in
their culture. I also learned what
an Amish wedding is like from the
start to finish ... a lot of eating
goes on throughout the day. And
often times the young people end
the day with a game of volleyball.

It wasn't too long before Perry
was able to join us. They are very
humble people and have quiet ways
about them. I had never really spoken
to an Amish family before so this
was very interesting to me and very
informative. I soon learned that we
have a lot in common. They put a
lot of importance on God, family and
being good people. It was such a
HUGE blessing to be able to spend
a warm summer evening with them.
This was truly a dream come true.

Rosemary and Chanel became good
little friends right away, even sharing
addresses to become pen pals.
Rosemary is about the same size as
Chanel and she offered to give Chanel
a ride in their buggy. She looks like a
delicate little thing but she is strong
and can handle those horses well.
She went into their barn and pulled
the buggy out, took the pony and
guided it to the buggy and harnessed

them together. These were heavy items she was dealing with but it looked as though it took little effort on her part. She took Nicole, Grant and Chanel in the buggy out on the country road. After they came back, Rosemary took the pony and let Chanel ride it with a summer saddle. Chanel got to help with the evening chores by feeding two baby calves milk from a bottle, feeding their chickens and cleaning the milk trays after the milking was done. It was a great learning experience for Chanel to see what farm life is all about. And it was a great learning experience for me (and the rest of the family) to see and learn what the Amish people and their culture is all about. They are just people trying to do the right thing in a quiet and humble fashion.

We had been visiting for a while and I noticed that Rosemary had gone in and changed her dress. Perry made a comment about Rosemary having just finished making her first dress that week, (the one she was wearing). She had done such a lovely job on this dress, it was beautiful. I was very impressed and told her what a nice job she had done. She just smiled. Perry asked Chanel if she had tried on any of Rosemary's dresses. It wasn't long before the girls were running off in the house and Chanel came out wearing one of Rosemary's dresses. She looked so cute. I asked Alma if I could take a picture of Chanel wearing the dress and she said that it would be fine. This is one of those times when I would have LOVED to capture every moment spent with this family on film but their friendship is too valuable to me. The Amish don't allow themselves to be photographed. I will have to rely on the memories in my mind and in my heart to recall this day.

After a while Alma asked me if I would like to go inside her home.

They had just gotten back from a family reunion earlier that day and she said things were a little out of order but if I didn't mind we were welcome to come in their home. Well, you can be sure I was not going to let an opportunity like that go by. So Marie, Jeanne, Nicole, Grant, Chanel and I went inside with Alma and Rosemary. I was thanking her for inviting us in and she said with a big warm smile," My home is always open for friends." I was so happy with meeting my new friends.

Chanel in Amish dress at the Nisley's.

Their home was nice and open. It was getting dusk outside and so their home was a little dim because they don't use electricity. I had seen that Perry had a couple of kerosene lanterns outside that I am sure he would be bringing in that night. The kitchen was very large with a big wooden table in the middle. I could only imagine the family meals enjoyed around that table. The living room was open as well. It was furnished with a couple of nice couches, a wood stove, two sewing machines in wooden cabinets, and bookshelves with a variety of books including a set of World Book Encyclopedias. They had a beautiful china cabinet filled with delicate china cups and good dishes. There were a lot of doilies, a few Precious Moments figurines, and wall hangings with Bible verses. Our favorite was of Isaiah 40:31. It was a nice wooden carving with an eagle. We told Alma that this was the Scripture that Bob would be preaching from in the morning.

She had a few men's pastel shirts hanging to dry in the house. There was also a man's black Amish hat that looked as though it had been washed and hanging to dry. I'm sure they had been prepared for church in the morning. But my favorite item in her home was seeing the freshly washed white Amish hats hanging to dry. Alma told me her sixteen-year-old daughter had played volleyball at the family reunion and had come home and washed hers out. Both Alma and Rosemary had bandanas on. They were in their chore dresses. As a matter of fact, yesterday Brenda, the Amish baker, had her bandana on. It must be customary for the women to wear bandanas on work days. There were several of these little caps drying on a special wired rack. They were so crisp and white ... and pure. I think the memory of those little white caps will forever be etched in my heart.

It wasn't long and we were getting ready to say our goodbyes. Chanel came up to me with a big smile on her face and a bag in her hand and said, "Rosemary gave me a dress!" She was so excited! I asked Alma if it was okay. She said that Rosemary was outgrowing that dress and that it was fine. What a very special gift this was for Chanel to receive such an authentic gift. She will treasure it always.

We thanked them for such a memorable evening. We told them how much we appreciated them setting aside the time for us and opening up their home. As I was giving Alma a hug and shaking Perry's hand I could tell they were both getting a little teary eyed. Perry got out his handkerchief and wiped his eyes. We felt that we had really created a special friendship with this family that evening.

Vic told us later that in the fifteen years he had known the Nisleys and of all the people he had brought out to their farm, he had never brought a family that connected the way we did. He said something very special had happened that evening. I, too, felt it was a very strong connection with this family ... a special bond ... a special blessing. Thank You, Lord, for this incredible day.

We went back to the motel and the kids all showered and then Bob took them over to spend the night at Vic and Marie's while I got our clothes ready for church. Jeanne went to the Graber's for the weekend.

I could hardly wait to call Betty tonight to tell her about my day at the Amish farm meeting my new friends.

Chapter 18

July 21 ~ Monday

We had about eight riders from the
Goshen church meet us at the motel
at 9:30 for a short bike ride on the
new Pumpkinvine Trail. Vic joined us
along with his ten-year-old grandson,
Tommy. It is a beautiful trail that
John Yoder has been very instrumental
in getting in place. John was from
the North Lima Mennonite church,
too. His wife, June, was a student
at Goshen when Jeanne attended. It
began raining and so we didn't ride
more than eight miles that morning.

We packed up and went over to Wal-Mart to get Marie some flowers. In the parking lot, they had a parking stall for the Amish buggies. Chanel and I went into the store and got behind a nice and friendly Amish lady named Ruth. We began talking and I told her that we had met Perry and Alma Nisley on Saturday. She said, "Oh, I know them, in fact, I just saw Alma in here." I couldn't believe it! With our roses in hand, we headed out to the truck and there was Alma talking to Bob! She was telling Bob he should come back and speak at their Amish school after we finish our bike ride in the fall. It was so fun seeing Alma again. She introduced me to her sister and by the time we left, Ruth came out of Wal-Mart and joined us.

We took the flowers over to Vic and Marie to thank them once again for the wonderful weekend and to say our goodbyes. I also told them of our

encounters of seeing Alma and Ruth.
They just smiled and again told me that
the connection we had with them was
very unusual. Especially when I told
them that Alma had mentioned how
wonderful it would be if we could
come and speak at their schools!
Vic was just amazed ... and I was
just excited! What a great meeting
we had at Wal-Mart, of all places.

Grandpa Vic

Cal and Betty Graber took Jeanne to the airport. We sent Jeanne home a week early so that she could help the last couple of weeks before Robby's wedding. She got to go home with a great send-off having just spent the weekend with old friends from North Lima. She left with a smile on her face.

We left Goshen and headed for Shipshewana. We had no idea what a beautiful and wonderful stop this would be for us. The Shipshewana area is the third largest Amish community in the world. And we were staying right in the heart of it! Our RV was built in that town and we wanted to stop at the office and schedule an appointment. They are going to be doing some repairs on it while we fly home for Robby's wedding and my family's reunion at Betty's. We stayed in a nice little campground near downtown Shipshewana. Bob, Grant and I rode in the country among all the

beautiful Amish farms. It was just
such a lovely ride on a warm summer
night. A dream come true bike ride. We
saw a lot of children playing outside.
I would wave and say ' hi.` Most would
wave back but usually wouldn't say
anything. These images are precious to
me. I wish I could snap a picture but
I won't. Most of the little girls were
in bonnets and bare feet. One little
girl was chasing after her kittens. It
is such a sweet, innocent picture in
my mind. We saw a lot of miniature
ponies. They seem to be a popular
thing in this area. They are so tiny and
cute. We saw horses of all sizes.
The Amish use horses a lot. Even the
Amish dogs are nice. We don't have
to worry about them chasing us on
country roads. Bob says it is because
Amish are pacifists and their dogs
are, too. I think he is joking. Of all
the rides we have taken, this truly
will be one of my most memorable.

We told Grant if he wanted to he could ride back to the campground and we would meander through the little quaint town. We stopped and visited with a couple on vacation named Daryl and Kathy. They were Christians and very interested in what we are doing. They took a couple of prayer cards and said they would be praying for us. When they left they were teary eyed and thought what we were doing was such a great thing. Next, we met a local bike shop owner who is a Christian and at one time was a fulltime pastor. It was a lot of fun just visiting with the people in this very cute town. Shipshewana is such a charming town with beautiful flowers, cute little shops and the Amish with their horse and buggies.

July 22 ~ Tuesday

We woke up to a day of riding in the Amish countryside. What could a country girl at heart want more than this? I was really looking forward to riding on this day but I really had no idea of the many blessings that I would experience in one day.

Bob, Grant and I left in the morning for a beautiful ride. Nicole and Chanel stayed back at camp and we had planned to have a fun afternoon together. Our ride began with passing several Amish in their buggies. We passed such well-kept farms; everything looked as neat as a pin. And they have such nice gardens, flowers and vegetables with their large white homes. You usually see buggies in the yards and/or bicycles. One of the reasons we love riding in the Amish community is the roads are great for bikes. Even though we have to dodge some horse droppings, we are on quieter roads that have a wide bike lane. The Amish ride bikes a lot so the people living in this area are already

used to slowing down and watching out
for cyclists. A great advantage for us.

We saw a sign that read " Rise-N-Roll"
bakery. We decided to take a detour
from the main road and go down the
country road and see what we might
find. We had no idea what waited for
us. What a blessing! As soon as we
biked up to the cute Amish bakery,
the owner, who was standing outside,
began to study us closely. He looked
a long time at Bob and finally said in
a serious voice," Interesting bike."
Bob looked back at him and said," Yes.
And an interesting man sitting on the
bike, don't you think?" He smiled and
came over to us and began talking.
His name was Orvin. He was in his
early thirties and very friendly and
interested in hearing our story. He
introduced us to a young couple that
was there with him. He told us later
that her husband of ten months had
died of cancer and the young man's

wife had been killed by a drunk driver.
This couple was handing out wedding
invitations and they were getting married
in two weeks. The widower had a little
two-year-old named Carol. She was so
cute with her little Amish dress on
and her little ponytails. We had a nice
visit with Orvin. His wife, Viola, was
out of town so we didn't get to meet
her. Grant and I went in the bakery,
some of the Amish girls came over
to us, and said Orvin had told them
what we were doing. We finally made
our choice of pastries. There were
so many yummy looking treats we had
a hard time choosing. We decided on
doughnuts and went to pay and the
girl said there was no charge for us.
We were so surprised and thanked
them for blessing us in this way.

Grant and I went outside and brought
out the doughnuts so we could
eat them with Bob. While eating
our doughnuts we heard singing

coming from inside the bakery. We looked through the window and the Amish girls were all singing while they worked. What a joyful sight.

There was an older Amish man visiting with Bob. I introduced myself and he told me his name was Ralph and he was Orvin's father. I said that was my dad's name and with a name like that he must be a nice guy. We talked for a while and Bob gave him a prayer card. He looked it over and asked if we took donations. He pulled out his worn wallet and he handed Bob a bill. We were so touched and felt bad taking it from him. But it was obvious that he believed in what we were doing and he wanted to bless us in this way. He was such a sweet, thin old man. He looked like your typical Amish grandpa ... named Ralph. We left the bakery with smiles on our faces ... we had just had some of the very best doughnuts I have ever

had ... and had made new friends in
the Amish community. We are really
enjoying the chance to fellowship
with them. They are special people
and we feel very honored that they
seem to welcome us in their circles.

During the whole time we were there,
people were constantly coming and
going out of the bakery. It seemed
to be the hotspot for baked goods.
I got to visiting with a guy from
Illinois who was staying in the same
RV park that we were and he told me
his name was Daryl and his wife was
Kathy ... that was the names of the
other couple we had met last night. I
thought that was a funny coincidence.

We went about 40 miles and then went
back to get showers and freshen up.
Nicole, Chanel and I found a little
place in Shipshewana to have afternoon
tea. Amish women served our tea. It
was a really nice time for we three

girls. It had been a very long time since we had shared tea together. They served the tea on Maryland china with pretty napkins. The tea consisted of hot tea and scones with Devonshire cream and jam. We had two chocolates, a piece of fruit and an orange sherbet-type dessert served in pretty glasses. Bob and Grant had gone over to the large flea market that is famous in this area. It is opened Tuesday and Wednesday during the summer. We met up with them and Bob had met up with my new friend, Ruth. She is working at one of the Amish baked goods stands. I couldn't believe that she was there! She is such a delightful lady. She is very bubbly and always has a smile. Her fifteen-year-old daughter, Marilyn (who has a twin brother, Marlin), was there, too. She will be starting as a teacher this fall and hopes that Bob can come and be a part of their school day. As we were saying our goodbyes, Ruth gave us her phone number to call when we come back through. She also gave us a box of chocolate chip cookies. These new Amish friends are just so giving.

Leaving the flea market, we stopped at the Blue Ribbon Kettle Corn stand and visited with the Amish owner. His name is Vernon and he is such a nice man. He was very friendly and outgoing. Probably the most talkative of the Amish men we had met. He was interested in our journey and our ministry. He gave us his card with his phone number and said to call him when we were in the area again. He hopes to hear us at one of his grandchildren's school when we come back. We bought some popcorn from him and then as we were leaving he gave us another bag and said we might need it for our trip! We definitely hope to see him again. Bob said he didn't see why we couldn't come back here on our drive home from New York. I am excited!

We went to the Blue Gate for dinner.
It is one of those nice Amish
restaurants. The atmosphere was
friendly and wholesome and the food
was good and plentiful. And we just
enjoyed our time being there.

I had loved our bike ride the evening
before and I wanted Nicole and Chanel
to have the chance of riding in the
area, too. So we went for a family
bike ride. I don't think we'll get a
chance for all five of us to ride
together again on this journey. Nicole
won't be coming back out with us
after we go home for the wedding
and reunion. She needs to get ready
for college. In my opinion, this was
the perfect ride to end our journey
with the whole family together. We
had fun riding on the country roads
through the Amish farms, seeing so
many Amish families around their

homes. They are so quiet you almost feel as if you should whisper.

We saw an old Amish man in his yard and he greeted us with a friendly smile and hello. It seemed as though several of the people knew about us. Vic had told us that their grapevine grows fast! We even had one family tapping at their window and waving at us as we rode past. We saw some more of the baby miniature ponies. One was so tiny we stopped and got some pictures of him with his mama. They are smaller than some dogs. We also saw a 'barn raising.' The Amish are very good about helping their neighbors.

Thank You, Lord, for giving me this great memory of riding on a warm summer night with my whole family in Indiana on a country road through the Amish farms. I couldn't have asked for a more perfect evening.

Wow! See why I thought Darla should tell you about Northern Indiana? None of us could express the events of the last five days as well as her. I hated taking Darla away from Shipshewana but our journey was not scheduled to end here. We packed up and moved camp to the east. This campground had Christmas in July, also. The next morning Vic drove out to see us one last time before we pedaled too far out of the area.

"I brought you a book that could be informative to you."

"That's kind of you. What is it?"

"In light of your new relationship with the Amish I thought you might like to learn more about them. Have you heard about the tragedy a few years ago at an Amish school in Pennsylvania?"

"The shooting? Yeah, I remember hearing that on the news. That was an awful thing to happen to such peaceful people."

"This book is about the shooting and the community's response. It is coauthored by three men considered experts regarding the Plain People. One of them is a professor here at Goshen College. The book has some good background into the history and doctrine of the Amish. It's called 'Amish Grace: How Forgiveness Transcended Tragedy.'"

It was impossible for Vic to stop being a pastor ... or an educator ... or a friend.

I took the book from his hands, "Thank you. I think the door is opening for our ministry to work in the Amish community and I need to learn more about them. I have had a couple of invitations to stop back and speak at Amish schools on the way home this fall. Last night I was in the Wal-Mart in Angola and started talking to an Amish man. He is on the school board in his district and wants me to come to his school. Vic, I have been speaking in schools across the country for over twenty-five years. I have never been in an Amish school. God is doing something here."

"I think so, too. I told Darla, I have never seen the Amish welcome an English family as quickly as they have welcomed you. You have been given an honor." The Amish refer to anyone that is non-Amish as 'English' no matter where you originated.

"We know we are being blessed and Darla is tickled pink. Thank you again, Vic, for all you and Marie have done. Not just for Hope and Courage Across America but for my family years ago. You made a difference in our lives."

"Well, I'm just glad I got to see what became of some of Harold's kids. I think your dad would be pleased."

We all said our goodbyes. It was especially hard on Chanel. She had adopted Vic as her grandpa. If she carried two baby toads in a jug for a week, you can only imagine how much she loved Grandpa Vic. Her tears were just a measurement of how close they had become in such a short time. I knew she would find a new BFF soon enough but Grandpas are much harder to come by. We decided it would be best to get busy to occupy our hearts. Nicole took Chanel down to a lake to play on the beach. Darla, Grant and I got on our bikes.

We headed east on US 20. The road had a good shoulder to ride on and was lined with farms and country lanes. The temperature and humidity hovered in lockstep around ninety. It was late July and everything was in full growth. The trees labored under the weight of their lush leaves. The crops filled the gaps in the rows and nudged against the fences. Pastures so green, horses and cattle barely wandered as they grazed through the afternoon. We were not in a hurry, either. We were satisfied with the road beneath our tires. The road ahead would wait for us.

A white steeple beckoned us off the highway. We took the side road that led to a long dirt lane up to the doors of the church. It sat on a knoll under the shade of a big oak tree. It had been sitting on that knoll since the 1800s. The mighty oak was much younger than the building it protected. The fresh white paint told wanderers, like us, that this place was not abandoned. Hope still dwelt here. The bell in the steeple still rang, calling all to come and find peace. And for several generations people have been coming off their farms, out of the woods, up this dusty lane to worship in this sanctuary. We parked outside its doors and borrowed the shade of its companion oak. Resting quietly we could faintly sense all the stories of hope and courage that had entered those doors in the last 150 years. We were definitely satisfied with the road beneath us.

A place of peace and hope.

Back on our bikes, we continued east. Rounding a bend, I saw a sign I had been waiting for, 'Welcome to Ohio.' We posed for pictures and said hello to Ohio.

The next day was my birthday. We moved camp again. And guess what? They were having Christmas in July, too. This was the third camp we had been in this month that celebrated this strange ritual. Oh well, at least it put everyone in a festive mood. Chanel decorated the RV – for my birthday, not Christmas, and we had a good evening.

Our next stop was Grace Church on the outskirts of Cleveland. It was one of the few places on our schedule that we did not know anyone. I had been in Germany with Grant speaking at an Air Force base. The chaplain there said a friend of his pastored a Christian Missionary Alliance congregation near Cleveland and might be interested in Hope and Courage coming to his church. A few emails and phone calls later had us on board. This would be the last speaking engagement before we flew back home for the wedding/reunion.

Grace Church was a large and active body of believers. More than three thousand people attended the Sunday morning meetings. They broke it up into three services to accommodate the size of the sanctuary. We arrived at 7:30 a.m. and were met by warm, wonderful people. There were no more strangers for us that day, only new friends. They handed us a box of Journey Bibles that had arrived earlier in the week. Our friend Mike had sent them ahead of us. Mike was the one who wanted to make sure we had Bibles to distribute along the way. We met him the first Sunday of the journey back in May. He had been buying and shipping Bibles to all of our scheduled stops. During the message, I would mention the availability of a Bible for anyone who did not have one already. The church set a table up outside the sanctuary for the Bibles, our Hope and Courage buttons, and our prayer cards. We offered all three for free. We did have a bucket on the table for people who wanted to give to the support of our ride. People were always generous. We were in a constant state of gratefulness to people's willingness to help us carry our message.

Preaching two or three services back-to-back is interesting to me. I know there are pastors who do it every week and don't think twice about it. I am less experienced at it but have made a few general observations. The first service is usually attended by fewer people and they lean toward the senior citizen age. The following services have a larger and more generationally diverse crowd. The speaker also has to watch the time closely in the earlier services because there is a whole new audience waiting to get started.

I say this is a general observation because Grace Church was an exception. The first service was well attended by people of all age groups. I was still aware of the clock but I was able to deliver my message completely and on time. I ended each service with two opportunities to respond. One was the chance to acknowledge Jesus as your Savior for the first time in your life and be forgiven of your sins. In church-talk we call that 'getting saved.' The other was putting all your hope in God no matter what mountain you are facing. And with that hope, have the courage to take the next step.

A woman who had been sitting near Darla came over and gave her a hug. She said she had a friend who needed to hear this message. Her friend had just lost a twenty-year-old son. He had been attending Seattle Pacific University and had really gotten into bicycling. Six weeks ago, he was on his way to work on his bike when a beer truck pulled in front of him and dragged him under the truck. It was an awful death. She told Darla she wanted to get a copy of my message and give it to her friend. Two other people came up and told Darla about the same accident. After the service, Darla and the kids stood at the table in the foyer to visit and hand out buttons and cards. And Bibles. Lots of Bibles. In a short time, the whole case of Bibles was gone and there were two more services to go.

"Grant, we're out of Bibles," Darla said with enough urgency to alarm Grant.

"What do we do?"

"I'm not sure. Were there any Bibles back at the RV?"

"Yeah. We had some leftover from last week. The Mennonites all had Bibles."

"We need to go get them. After Dad introduces us in the second service we'll sneak out and drive back to the RV."

At the beginning of the second service, I introduced Darla, Nicole, Grant and Chanel. They all stood and gave a smile to the audience. Shortly afterward Darla and Grant quietly slipped out and made a dash for the RV. They grabbed a nearly full case of Bibles from the week before and any others that had been left over.

That should be enough, they thought as they set them on the table.

The second service ended and by the time the third service began all the Bibles were gone again. Grace Church was such an active church. There were new people every Sunday. And new people were anxious to get the Word of God. I did not mention the Bibles in the last service.

I sat in the foyer after three consecutive sermons. I was drained as I greeted people. I have to confess I was thinking more of getting away from the crowd and relaxing than I was shaking one more hand. A woman and her college-age daughter timidly came over to me. I extended my hand out of habit and the mother took it. Instead of a quick shake and release, she prolonged the grasp. That was enough to snap me out of my complacency and bring me back to focus.

"A friend called me this morning and said I needed to get over here and listen to your message. My daughter and I were able to make it here before the last service started. We needed to hear everything you said. Last month my son, her brother, was killed on a bicycle in Seattle. He was going to college at SPU and was hit by a truck. His death has been extremely hard on us, especially my daughter. They were very close. Your message of hope and courage was exactly what we needed today. It has really helped us."

My eyes watered and my voice cracked as I encouraged them to take what God has given them and face each minute together.

That morning we saw hundreds of hands raised to say, "I am putting my hope in God and having the courage to face the mountain before me." We saw thirty or more get saved. But it would be the memory of this mother's hand in mine that would symbolize the meaning of this journey so far. Grace Church, amazing Grace Church, was the last stop before our break. God could not have given us a better one.

We pulled the RV 200 miles back to Shipshewana to leave at the manufacturer. They would fix it and park it until we came back. We packed a few bags of clothes and drove the truck to the Fort Wayne airport. Darla, Nicole, Grant, Chanel and I boarded a plane bound for Seattle. It was time to go home for a break. Darla's sister, Betty, was hosting a family reunion and Jeanne's son, Robby, was getting married. We could attend both events and be back to our bikes within ten days.

I sat in an airplane flying back over the same ground we had just pedaled across. What took seventy-six days on a bicycle would take four hours by plane. It was impossible not to reflect on our journey so far. We had come through the west and were pushing deep into the heartland of America.

I used to think of America as a patchwork quilt. Separate states sewn together in a colorful blanket. Just like the maps show in our schoolbooks. Every state a different shade defined by clear and distinct borders. Then I started travelling by car and airplane from coast to coast. Looking out the window of a plane at 30,000 feet, you realize there are no actual borders. I began to see our nation as a huge tapestry. One big design flowing north to south and east to west. This bike ride is changing my perspective again. I now see America as both a patchwork quilt and a tapestry. Separate pieces sewn together and interwoven by common threads. Different people with different customs connected to the others by over two centuries of shared history.

Another thing I have come to realize is most of the geography of America is made up of small towns. Small towns with small churches. I think it is the stitching and fiber of these small towns that keep this nation from unraveling at the edges.

The cockpit radio crackled, "We are making our final approach to SeaTac Airport. Flight attendants, please prepare the cabin for landing."

Chapter 19

It was strange being at home. We didn't feel like we belonged here now. We belonged on our bikes. The house seemed huge to us. And after eleven weeks in an RV, most of what we had in the house seemed unnecessary. However, there were benefits to being in our house again. We could spread out and have a little privacy. The kids could actually be in their room and not be able to see everyone else's room at the same time. As soon as we got in the house, everyone separated and went to their private spaces. It wasn't long, though, before we all congregated in the same room. We had gotten used to each other's company. That is not a dysfunctional thing in a family.

As I said, it was strange being home, being in Gig Harbor. We felt awkward running into people and explaining why we were here and not in Ohio. It wasn't so bad that we avoided people. We just didn't go out of our way to see them. We didn't have a lot of time for random socializing anyway. We had mail to catch up on, bills to pay, and laundry to do. On top of that, there was the Hollis reunion and Robby and Marlo's wedding.

The first weekend was the reunion. As I had mentioned earlier, Darla is the youngest of seven. Ralph and Myrtle Hollis had children between 1940 and 1960. Four boys and three girls. Ralph was raised on a farm in Kansas and Myrtle's family lived nearby. They, too, were from large families. Ralph had ten siblings, Myrtle had seven. Born at the time of World War I, they came of age through the Great Depression, and started their family during World War II. The Dust Bowl of the '30s forced them from Kansas to seek work in California. For Ralph and Myrtle, hope and courage across America was not a bike ride. Hope and courage was a way of life.

Ralph became a skilled carpenter. His five brothers became Assembly of God ministers back in Kansas. Both professions were familiar to Jesus. I had never met him but when I would ask about Ralph people said, "He was a man of few words. But when he spoke, people listened." Myrtle would become a gifted homemaker. Not because she couldn't do anything else. Myrtle had proved herself a strong worker on the farms in Kansas and the chicken ranches of California. She was a homemaker because that is what she wanted to do with her life. Her family was her passion.

Ralph moved the family to Washington State in 1969. He built a home on the lake and went to work for a local cabinet maker. In 1975 Ralph would suffer a fatal heart attack and leave Myrtle with three children still at home. Darla was two weeks from her fifteenth birthday. Myrtle would continue her passion as family homemaker for twenty-two more years. In 1997, she would join Ralph in heaven to watch over the fruit of their lives. When she left this earth there were seven adult children, fourteen grandchildren (Darla was three months from delivering the fifteenth grandchild, Chanel, at the time), and six great grandchildren. It is a legacy that is still growing today.

A few decades ago, those seven adult children started hosting a Ralph and Myrtle Hollis Family Reunion. Every two years a different sibling is the host. They started with the oldest, Betty, and went down the line to the youngest, Darla. Darla had to wait twelve years for her turn in 2006. This year we are back to Betty's turn again. There is a lot of Myrtle in Darla, and missing a family reunion was not an option. Besides, Ralph and Myrtle's newest great grandchildren were making their reunion debut. Darla's sister Juanita's daughter Cheri had twins, Jackson and Jensen. Did I lose you on that? Sorry, but it is the reunion's first set of twins and they deserve mention. We spent a few days eating and visiting out at Betty and Dave's house on Silent Lake. We had a great time. It was a little strange though. It felt like we had traveled across the country to a reunion that was only sixty miles from home. Which is exactly what we had done.

The next weekend was Robby and Marlo's wedding. The ceremony was beautiful. Robby had found himself a wonderful young lady to marry. And Marlo was getting a great young man for a husband. Jeanne had come back a week earlier and had used that time well to prepare for her son's big day. The reception gave us a chance to see all of my side of the family. It was especially good to see my mom. We caught up on everything that was going on while we were gone. The world at home had not come to a screeching halt just because we decided to take a bike ride. People wanted to know details about the journey and we told some of the more interesting stories, mostly about people we had met along the way. We discovered it was difficult to fully express what we were seeing and feeling out there. It was as if our brains had not processed it enough to make sense yet.

The day after the wedding was Darla's birthday. She turned forty-eight. The kids and I put together an afternoon tea to celebrate. Darla loves afternoon teas. It consisted of quiche, cucumber and cream cheese sandwiches, fresh fruit, scones with Devonshire cream and jam, chocolate covered strawberries, and lemon bars. We displayed the goodies on tiers and served them on nice china plates. These were Darla's own real plates on her own real table in her own real house. Not paper plates on a worn out picnic table in a campground a thousand miles from home. To be fair, Darla did not care where she celebrated her birthday. She was just happy we were all together.

Family photo before we headed back to our bikes.

The rest of the day was spent packing and preparing to catch the midnight flight to Fort Wayne. We went over things with Nicole. She wasn't going back out with us. College was starting in two weeks and she needed to be prepared. Man, she is going to be missed. I will miss her because she amuses me to no end. She is leaps and bounds ahead of where I was at twenty years old. I love watching her grow into a young adult. Darla will miss her because Darla is her mother and loves it most when her children are near. She will be missed most by Grant and Chanel. They totally love being with their big sister. It is different for them when she is not there. We told Nicole to check her class schedule and see if we can fly her to New York City to cross the finish line with us. That evening the cab to the airport pulled into our driveway. We loaded the bags and turned to say our farewells. Leaving the house was not difficult. Leaving Nicole was very hard. Especially for Darla. You should know by now that family is very important to Darla. It breaks her heart that we are not all out there together. She wiped her tears all the way to the airport.

A similar scene was playing out at the Oesch home where Jeanne was bidding farewell to Don and their daughter, Jenny. She was leaving them and would not be back until the end of the ride. We were very aware of the sacrifice she was making to support us on this journey. We met her at the airport. Darla, Jeanne, Grant, Chanel and I boarded the plane. This was our team. Hope and Courage Across America left home again. This time we were not coming back until we reached the end. I looked over the schedule of speaking engagements left on our route.

August 17 AM North Lima Mennonite in North Lima, Ohio

August 17 PM Tabernacle Evangelical Presbyterian in Youngstown, Ohio

August 20 PM South Hills Assembly in Bethel Park, Pennsylvania

August 23 Portland CityFest Waterfront Park in Portland, Oregon (I'm on stage around 5:00 PM)

August 24 PM River of God Church in Enola, Pennsylvania

August 27 PM River of God Church in Enola, Pennsylvania

August 31 AM The Power Place in Kennett Square, Pennsylvania

September 7 AM Hopewell reformed Church in Hopewell Junction, New York

These stops represented the rest of our journey. Except the CityFest in Portland, Oregon. That was definitely off our route. Luis Palau was having a huge Christian festival in Portland and wanted me to be a part of it. Luis is a friend and has been good to our ministry in the past. I was more than willing to fly out to Portland and be a part of CityFest. I smiled realizing the last church Hope and Courage had scheduled was in Hopewell Junction. I put the list away and closed my eyes to try to sleep. The drone of the jet engines covered all the noise around me.

Lord, it is August 11. In one month, we plan to be at the Statue of Liberty. There are a lot of miles and a lot of stops to get there. I hope we can make it.

A familiar voice joined my thoughts, *Haven't you learned yet? It is not about the miles, it is about the message. Get some rest. You will need your strength to carry My message.*

We landed in Fort Wayne and loaded our gear into our truck. We drove back to Shipshewana to get the fifth wheel from the manufacturer. They had repaired the minor fixes on our list and had done more than we asked. They were a great group of people. They really liked the Hope and Courage logos we had on the RV. One of the guys came up and said he had visited our website and really appreciated what we were doing. We decided to stay overnight and show Jeanne Shipshewana before driving to Ohio to resume our ride. We parked at the same campground we had stayed at before.

After we were settled back into the RV, Darla and I went out for a bike ride. It felt great to be back on our bikes. These were the same Amish roads we had enjoyed so much three weeks earlier. As the sun started to set, we turned around and headed back toward camp. We pulled into a convenience store to buy some juice for the morning. Darla was dismounting her bike to go in when a woman walked right up to us.

"My daughter-in-law just got her handcycle today. She loves it!"

In the next thirty minutes the story unfolded. Three years ago, her daughter-in-law was the victim of an attempted carjacking. When confronted by the attacker, her instinct or fear kicked in and she tried to speed away. The attacker shot at her. One bullet passed through the flesh of her arm, entered her side, and lodged against her vertebrae. The bullet would paralyze her from the waist down. She was five months pregnant at the time.

Lying in the hospital, the young girl's prayer was simply heartbreaking.

"Let me live long enough to give birth so my baby can live and then take my life. I don't want to live in this condition."

I love how God answered her prayer. You see, God is not in the business of taking lives. He is the giver of life.

Jesus said it so clearly in the Gospel of John, "I am come that they might have life, and that they might have it more abundantly."

God gave life. First, He gave her the baby's life, a son. Then He gave the woman her life. I can only imagine when her prayer changed from give me death to give me life. I picture her cuddling the baby in her two arms and realizing there is no other woman on this planet who is more physically able to raise this child than her. There is hope and courage. Hope that God can hear your prayer. And courage to accept His answer. Again, Jesus says it best, "Not my will, Father, but Your will be done."

The woman continued her story about her daughter-in-law. Her son stands beside his wife as she adapts to her new abilities. She has just finished a twenty-six mile ride on a borrowed handcycle. The next ride will be on a handcycle of her own. I can imagine her husband riding on a regular bike next to her … with their two-year-old son in the baby seat. Hope and courage is all around us. And it's all around you, too.

We spent the next morning at the very large and popular Shipshewana Flea Market. While browsing through the stands Darla saw her good friend Ruth Miller. She was working at the bakery, "Darla! What a treat to see you."

"It's good to see you again, too, Ruth."

Darla introduced Jeanne to Ruth and they all visited awhile. "What are you doing in Shipshewana? Shouldn't you be on your way to New York?"

"We went home for a wedding and left the RV here for repairs. We just got back and are camping next door. We are leaving this afternoon." Darla explained. "Oh, we saw your daughter Marilyn before we flew home a few weeks ago."

"I know. She told me all about it. She said, 'Mom, there is something different about those people. I feel such warmth when I am with them.' I told her that warmth was our connection through God. Marilyn is really looking forward to Bob speaking at her school on your way home in September. You all need to come over for supper that day."

"We'd love to," Darla replied without trying to hide her excitement.

Ruth gave Darla a big hug, "I've had a difficult week. Seeing you has been an encouragement to me."

Darla had no idea what it was she had said or done to bring encouragement but that was okay. We had learned that the purpose of Hope and Courage Across America was to interact with people. God would take care of the who, when and why.

As we were leaving the flea market, we stopped by Vernon Miller's Blue Ribbon Kettle Corn. We had met Vernon before. He had his ten-year-old grandson, Michael, helping him. Michael was the oldest of seven children. Ten years old and the oldest of seven. That amazed me. I talked to Michael as Vernon finished popping a batch of kettle corn. The smell of fresh popped corn mingled with melted sugar was more than I could resist.

"Vernon, I'll buy a large bag of that corn," I said, reaching for my wallet.

Vernon scooped the warm corn into a bag so full he couldn't close the top. "I won't sell you anything but I'll give you something if you answer a question for me."

"For popcorn you can ask anything you want."

"How did you lose your legs?"

It was not the question I was expecting, but at least I knew the answer. I told him about the car crash and meeting Darla four years later. I did not give him the full version but I must have given him enough because he handed me the bag of kettle corn. Holding the long sack close to my body, I felt the warmth and smelled that sweet-salty aroma. I tried not to eat it by the fistful but popcorn is a weakness of mine. I was powerless. Darla and Vernon visited while I munched away. Vernon is really hoping that we are able to come back and speak at Michael's school. He wants to come and listen as well. He said when we come back he really would like to have us over to his house and meet his wife, Betty.

Darla carried the conversation long enough for me to satiate my popcorn craving. I started talking to Vernon about the book Vic gave me.

"Vernon, a friend gave me the book, 'Amish Grace.' It is about the shooting in Pennsylvania. I'm looking forward to reading it because I want to know more about Amish beliefs."

He finished filling a bag of corn. "You can't believe everything you read in books about the Amish," he said. "We are just like you. We believe Jesus died on the cross for our sins. We feel if people lived their lives by the Sermon on the Mount and the Lord's Prayer the world would be a better place."

"Amen." I couldn't think of anything else to add.

Bidding farewell, we went back to camp. Grant and I hooked up the truck, the girls prepared the RV, and we drove to our next camp in Ohio. Hope and Courage Across America was well on its way again.

Grant and Chanel at Vernon's popcorn stand.

Chapter 20

"So," Grant asks, "if a tornado were to hit the RV we'd all be killed, right Dad?"

We are very accustomed to Grant asking random questions that seemingly have nothing to do with anything going on. We were sitting in a local restaurant and the waitress had just delivered the closest thing to home cooked food you could find away from home. Darla and I had ordered Swiss steak and mashed potatoes that reminded us of her mom. A question about death and tornados could seem out of place at this moment.

However, I knew where this question originated. We had cycled through most of Ohio and were camped at West Branch State Park. Earlier in the day, we were looking at the clouds to see if it was going to rain before we got on our bikes. I pointed to the dark bank of clouds and showed Grant how to tell the direction they were traveling.

"You mark their progress against the tree tops or hold your thumb steady as a mark if there aren't any trees." I said. "The interesting thing about these clouds is they are moving in a different direction than the wind was blowing at ground level. That can make for some dramatic weather ... possibly a tornado."

Relax, there was no tornado. However, within minutes we were in the heart of a great thunder, lightning, wind and heavy rainstorm. Very dramatic weather indeed. And it made me look pretty smart in front of my son. Sometimes you get lucky.

Back to Grant's question, "So, we'd all be killed, right?"

I figured I could turn this into a learning moment. The cloud thing had bolstered my confidence. I finished my bite of Swiss steak and put on my 'motivational speaker' hat.

"No matter what you are facing you should always have the attitude that you will live through it."

That statement was bolstered by recent events. You see, while camped out in the state park we had several visitors stop by the RV. Our RV is somewhat of a magnet. There is something about the words "HOPE and COURAGE" and "SEEK . FIND . LIVE" emblazoned all over that draws people. Howard came by using a cane, staring at the graphics. He said he didn't know what we were doing but he liked the message. We talked and he told me about a long list of ailments he had gone through.

I said, "Yeah, but you didn't let any beat you, did you?"

He said he felt he met a band of angels today. We parted with brotherly hugs all around.

Next was Allen. He was missing a hand from a childhood farm accident. He wanted to talk about the lift I used to get in and out of the RV. He had worked on them and had some real knowledge to share. I appreciated the free tech support and carried the conversation deeper. He was a good man on a good path. He was in the park enjoying his grandkids from a good life. Obviously, he had the 'live through it' attitude for quite some time.

Our third visitor was Tina, around thirty years old I am guessing. She came toward the RV slowly with her arms on the shoulders of two ten-year-old boys. They were assisting her walk.

She was fighting back tears when she pointed to our logo and said, "I like that. Hope and Courage. I need that."

She had come through cancer and was dealing with kidney failure. She had just come back from dialysis. The two boys were her little brother and his friend. We are dedicated to taking time to talk to whomever God sends our way on this journey. It is the primary reason people sent us out here. We took time with Tina. I explained the logo. Hope in Christ and the courage within you to use that hope to take the next step. We talked about leaning on Christ to help her through her day. She could relate to that. She was leaning on two boys when she came into our campsite. She began to believe she could 'live through it.' We prayed with her and gave her a Journey Bible to help guide her next steps.

No matter what you are facing you should always have the attitude that you will live through it. I don't say that just based on three visitors in a campground. I do have a little experience on this subject. Take a stroll down memory lane with me.

April 25, 1976 ... A rhythmic beeping stirs me awake. Beep ... beep ... beep ... beep ...

Did Tom set an alarm? Are we late for work? I blink my eyes to bring them into focus. *Whose room is this? What are these tubes and wires? Where is this pain coming from?*

I turn my head and see the blurry outline of someone sitting in a chair next to my bed.

Mom?

I can't keep my eyes open. I slip back into unconsciousness.

Beep ... beep ... beep ... beep ...

Why doesn't someone stop that alarm?

My mind forces itself into consciousness. I turn my head toward the sound. A light blinks in sync with the beeps on a machine close to my bed. Wires come from the machine and attach somewhere to me. I am lying flat on my back in a narrow bed. I can see other tubes coming from my body but cannot see where they go.

A hospital. I'm in a hospital. What am I doing here? I turn my head toward the chair again.

Mom! She is wearing a white gown and her face is covered with a white mask but I can see her eyes. *Yeah, that is Mom.*

I open my mouth to speak but my throat locks. I push the word out but I don't recognize my voice, "Mom."

Mom comes close to my bed, "Bobby! You're awake! Thank God you're awake."

Tubes running down my throat make speaking an effort. "Where am I? What happened?"

"You're in the hospital. You've had an accident."

I lower my eyes to look at my body but can only see my chest. A patchwork of burns and open wounds come into view. *Whoa! Where'd my skin go? What kind of accident does this?*

I faded back to sleep.

I awake again and immediately turn my head toward the chair. There is someone there but it does not look like Mom. I blink to adjust my eyes.

"Is that you Tom?"

"I'm right here Bob." Seeing him brings an instant smile to my face. I cannot help it. He has always made me smile.

Even through his mask, I can tell he doesn't smile back. He has a look on his face I had never seen before. And I have seen about every look he has.

"How ya' doin', Tom?"

"I'm alright. How about you?"

"I don't know, Bro. I'm messed up. What am I doing in this hospital?"

"You don't know what happened?"

"No. I don't know anything."

"What's the last thing you remember?"

"I remember getting off work and coming home. We got paid, didn't we?"

"Yeah, we got paid. You really don't remember anything else?"

I search my mind for more. "No. Nothing. I remember waking up in this bed." I look into his eyes and ask, "Tom ... why am I so beat up? What happened?"

He looked at me with that look on his face again. *What is that look?* I could tell he was struggling for words.

"I'm sorry, Bob. I am so sorry."

"Sorry? Sorry for what?"

He opened his mouth but nothing came out. I waited. That look on his face became so intense I forgot my question. Tom abruptly got up and left the room.

Mom came back in the room a little later. It could have been minutes or it could have been hours. I drifted in and out so often, time was irrelevant. My sister, Jeanne, was with her.

"Hey, Jeanne, good to see you. How many more of you are out there?"

"Oh, everyone's out there. Don and Reenie and Pat and Lana have been out there for quite a while. They are so glad to hear you are awake."

"Really, they're all out there? And Tom? Is Tom still out there?"

"Oh yes. Tom is out there. He's been out there the whole time."

"How long have I been here? And why am I here?"

Mom and Jeanne realized I had no clue about the car crash and the electrocution. You see, I have been given a gift. I have had twenty-four hours of my memory erased. Twelve hours before I touched the power line and twelve hours after I touched the power line do not exist in my mind. And to be honest, if I was going to choose twenty-four hours to forget, I think those particular twenty-four hours would be pretty high on my list.

That story I told you earlier about our trip to Olympia and the night on the dark highway is from Tom's memory. It is from the police investigation. It is from common sense. But it is not from me. As I said, I have been given a gift, a wonderful gift. My first memory of this event is waking up at Harborview Medical Center in Seattle, tubes and wires are hooked to my body, and there is a chair next to my bed.

Mom and Jeanne told me what they could about the night before. The trip to Olympia, the crash on the way home, the downed wires, the electrocution, Tom pulling me off the wire –

"Wait! Tom pulled me off the wires? Is Tom okay?"

"Yes, Tom is okay. He got you off the wires and kept you alive until help came."

"Why didn't he tell me this stuff when he was in here?"

"Tom's had a rough night. He was driving the car. He is blaming himself for hurting you."

"Hurting me? He saved my life."

That explains the look he had on his face. That was the look of someone who thinks they made a mistake and ended up hurting someone they loved. He felt guilty and wanted to trade places with me. I have been telling Tom ever since that day this is not his fault. He did not hurt me. I was the one who walked into those power lines. He saved me. I owe him my life. He is, after all, my favorite brother.

I lay there a moment and let everything I had just learned find a place in my mind. I was glad Mom and Jeanne were in the room. God has blessed my life with strong women. You already know about Darla. But this was before I met Darla. This was the time of Mom and Jeanne. They left their tears and fears in the corridor and brought strength into the ICU. I needed that strength. I turned my head to look at my left arm. I had not noticed it before. I did not recognize what I saw. From fingertip to elbow it was shriveled, curled, and scorched. From elbow to shoulder, it was swollen to three times its original size. I lifted the limb over my chest and turned to Mom. My gaze went from her eyes to my arm and back to her.

"Mom … I hurt. I'm in a lot of pain."

"I know, Bobby." She takes my right hand into hers, "You've been hurt real bad. But you're going to be okay. You're going to be okay."

If she is calling me 'Bobby' it must be bad. She doesn't use that name often.

But I've known the touch of those hands since the moment I was born. And that voice has comforted me even longer than that. If Mom says I will be okay, I guess I will be okay.

As we were talking, a doctor came into the room and stood next to my bed. He had a clipboard in his hand.

"Bob, I'm sorry. I have to ask you to sign this release form. We need to amputate your left arm right away."

The doctor explained the medical details. The lower part of my arm was not viable anymore because of the extreme electrical shock. Body fluids were backing up in my upper arm because they had no place to go. In order to spare the upper arm, we needed to remove the non-viable part of the lower arm. In simple terms: If I was going to save anything, I needed to give up something. That could be a message for someone reading this book right now. You could be in a situation that has gotten out of control and threatens to destroy the good things you still have in your life. Sometimes if you are going to save anything, you may need to give up something. I signed the release form. They immediately prepared me for surgery to amputate my left arm above the elbow. Mom and Jeanne went out to the corridor to be with their tears.

Two weeks later, I am lying in bed and the doctor came in with a clipboard in his hand.

"Bob, I'm sorry. I have to ask you to sign this release form. We need to amputate your right leg."

I didn't know how bad my legs were. I lay on my back for three months. My back was the only part of my body that did not have burns. I could not sit up and I could not see my legs. If I could have seen my legs, I would have realized my right leg was so damaged it was only attached to my body by the flesh behind the knee. I could not see the damage but I could feel the pain. After two weeks, I knew anything that could cause me that much pain I needed to get rid of. That could be a message for someone reading this book, too. You need to identify the source of your pain and take healthy steps to remove it. A good place to start is to talk to someone. Talk to a friend, talk to your spouse, talk to your pastor, talk to God. It is not easy to face issues but it is better than living with the pain. I signed the release form and they took me in and amputated my right leg above the knee.

Two weeks later, I am lying in bed and the doctor came in with a clipboard in his hand.

Does anybody notice a pattern developing here? Well, I noticed a pattern. This time the doctor surprised me, though.

He said, "Bob, what would you like to do with your left leg?"

That was a question. I picked up on that right away. I was twenty-one years old and in the span of two weeks they had amputated two of my limbs and nobody had ever asked, "What do you want to do?"

What do I want to do with my left leg? "I want to keep it, sir."

I surprised the doctor. He hid the clipboard behind his back. "We'll try," he said. "We'll try."

I tried. I tried hard. The exit point of the electricity from the power line had taken my kneecap and all the supporting ligaments. It had also taken the flesh and some muscle. We came up with a plan that would require my upper and lower leg bones (femur and tibia for you med students) to fuse together and make a stiff leg. Once everything healed, we could graft skin over the exposed areas. With an artificial leg on the right side and possibly a brace on the left I might be able to walk. That is what I worked and fought toward. But as many of you have learned in life, sometimes, no matter how hard you try or how hard you fight to keep something, it can still be taken away. While recovering and working on the plan, I fell out of my wheelchair. The fall onto the sidewalk snapped my lower leg in two. The doctors used screws to reconnect the break. We watched to see if the broken pieces would bond together. After two months, it was clear that the bone was dead and was never going to heal.

I said, "Bring the clipboard. Let's get this over with."

I signed the release form and they took me in and amputated my left leg above the knee. It was the best thing I could have done. In fact, I really should have done it the first time the doctor asked. But I was stubborn. I had just lost two limbs and if there was any chance of keeping my leg, I wanted to try. I do not regret trying but after amputating my last leg, I got healthier. My body did not have to use all those resources to support a dead limb. Sometimes you have to lose the fight to win the battle.

I would spend six months of my life in Harborview. The first three months would be in the Burn Unit. During that time, they would skin graft the front of my body. The last three months would be on the Orthopedic Rehab Floor. I'm not going to tell you much about those six months. I will tell you that during those six months I had visits from my family every day. During the week it was usually my sister, Jeanne, driving forty miles from Puyallup. On weekends, the rest of the family would come a hundred miles from Hoquiam. They helped me adapt and accept.

There were several other things that helped me adapt and accept but that is for another book.

Back on April 25, 1976, the day I woke up at Harborview and realized I had been electrocuted by 12,500 volts of electricity, I knew one thing for sure. No matter what they had to do ... amputate my arm, amputate my legs, skin graft my chest, I do not care ... I was alive. And I was going to do everything in my power to stay that way.

Now back to Grant in that restaurant in Ohio. Remember his question?

"So, if a tornado were to hit the RV we'd all be killed, right Dad?"

You can appreciate my answer a little more now.

"No matter what you are facing you should always have the attitude that you will live through it."

Here is the real beauty of that statement. If you can adopt that attitude all your life ... you will only be wrong once.

Chapter 21

After dinner, we drove back to the state park to turn in for the night. Jeanne set up her room in the back while Grant and Chanel prepared their beds up front. When Darla went to get our bed ready she discovered we had left the window open. The storm earlier that day had blown water in and gotten our blankets and sheets wet. Back in May these kinds of surprises would wear us down. But this wasn't May anymore. May was three months ago. We had pedaled two thousand miles and adapted to everything thrown at us since then. Let's be real here. We're talking about wet blankets. As Jeanne was fond of saying, "Well, nobody died." Darla bundled them up and put them in a pile to be handled tomorrow.

The next morning was spent doing housekeeping chores. Our house was only three hundred square feet but it still needed to be kept. We couldn't become lackadaisical about it. (I'm sorry, Grant just showed me the word 'lackadaisical' and I wanted to use it in a sentence.) We picked up and swept up. Everything has its place in the RV and needs to be put there. Sweeping was a continual chore. It was impossible not to track the outdoors indoors. On top of all that was laundry. Between all the cycling clothes, camp clothes, and church clothes, we had lots of laundry.

Our spaces for clean clothes emptied and our spaces for dirty clothes filled. Sometimes we would make special trips into town to the Laundromat. Other times we would use the washer and dryer at the campgrounds. This campground had a good laundry facility so Darla was able to do the necessary loads here. Jeanne volunteered to iron our church clothes while the rest of us went off on our bikes. Yes, Darla and Jeanne are from that generation that was taught how to iron clothes. They are a dying breed. We were able to get thirty miles of riding in before it was time to load up the RV and move out.

Jeanne and I were especially excited about our next stop, North Lima. We were going back to where we grew up. North Lima is a small Ohio farming community near the Pennsylvania border. It is not on the north side of Lima, Ohio. In fact, it is 200 miles due east of Lima, Ohio. It is north of Lima, Peru, but I doubt that is how it got its name.

We drove Jeanne out to Columbiana to meet up with Don. He had flown back to spend a few weeks with her. They were going to stay at Don's family farm. Jeanne and he had lived there in the early years of their marriage before moving west. Don's sister, Margie, had the farm now. After a few days they were going to Philadelphia to see some old friends. We dropped Jeanne off and headed toward Boardman. We had two churches to speak at on Sunday. One was in North Lima and the other in Austintown. Boardman was between the two towns. There was not a good campground in the area so we booked a hotel for the weekend.

Driving down State Route 7, we came to the "Entering North Lima" sign. I had crossed in and out of North Lima scores of times in my life. There were the times Dad would take us on family trips to New England or Gettysburg. There were the times I crossed with Tom, hitchhiking or by Greyhound Bus. There were the times I took my own family through here as we ministered on the east coast. But this time was different. Not just because we were on bicycles. I felt this time into North Lima was the completion of a journey that I began thirty-eight years earlier.

During the summer of 1970, my dad realized he needed to change. He had allowed prescription drugs to creep back into his life and had lost control again. Thinking a change of address would help, Dad embarked on his own journey of hope and courage. He accepted a job in Rapid City, South Dakota, and led his family (Mom, Reenie, and I were the only ones still at home) out of North Lima. Unfortunately, changing your address does not help if it is the only thing you change. Nine months later, I would open the bedroom door to wake Dad for work and find him dead. Years of alcohol and then prescription drugs had put too much strain on his body. I do not know what measure of hope or courage leaving North Lima brought my dad. I just know that at the age of forty-one he found his peace. The rest of us had to keep seeking. More on that later.

Including North Lima on the route of Hope and Courage Across America was important to me. Yesterday I was talking to Ichabod on the weekly KMPS radio update. I told the listeners I was hoping to come back to North Lima a better person than when I left. That is not a bad thing to hope, is it?

Coming up to North Lima Mennonite Church, Darla pointed to the reader board next to the highway, "Look at that."

Hope and Courage with Bob Mortimer
Sunday, August 17 at 9:30

North Lima Mennonite Church was where Vic Stoltzfus was the pastor when I was young. It is where Dad took us after he became sober. It is where I sat in Sunday school classes and learned that Jesus was more than a babe in the manger. Seeing my name on the board as a guest speaker was something I would have never expected.

"Wow. Who would've thought I'd ever see that," I said to Darla and the kids.

Maybe I am coming back a better person, I thought to myself.

We spent the Saturday visiting friends and relatives. We drove back out to North Lima to see my friend Jeff and his family. Jeff and I have been friends since elementary school. He grew up about a mile from where I lived. Back then a mile was like living next door. We would walk or ride bikes back and forth to spend our Saturdays together. Like a lot of boys, we tried to balance our time between staying out of trouble and getting into trouble. It was always surprising how quickly we could move from one to the other. Some of our best memories of the latter were sneaking his Grandma's 1957 Corvette out late at night and cruising the country roads. I know. It sounds shocking to me, too. His grandmother had a '57 Corvette. Unbelievable.

Jeff was one of the few people I stayed in contact with over the years. He was a hard working guy doing his best to raise his family. Jeff and his wife, Mary, didn't live far from where we grew up. I had not seen Jeff since 1992. We pulled into their driveway and surprised them. They were glad to see us. Mary said Jeff was keeping track of our journey online and was beginning to think we had passed them by.

"No, way," I said. "We wouldn't pedal through without seeing you guys."

"You better not," Jeff quickly added.

We reminisced about old times and brought each other up to date on the new times. They were facing some steep mountains. Jeff has had his back against the wall for several years. I asked him how things were going.

"I got some good advice from someone last year," he said.

"Really? What'd they tell you?"

"When you feel like you can't go forward, just stand still and fight."

"That's good advice," I said. "Who told you that?"

"You did, you goof. Don't you remember?"

Actually, I did remember. A year earlier Jeff had called me while I was out on the road somewhere. He was as close to the end of his rope as a man could be without letting go. He talked and I listened. That is what friends do for each other. Talk and listen. I could tell he was struggling with his last step and his next step. Moving ahead seemed impossible and moving back was a dead end. The only advice I could give him was to stand still and fight. Standing still allowed the path ahead to clear. Jeff could then see better to fight the discouragement that was smothering his life. Discouragement is the enemy of courage. And hope is the greatest weapon against it. Visiting Jeff reminded me that our journeys are not ours alone. We share them with friends.

We spent the rest of the day at my Uncle Don and Aunt JoAnn's house. Don is my dad's only brother. Seeing him gave me a glimpse of what Dad might be like if he were still alive. They invited other relatives over. We rarely get to see this side of our family. Darla loved talking to all the cousins from the generation before us. Darla loves the elderly. Don't get offended by that, cousins. Let's admit it. When you are in your seventies and eighties there are not too many people left to refer to you as the young ones. Embrace the glory of your age and pass some of your wisdom down to the next generation. We learned a lot from you. Grant was glad to see other young men with the last name of Mortimer. And Chanel immediately adopted Uncle Don and Aunt JoAnn as her new Grandpa and Grandma. We share our journeys with family, too.

Sunday morning we headed to North Lima Mennonite Church. Pulling up to the front of the church reminded me of when I was a little boy. Only this time I was the dad getting out of the front seat, not the child getting out of the back seat. I entered the doors older but not taller. Old friends greeted us. Their faces slightly resembled the faces I knew as a boy. The same was true about my face, also. (Cousins, this is where I admit that I am aging, too.) I presented our message of Hope and Courage. Many people connected and responded to the message.

Afterward, the ladies of the church had prepared a potluck for everyone in the fellowship hall. I don't know if I can fully describe this potluck in the way it deserves. We have been well hosted by other church potlucks across America but this was over the top. If you are not familiar with church potlucks let me give you a quick description. The ladies of the church bring their favorite meat dish, casserole, salad, dessert, etc. The men of the church can bring something but my experience has been it is best to leave it to the ladies. This comfort-food buffet is laid out on banquet tables to be shared by all. People fill their plates and then sit down and visit until the food or conversation runs out. I have never been to a bad church potluck.

North Lima Mennonite, though, took potlucking to a whole new level. It was mid-August and gardens were starting to produce fresh vegetables. There were several potato dishes. From mashed to shredded, au gratin to sweet. Green beans, sweet peas, corn and carrots all prepared home-style. Sauerkraut, coleslaw, cucumber salad, fruit salad and taco salad. I don't even know how to describe the casseroles. Remember your favorite hot-out-of-the-oven casserole? I'm sure it was there. Meat? We're talking about beef, ham and chicken. But the best was the roasted turkey, yes, roasted turkey. Thanksgiving-style roasted turkey in August. Now, I have already confessed my weakness for popcorn in an earlier chapter. My weakness for popcorn is only second to my weakness for roast turkey. I can't help it. Just the aroma is enough to make my head spin. My favorite part of the turkey is the drumstick.

A psychologist would say, "He desires the leg of the turkey because he feels remorse for the loss of his own legs." Not true. My love of drumsticks started long before I lost my legs. It is more likely my passion for drumsticks stems from being the youngest of five boys. By the time the Thanksgiving turkey made it to me the two drumsticks were gone. Their scarcity made them precious to me. When I think turkey, I think drumstick. And even if there were only two at the potluck, it didn't matter. I was the guest speaker and they let me go first.

As I enjoyed the banquet on my plate, Darla kept her eyes on the part of the meal that most interested her. Past the 'real food' stood a table spread with desserts. Darla loves sweets. People that just meet her might find that hard to believe. But she doesn't fool those of us who know her. Her sweet tooth didn't stand a chance against the Mennonite ladies' dessert table. Her plate of hot dishes seemed small in comparison to mine and took little time to finish. She excused herself and headed toward the sugary end of the potluck. A few minutes later she returned with her plate covered with treats. "Everything looked so good I couldn't make up my mind. And everybody was so nice over there they told me 'try a little of each.' So I did."

To be fair, everything did look good. There were a variety of cookies, cakes and pies. Lots of pies. But only one pie caught Darla's attention. Shoofly pie. Shoofly pie is a molasses and sugar filled creation so sticky it got its name from having to deter winged pests. Anything that sweet is a perfect pie for Darla. She 'oohed' and 'aahed' over every bite. Darla made the lady that brought that Shoofly pie feel great.

Jeanne and Don had come to church that morning, also. Jeanne talked with people she hadn't seen in decades. She was actually more involved with the church than I was because she was a teenager when we started there and I was just a little kid. Her closest friend in high school, Kathy, drove up from southern Ohio to see her. It had been thirty years since they had visited. The emotions of the day were overwhelming at times. After the potluck we headed back to our hotel. We needed a nap after that feast before going to our next church that evening.

That evening we spoke at Tabernacle Evangelical Presbyterian Church in Austintown. This came about because two of our cousins, Joy and Marian, had brought an article about us to their pastor. They were pleased to have us at their church. Uncle Don, Aunt JoAnn and the other cousins showed up, too. The service went great. I am always grateful to God that He uses our journey for His purpose. After the service the church had snacks in the fellowship hall.

While visiting with people, one of the men came to me. "There is a couple that would like to speak to you."

"Great. Which couple?"

"They're not in here. They are out in their car in the parking lot. They got lost trying to find the church and just made it here."

"Can they come in?"

"No. They are quite a ways from home and need to get started back. Besides, they have some disability issues and it would be difficult for them to come in for such a brief time. They asked if you could come out to the car."

"Of course I can come out."

If we are willing to pedal from Seattle to New York to share Hope and Courage, I can surely roll from the fellowship hall to the parking lot. They were a nice couple. They felt bad that they had missed the message.

"You didn't miss it." I said. "I can tell it to you right now. Our hope is in Christ. You have hope in Christ, don't you?"

"Yes, sir. We do."

"Good. That is the most important part. The other part of the message is about courage. Your hope is in Christ but the courage is in you to do something with that hope. Courage to face the mountain in front of you. Are you facing any mountains?"

"We are, sir, but we figured if a man like you can pedal this far with one arm we don't have anything to complain about."

"Oh, I wouldn't say that. Your mountains are your mountains. They are as big to you as mine are to me. That's not the point. The point is, do you have the courage to take the next step toward your mountain?"

"I think we do. I hope we do."

"Of course you do. That is the message. Keep your hope in Christ and have the courage to take the next step. You didn't miss a thing."

"Thank you, sir. And God bless you."

"He does. Thank you."

The next morning we loaded up the RV and moved camp out to Don's family farm. His sister invited us to park there for a few days. Don showed us around the yard and house. He pointed out the barn peak I painted when I was thirteen. It still looked very high.

Staying at Margie's was fun for Chanel. While Darla, Grant and I pedaled she stayed back on the farm. Margie had her help with chores. When we left she was hanging clothes outside on the clothesline.

Chanel said, "I learned about hanging clothes on the line from 'Little House on the Prairie.'"

Grant got our bikes out and we loaded our packs with water and snacks. We put our helmets on and headed down the country lane. We were able to pedal through North Lima. I enjoyed riding to the school I went to as a boy. A man there said they would be closing it down and building a new one next year. I guess we came at a good time. The rest of the town brought back memories and I regaled Darla and Grant with tales from my youth. It was good to be on our bikes. The rest of the miles that carried us through Ohio were a mixture of county roads, state highways, and bike paths. We loved them all. The hot August weather was a nice change from the summers we had in Washington. We didn't even complain about the humidity.

Coming through Ohio was not a mistake. Stopping at North Lima was not a mistake, either. Hope and Courage touched a lot of people here. And a lot of people touched us. I had thought that coming back to my roots would complete the journey started thirty-eight years ago. It didn't. I feel I have learned a valuable lesson. Roots are not a journey meant to be completed.

Roots are a journey to be continued. Pedaling down State Road 14, we came to a little sign that said 'Leaving Ohio.' Crossing into Pennsylvania I knew that there was a part of me that would never leave Ohio.

The country lanes hadn't changed much in forty years.

Chapter 22

Ohio State Highway 14 becomes Pennsylvania State Highway 51 as soon as you cross the border. That could be confusing if you are giving interstate directions but it doesn't matter much when you are on a bicycle. A lot of things don't matter much when you are on a bicycle. Darla, Grant and I rode along enjoying the wide shoulder for our bikes. We realized we were less than 500 miles from the Statue of Liberty. It is hard to believe the end of our journey is so near. I know I haven't written about the actual bike riding lately. I've focused more on the people and the ministry and the memories. But pedaling is still a big part of this journey.

We have pedaled about 2,000 miles, so far. Not as much as we had hoped. While planning Hope and Courage Across America I had overestimated how many miles we could pedal in a week and still make it to our speaking engagements. We have personally struggled with that and have prayed more than once for God to help us keep our attitude and spirit in alignment with His purpose for this journey. (It's not about the miles, it's about the message.) We have been able to ride all the miles since Indiana. That makes us feel good. But more importantly, we don't think we've missed any ministry opportunity since we left Gig Harbor on May 17. That makes us feel great.

As I said, we crossed into Pennsylvania. We were soon reminded of a geographical fact. Not all the mountains on our route are in the west. Pennsylvania has mountains, too. They are not the big towering peaks of the west. In Washington we would call them hills. But what they lack in height they make up for in quantity. On top of that, their steepness can match anything we've seen yet. Our first encounter came upon us suddenly. We pedaled up Highway 51 and the road started to climb. We looked ahead at a long, steep road stretching as far as we could see.

"Whoa. What's that?" I hollered to Darla and Grant as we stopped our bikes.

"That's a pretty big hill, Dad."

"What should we do?" Darla asked.

"I think we should take a break. Do you have any of that trail mix in your pack?" I figured we were going to need some nourishment to get up that hill. We rested in the shade and drank a bottle of water.

A well-earned break.

"How far do you think that hill goes before it reaches the top?" Darla wondered.

"I don't know. It's been a long time since we've run into a real climb. I forgot Pennsylvania was hilly. I can't imagine it goes much past what we see though. Let's get our helmets on and find out."

Starting up the hill brought back memories of Snoqualmie Pass. It was three months earlier when we struggled over our first mountain. It took us a few days and several attempts to cover thirty miles. Rain storms, equipment problems and bruised spirits tried to keep us from the peak. Along the way, God used Nicole to save a baby's life and taught me that I was not in charge. We'd come quite a ways since then. This hill was steep and steady but didn't wear us down as much as Snoqualmie. We were definitely in better physical and spiritual condition now. After two miles we took a break. The ninety degree weather and humidity depleted our liquids quickly. No problem. We always carried enough water. We sat on the side of the road enjoying the beauty of Pennsylvania. It is truly one of our most beautiful states. We all commented on how fun the riding is now. Sure we had aches and pains. You can't expect to spend this much time cycling without a few aches and pains. Generally speaking, riding a couple of thousand miles on a bike is good for your physical health. We are definitely building the muscles we are using. It's the joints and ligaments that are taking the beating. Darla and Grant will feel it in their wrists and neck. I feel it in my shoulders and elbow. It has never been so bad that it has kept us from getting back on our bikes the next day, though. Even this hill was just a reminder that we were pushing our bodies to new levels. We continued our climb three more miles before we came to the top. Then came the fun part. The next four miles were all downhill and then the road flattened out as it followed the valley.

Several miles further we came into the town of Bridgewater. It is where the Beaver River feeds into the Ohio River. The road crossed both rivers in the span of a mile. There was a huge construction project up ahead. It looked like they decided to work on both bridges at the same time. Traffic was congested as they funneled four lanes into two. I pulled to the side of the road.

"What do you think of that, Darla?"

"It looks bad. Is there another way?"

"No, those bridges are the only way over the rivers. Grant, can you see any of that construction up there? What do you think?"

"Other bikes have had to go through it. I don't know why we can't."

"He's right, Hon. They had to figure bikes would ride through there."

"Maybe we should ask those workers," Darla said, pointing to the construction crew.

"Fair enough," I said. "Let's go." We pedaled up to the closest one.

"Excuse me, are they still letting bikes cross the bridges during construction?"

"It's the only way to get across around here," he said. "That's a pretty interesting bike. How far you going?"

"Well, we're going to the Statue of Liberty."

"Statue of Liberty? Where'd you start?"

"We started near Seattle three months ago."

"Seattle to the Statue of Liberty. Are you part of a group or something?"

"It's me and my family. We call our ride Hope and Courage Across America. Our hope is in Christ and the courage is in us to do something with that hope."

"That's pretty impressive. Looks like a lot of hope and courage to me."

"Thanks. But right now we'd be glad to get over those rivers," I replied. "Any advice?"

"Stay on the shoulder up to those barricades. Then you are going to be on one lane each way until you get over the bridges. There are no shoulders so you have to be very careful. We call it the dead zone."

I wasn't exactly sure why they called it "the dead zone" but I didn't want to ask. If it was what I expected it was better off not said out loud.

"Okay, guys, let's stay real sharp here. I'll lead, Grant next, and you bring up the back, Hon." We squeezed between the traffic and the barriers. This was way too close to the cars. I kept my right rear wheel up against the edge. My bike never felt so wide. Grant and Darla were just as tense. I was crossing the Ohio River and should have been able to enjoy it. Instead I couldn't wait to get it behind me. The mile seemed to go on and on. Finally we got out of the construction. We pedaled on another mile with a narrow shoulder and heavy traffic. We rode into a shopping center and stopped our bikes in front of a grocery store.

Grant said, "That was interesting."

Darla said, "Yeah. Too interesting."

"Listen, this road is really bad for bikes. We're getting into rush hour and this traffic isn't going to get better. Let's call Jeanne to bring the truck and get us out of here."

Darla and Grant didn't have any problem with that plan. They got off their bikes while I called Jeanne back at the farm.

"She'll be here within the hour," I reported after getting off the phone.

"Grant and I are going in the store for a few things. We earned ice cream on that road. Do you want anything?"

"No. I'm good with what's in my pack. I'll wait out here for you."

As they went in I noticed an old man sitting on a bench outside the store. I rolled my bike closer to him.

"How's it going today?"

"I dunno. My hip hurts and I can't walk too far. I feel like I'm not much good." His answer concerned me. I wondered if he was here alone.

"Do you have anybody with you?"

"Yeah, my wife's in the store. I was goin' to shop with her but realized I'd just slow her down. My walker's in the car."

"My wife is in the store, too. This bike isn't good for grocery shopping. I guess we'll both wait out here for the women. My name's Bob. What's your name?"

"My name's Ben. I saw you guys ride up here. Where you goin'?"

I explained about our ride and the message but I was more interested in knowing Ben's story. He was old but I knew he hadn't always been old. It is an often forgotten fact that old people were young people once upon a time. I may be more aware of this now that I am in my fifties than I was in my thirties. I asked Ben a few questions and discovered he was retired from the post office, married a long time, raised a family, had numerous grandkids, and an equal number of aches and pains. I heard about feet, legs, knees, backs and shoulders. There was something wrong with one of his eyes but he forgot to mention that problem. He was grumbling because he didn't think his life amounted to much.

"How old are you, Ben?"

"Oh, lemme think." His pause made me realize he actually had to think about it. "I turned eighty-five on my last birthday."

I quickly did the math in my head. If he is eighty-five he was born in 1923 and turned eighteen in 1941. My next question came out of true interest not just the desire to make small talk.

"What'd you do during the war?" I knew if he was eighteen when the war started, he had to be involved somehow.

"I was a paratrooper with the 101st Airborne."

"101st Airborne? Did you get to Europe?"

"I was in France. We dropped in on D-Day."

Ben said it so matter-of-factly my look of awe must have bewildered him. I had read about these guys in history books. Grant and I had watched movies about them.

"You were one of the guys that parachuted behind the lines on D-Day?"

"Well, it was really the night before D-Day. They wanted us in there before they started landing on the beach."

"I've read about you in books. I've seen that drop portrayed in a dozen movies. They did a whole series on TV about the 101st. Ben, you guys are heroes."

"I wouldn't call me a hero. I was only there a little while. I got shot in the eye and they sent me back to a hospital."

"Ben, people say I'm courageous leading my family across America on bicycles. What I am doing is child's play compared to what you did."

"I didn't do nothin'."

"Really? You served your country in World War II, parachuted behind the lines on D-Day, lost an eye freeing Europe, came home and got married, raised a family, faithfully worked the same job for decades, and helped build America into a world leader. You call that nothin'?"

"I still didn't do nothin'."

"Well, your 'nothin'' is more about hope and courage than my bike ride."

Grant came out of the grocery store and came over to us. He smiled politely and said hi to Ben.

"Mom's buying a few things and will be out in a minute."

"Grant, this is Ben. You might want to shake his hand."

Grant politely extended his hand. I'm sure he was thinking, *Great, Dad. I'm glad you found a new friend who is older than you. That's not easy at your age.*

I quickly added, "You know those books and movies about the 101st Airborne in Europe? Those aren't just stories to Ben. He was one of those young paratroopers that dropped into France the night before D-Day."

Grant straightened up and took Ben's hand, "Wow! You were there. That's amazing. Thank you."

Ben pointed to a lady taking a cart of groceries to a car parked nearby, "There's my wife. I have to wait for her to bring my walker."

Grant said, "I'll go get your walker. It's an honor to meet you, sir."

There are seven decades between Grant and Ben but both were reminded of that often forgotten fact: All old people were young people once upon a time and, God willing, all young people will become old.

Darla came out from the store and I introduced her to Ben. Grant brought his walker and we watched him climb into the car. It wasn't long before Jeanne and Don arrived with the truck. Chanel had stayed back at the farm with Margie to help prepare dinner. We had farm fresh corn and tomatoes with chip-chopped ham sandwiches. After dinner we took Chanel for a bike ride on a local trail. It was quiet and much safer than the roads we had been on earlier. Darla saw a bunny. She gets excited when she sees bunnies and has been counting them ever since we left home in May. This one was number seventy-five. We went back to the farm and turned in for the night.

The next morning we hooked the truck to the RV to move camp. We were scheduled to speak in a church at Bethel Park near Pittsburgh. The pastor had contacted me from an article he read before we started our journey. I'm glad it worked out for us to stop. He and his wife were wonderful and the people made us feel at home. It was a Wednesday evening but the crowd seemed like Sunday morning. When we arrived at the church there were two packages waiting for us. One was a case of Journey Bibles to give to the congregation. The other was 1,000 postcards we ordered. We wanted to send a postcard to all of the people we had met and the people back home. It was just a reminder that we were getting close to the end and appreciated all they had done. We had taken a group picture while we were at home and sent it to Tim Smith. Tim had designed all the graphics for Hope and Courage, including the RV. He put our picture in front of a barn and silo with our greeting printed on the back. We had ordered 500 but the printer added another 500 at no cost. The postcards looked great and we passed some out to the congregation.

Chanel was met at the church by Kristen, a girl she had met in a campground in Ohio. I told you she makes a new BFF (best friend forever) everywhere we go. Kristen had been at the camp that had the tremendous rain and thunder storm. She was there several days before we arrived and was too shy to mingle with the other girls in camp. That all changed with Chanel. She has that effect on people. The two girls were soon inseparable as they played and rode bikes all around the park. Kristen lived near Bethel Park and got her dad to bring her to see Chanel. She even brought a batch of home baked chocolate chip cookies. They were delicious. We all had a difficult time saying goodbye, not just Chanel. It was becoming evident there weren't many churches left on our schedule. Our conversation and our thoughts all pointed to the end of the journey.

Chapter 23

The next morning we packed up to move camp again. Darla was looking forward to our next stop. We were going to her brother Paul's home in Harrisburg. Now Darla would never say she has a favorite brother and that is the truth. She does not have a favorite sibling. Each one has a special role in her life. Paul is the brother who helped fill the void after Darla's father died. Paul was earning an engineering degree at the University of Washington in Seattle at the time. He left the dorm and moved back home to be with his mom and Darla. He would rather commute to campus than leave them alone. Paul took a job in Pennsylvania after college and started his engineering career. He later married Karen and they've settled there ever since.

As an older brother he is nurturing and protective. I was very aware of that protective nature. He was visiting his mom when I first started dating Darla. Paul and I are the same age and although it was never said, I could sense he was sizing me up. Who was this man coming around his little sister? What are his intentions and where did he come from? I don't blame him for being cautious. My resume didn't look too good. When Darla and I got closer to marriage, Paul asked her the tough questions. Is this guy going to be the spiritual leader in your home? Will he be able to support you? Are you willing to be the one to change light bulbs for the rest of your life? He never interfered with our relationship but I know Darla respected his opinion. I must have passed inspection because at our wedding he walked Darla down the aisle and put her hand in mine.

We knew we would enjoy our time with Paul and Karen. Our plan was to be there a week. Grant and I had to fly back to Portland, Oregon, for the Luis Palau festival over the weekend. Darla and Chanel would stay in Harrisburg. We were scheduled to speak at Paul's church the next Wednesday. Jeanne and Don were renting a car and driving down to Baltimore to see old friends. On top of that we needed to cover quite a few miles on our bikes.

I drove the winding country road to Paul's and parked the RV next to his house. Paul and Karen came out to greet us. It was great to see them. They are our most distant relatives and we have always enjoyed every minute with them. Paul's neighbor walked over and said we could hook our power cord up to her place. What a nice, neighborly thing to do. We unhitched the truck and leveled the RV before going in the house. Karen had made a peach pie and coffee. She added a few scoops of ice cream and we were in heaven. Their son, Brenton, came home from work and we told tales of the journey. After dessert I drove Jeanne and Don to a motel for the night. The rest of us slept in the RV. I figured we brought our own beds so we might as well use them.

In the morning we woke early to warm weather and fresh coffee. It was a beautiful day to ride bikes but there wouldn't be any bike riding this weekend. Grant and I had a plane to catch. We finished packing our bags for Portland and Darla drove us to the airport. It was strange flying back to the Northwest to speak at a festival. Usually I fly from the Northwest to work with Luis Palau. Luis has an international evangelistic ministry based in the Portland area. I first started working with him a decade ago.

I was traveling with another evangelist, Steve Jamison, at the time. Luis invited Steve to help him do a series of meetings on the east coast. Well, when he invited Steve he got me as a tag-a-long. I told my story to the audience before Steve got up and brought the Gospel message. I didn't actually meet Luis there but he heard about my message. In the spring of 1999 I got a phone call.

"Bob, I'm calling on behalf of Luis Palau. We are doing an outdoor event in Portland, Oregon, next month and Luis is wondering if you would come and share your testimony?"

"I would love to. Where is it?"

"We are holding it downtown at Waterfront Park. I'll send you the details. Thank you. Luis really liked your story. In fact, he has retold it several times since then."

"Wow. I wonder if he tells it better than I do. I look forward to meeting him."

I had done open air meetings in parks before. They can be a little challenging. It is hard to get a good sound system, weather is a big factor, and people are busy doing other things. After all, people don't usually go to the park to listen to a preacher.

I thought, I'll go and speak but I doubt there will be very many people there. Oh well, it's never been about the size of the crowd, anyway.

Darla and I dropped Nicole and Grant off at her brother Daryl's house near Portland and drove to the park. We kept Chanel with us. She was still a baby. Getting close to downtown we noticed heavy traffic and a lot of people walking around.

"Must be something going on in the city today," I told Darla as we followed directions to the parking spot the Palau team had sent us.

As we came around the last corner, we saw a crowd of people that stretched all along the river to a huge stage with massive speakers and twenty-foot video screens. Officials later estimated the crowd at 40,000. We were awestruck. We had never been invited to anything like this before.

"Darla, I don't think we're in Kansas anymore."

Our directions led us to a restricted entrance behind the stage. We were running late, so Darla dropped me off and went to find a parking space. I went behind stage and was introduced to Colin James. Colin was part of the Palau team that put this whole thing together. He told me I would take the stage right before Luis Palau, I had fifteen minutes, and Luis would like me to stay out there while he preached. I was shown a spot where I could wait.

Darla, in the meantime, had found parking a few blocks away. She put Chanel in the stroller and waded into the crowd. One of her favorite performers, Bob Carlisle, was on stage and she didn't want to miss him singing "Butterfly Kisses." And she didn't. After he sang her favorite song, she remembered she needed to get backstage to me. She spotted a break in the fence just left of the stage. There was a security guard monitoring access to the area. The security guard wasn't her biggest concern. There was a sea of humanity between her and the gate and she was pushing a stroller. The park ground was covered with families on blankets, picnic baskets, and lawn chairs. Darla had to maneuver a stroller with a one year old inside across that landscape. And Darla's nature is to be quiet, shy and non-intrusive. She doesn't even like to ask for more bread at a restaurant. She was way out of her comfort zone.

But I know that no matter what her comfort zone is, Darla will step up and do what needs to be done. She bravely nudged the stroller forward, apologizing profusely to anyone near her. When the people cleared away she struggled with the bumpy, uneven ground. The closer she got to the stage the thicker and noisier the crowd became. Her progress came to a standstill and people closed in around her and Chanel. She was still a long way from the stage. Panic began to set in. A tap on her shoulder turned her around.

"Where're you trying to go?" The woman's calm voice and bright smile brought assurance to Darla.

"I've got to get to that gate. My husband is speaking on stage in a few minutes and we need to be there."

The lady stepped in front of the stroller and said, "Follow me."

With a strong voice she led the way. "Clear the way, please. This lady's husband is going to be on stage. We need to get her back there. Clear the way. Coming through. Here, let me help with that stroller. Coming through. Excuse us. Her husband is the next speaker. Move, please."

Before Darla knew what was happening she found herself at the gate. She quickly turned to thank the lady. Searching the hundreds of faces around her, she couldn't find the one that rescued her. The lady was gone. Now, I have previously mentioned people that Darla has met along our journey that she likes to refer to as 'angels.' Darla has been meeting these angels long before taking a bike ride across America. Are you wondering why she seems to meet so many of them? I think it is because she notices when people do something kind. She acknowledges good behavior. A bottle of cool water or a helping hand is always appreciated. She knows that they are just kind-hearted people, but I've got to be honest with you, it happens so much to her I wouldn't be surprised to get to heaven and discover a few of them really were angels. All I know is that she made it backstage.

Darla joined me and they escorted us to a spot just off stage to await my introduction. I was glad Darla was there. I try not to get nervous but this was out of my league. We said a quiet prayer together and then I heard my name. Rolling from behind the curtain, 40,000 people covered every open space in front of me. I headed for the microphone.

My mind raced. *Thank God I'm sitting in this chair with no legs. I don't have to worry about falling down or my knees knocking. Maybe they can't tell how scared I am.*

I leaned into the microphone and forced words out of my mouth. My opening statement got a roar of approval from the crowd that relaxed me. The story of my crash and surrendering my life to Christ came out quickly. I couldn't help but mention Darla's role in my life. Looking over, I saw her standing off stage. A thought came to my mind I knew I would pay for later.

I addressed the audience, "Darla is waiting backstage for me. In a second I am going to ask her to do something she is able to do but really doesn't want to. I am bringing her out here. And then I am going to ask you to do something for me that I am not able to do but have always wanted to. Could you stand to your feet and put your two hands together to show Darla how much I appreciate her?"

At that I turned to Darla and asked her onto the stage. She was as pale as I have ever seen her. She knew she couldn't refuse in front of all these people but she really didn't want to come out there. She told me later she almost forgot how to walk. As she timidly came and stood next to me, 40,000 people stood to their feet and clapped and cheered as loud as they could. It was the greatest standing ovation I have ever seen.

Since then, Luis has used me many times throughout America. The largest groups of people I have ever spoken to have been at Palau festivals. The biggest being 200,000 on the beach in Ft. Lauderdale during spring break. When Luis asked me to come back to Portland for another festival in the summer of 2008, I couldn't refuse. Which brings me back to Grant and I flying out to Portland. I was scheduled to speak the next evening, and we would fly back to Pennsylvania on Sunday. Sunday also happened to be Grant's sixteenth birthday. We planned to celebrate with everyone when we got back to Harrisburg.

While we were gone, Darla and Chanel got to spend some quality time with Paul and Karen. Chanel immediately promoted Karen to BFF status. Karen brought out a box of her old dolls for Chanel to play with and actually gave her one as a gift. Darla spent the day stamping and labeling the postcards we had picked up on Wednesday. She was able to take 500 of them to the post office. That was a big chore to finish. When Paul came home from work they had chicken and gravy with biscuits. Darla loved being with Paul and Karen and enjoyed their hospitality. That night Darla and Chanel slept in their guest room. This was the first time Darla had slept in someone's home on this journey. She couldn't have hoped for a better place to be while Grant and I were gone.

The next day Paul took Chanel fishing, which she'd been waiting for a long time. Years ago he had taken Nicole and Grant fishing. Chanel knew that and wanted her turn with Uncle Paul, too. He is the best fisherman in our family. Paul would never say he is the best but I know better. His family usually fishes the rivers of Pennsylvania or the lakes of New York. However, they do have a small pond in their neighborhood that is perfect for out-of-state nieces and nephews. Paul walked Chanel down to the pond and initiated her into the world of hook, line and sinker. The pond had a fair number of large-mouth bass and sunfish. Chanel was proud to tell her Mom she caught six: two with the help of Uncle Paul, three all by herself, and one that got away. It is interesting to me that she would claim the one that got away as being caught. I think she has the makings of a true fisherman … or fisherwoman … or fishergirl. I'm not sure what the proper term would be.

Chanel and Uncle Paul fishing.

In the meantime, Grant and I were 2,000 miles away at the Luis Palau festival in Portland. Grant's friend Dustin came to Portland and spent the weekend with us. My brother Tom and his wife, Cindy, came down also. Robby and Marlo were there as well, and stayed at the hotel. It was great to see them all again. The festival went really well. I was able to tell a brief version of my testimony in front of 100,000 people. Even with such a brief message, God blessed it and many people joined me in a prayer to surrender their lives to Christ.

Sunday we woke up to Grant's birthday and got a ride to the airport. We flew back to Harrisburg and connected with the girls. Darla met us at the airport and took us directly to Paul's church. They were having a special outdoor service with ice cream and fireworks. We got there too late for the ice cream but did not miss the fireworks. I spoke briefly to the audience and invited them to come hear more about our journey on Wednesday.

Afterward, we took Grant to the Dairy Queen for ice cream. It wasn't quite what he deserved for his sixteenth birthday but it was the best we could do with the schedule. We planned to celebrate more the next day.

Monday we met Don and Jeanne at the Harrisburg airport. They had been in Baltimore visiting old friends. They returned their rental car at the airport and Don caught a flight to Seattle. Jeanne stayed back with us to finish the ride. We then met Paul, Karen, Justin and Brenton for dinner. We let Grant pick the restaurant as part of his birthday. He researched his options and settled on a place called Flinchey's. He liked it because it had a feature we discovered in Germany while speaking to our troops. You order a steak and they bring a super-heated flat rock to your table with a raw piece of meat. You cut the meat and grill it yourself on the rock. It is a fun and tasty treat. Grant, Paul and I ordered a hot rock meal. The others chose ordinary selections from the menu.

I said, "You could have been more adventurous."

They said, "Why go to a restaurant if you have to cook your own meal?"

Either way everybody got what he or she wanted.

Grant enjoyed the night as he opened his cards and gifts. Earlier in the day his mom and I gave him a ring inscribed with "TRUE LOVE WAITS." He wears it as a symbol and reminder of his commitment to the girl he will marry someday. Nicole wears a similar ring. I gave it to her on her thirteenth birthday. Girls mature quicker than boys (in case you didn't know this). Anyway, I presented hers on the Narrows Bridge that spans the Puget Sound between Gig Harbor and Tacoma. As part of her birthday celebration, I walked her across the mile-long bridge. When we reached the midpoint, I stopped and took her hand. I used the metaphor of the bridge to explain how she was crossing from childhood to teenager. From little girl to young woman. The other side of the bridge would offer new opportunities, new choices, and new temptations. Many of the choices she would make would be based on principles she established now. We specifically talked about sexual purity and waiting until marriage. I took the ring from my pocket and offered it as a symbol of a promise. She willingly took it and wears it well. Grant did not receive his ring while crossing a bridge. He got it while crossing his nation on a bicycle. How cool is that? I was reminded of how proud I was of him. He is my hero.

We got back on our bikes the next day. The weather was hot and humid. This was what we had expected for this part of the country. After the last few months we had become very smart about drinking plenty of fluids and staying in the shade. (We were not working on our tans.) We rode a bike path through Harrisburg. There were times the path would dump us out onto city streets. The neighborhoods were always interesting. Even in the rough ones we never felt threatened. God always had His hand on us. Besides, people were more interested in a one-armed man pedaling a strange bike than they were in causing us any problems. The vast majority of people are good people.

After getting back to Paul's we cleaned up and headed over to the church. They were having a seniors' dinner and wanted me to speak briefly to invite folks to the next night's service. We were glad to spend time with the people and get to know Paul's pastor better.

On Wednesday morning, we loaded our bikes into the truck and headed out for our starting point. Today's ride brought us to a long stretch of road on the outskirts of Harrisburg. The road had pros and cons. On the pro side, it went through a beautiful forest, quaint towns, and had relatively light traffic. On the con side, it had very narrow shoulders, lots of hills, and the few cars on the road tended to drive very fast with little regard to cyclists. Between the hills and the stress of fast-approaching cars, we felt as though we were getting a real workout. Jeanne helped refresh us by getting delicious oatmeal cookies from a local farmers market. All in all it was a pleasant day.

We showered and headed over to the evening service. The crowd was good and I presented our message of hope and courage. The church had a cycling club and was very interested in my handcycle. I actually brought my bike onto the platform and delivered part of the message from the bike seat. I must admit it felt a little awkward but it didn't seem to hurt the message. We spent quite a while visiting with people before heading back to Paul's.

We spent our last day in Harrisburg with Paul's family. Paul took the day off work and we went to a neighboring town to take a scenic train ride. It was fun being with them. When we got home, Paul took Chanel for her first motorcycle ride. It was a family tradition. He had given Darla, Nicole and Grant their first motorcycle rides over the years. In fact, years ago he had given me a ride on the back of his BMW, too. I was more daring then and clung tight with my one arm as we wound through the Pennsylvania countryside. When Paul returned with Chanel, he helped me with a few maintenance chores I had put off. He helped us get air in the truck tires, fix a few items in the RV, and build a part for my bike I had lost along the way. Paul is a pretty handy brother-in-law to have around.

Our time with Paul and Karen was coming to an end. Darla and Chanel were quite emotional as we approached the inevitable farewells. Darla truly loves her brother and Chanel is a lot like her mother. Just because we have had many farewells on this journey doesn't make them easier. Grant and I busied ourselves with getting the gear together. It beats crying. We hooked the truck up to the RV and headed toward our next stop.

Kennett Square is west of Philadelphia. It is also where Darla's cousins, Greg and Kristie Hollis, pastor a church. They had started Power Place four years earlier with their two sons and one daughter. They met in the basement of the VFW hall. Their congregation had grown to a few hundred and they were doing a great job. The two sons were on staff at the church. Their wives and sister served there as well. We had scheduled to speak there early in our planning stage. We found a KOA campground nearby and settled in for the weekend.

On Saturday, we loaded up the truck and drove into Philadelphia to be tourists. We saw the Liberty Bell, visited Ben Franklin's grave, and ate pretzels from a street vendor. How much more American can we be? After that, we met Greg and Kristie at the church. It was a joy to see them. We went through the church and made plans for the morning service. They showed us the Pentecostal Evangel with our picture on the front. We had almost forgotten about the reporter who'd met us in Montana in June to do the article. She had said it would be in the Labor Day weekend edition. I guess it is Labor Day weekend. The article and pictures were great and brought back a lot of memories for us. Greg gave us a few copies to take back to camp.

On Sunday we arrived at the church for the two services. We had coffee and pastries greeting us in the foyer. People came and filled the rows of folding chairs. When Greg and his family started the worship service, we realized we were in for a treat. This family has an abundance of musical talent. They used to travel around the country singing and preaching in churches before starting Power Place. We have experienced many worship styles on this journey but Power Place was the hippest we had heard. They were lively, loud and very spiritually sound. I was sad to see them stop so I could preach. Both services went well and people responded to the worship and the message. The real test of a

ministry is in its fruit. That morning ten people put new hope in Christ. We have seen a wide variety of worship on this journey and they have all been good. Churches have so many different styles of worship because there are so many different styles of people. Don't worry, there is a style that fits you, too.

Chapter 24

Today is September 1, Labor Day. As the navigator and cartographer for Hope and Courage, I am always the one most aware of our intended route. However, on this day Darla was very in tune to our location. Our riding would take us right through Lancaster County, Pennsylvania … Amish Country. As the navigator, it is also important that I factor the nature and desires of the riders into our expectations for the day. I know I cannot rush Darla through the Amish.

"Hon, this is your only day in Lancaster. We are going to take it slow. We can always make up the miles on another day. Enjoy it."

I'm not only the navigator and cartographer, I'd like to think I make a pretty decent husband, too. Now, as before, I think it is best if I let Darla tell you about our Amish adventures.

September 1, ~ Monday, Labor Day

How does one put into words what happened today? After preparing for our day and getting some corresponding done, we began our ride. We drove about 30 miles, unloaded the bikes near Wagontown, and started pedaling into Intercourse and Bird-in-Hand. We hadn't gone too far before Jeanne and Chanel came toward us in the truck shaking a fresh loaf of bread out the window.

"We got fresh Amish bread!" Chanel yelled.

They had stopped at an Amish farm stand and bought a loaf. We pulled off the road up ahead and they drove in behind us. We all tore off pieces of fresh bread and enjoyed every bite. What a fun and memorable way to eat a loaf of bread!

I can't imagine a better way to begin
the month of September than riding
bikes in the golden warm sunshine
down Amish country roads. We are
beginning to understand and appreciate
the Amish ways. They truly live a
quieter, simpler and slower lifestyle.
As we were pedaling through the
area, Jeanne and Chanel noticed a
home that had quilts hanging on the
front porch. We all stopped there
and a nice 80-year-old Amish lady,
Rebecca, came out and welcomed us
warmly. When she told us her last
name was Esh, we thought Jeanne
was going to faint. She could not
believe it. They had the same last
name just spelled differently.

We began talking with Rebecca and
told her of our Hope and Courage
Journey. She was fascinated with
what we were doing and quickly
offered a glass of cold water. Then
she said her husband, Samuel, was

taking a nap but she wanted to go wake him up so that he could see us. In the meantime, she showed us where her quilts were. They had a little gift shop downstairs that her 15-year-old granddaughter, Rachel, was tending. On the way to the shop we saw about fifteen cats (some kittens) running around. We had never seen so many cats in one place.

Around the corner was a cute little garden filled with shoes. Each shoe had a plant growing in it. A sign read "Mom's Shoe Garden." The garden belonged to Rachel's mother, Anna. The shoes were of all sizes and well worn. They represented the chores and growth of many children. How sweet.

The shop was filled with beautiful handmade quilts. Chanel and Rachel became instant friends. Rebecca went upstairs to wake Samuel. He came out and joined us on the front lawn. He

sat on a chair while Rebecca sat on
the grass beside him. They were both
interested in Bob's story. Before long,
Rebecca brought out cheese, crackers,
little Snickers bars and root beer.
Then she wanted their son, Jacob, to
meet us. He was milking the cows
in the barn. We felt bad interrupting
Samuel from his nap and Jacob from
milking. But they sure didn't seem
to mind. Then they brought Anna,
Jacob's wife, out for us to meet
and she had little Samuel, who was
four and very shy. We talked and gave
them Hope and Courage prayer cards.

Samuel and Rebecca said that Jacob
had been in an accident and then he
began to tell his story. He had been
run over by a hay bailer. He made a
comment that I really admired. He
said, "You can either become bitter
or you can become better." Jake was
a really nice guy and when he came
over to Bob, he got down on his

291

knee to be eye level with him. They had seven children and were doing a great job raising them. Jake and Anna were taking over the farm and living there with Samuel and Rebecca.

It had been Samuel's 81st birthday last week and he said he had two birthday cakes. One was from his family and one from his church. The way they do birthday cakes at their church is whoever has a birthday receives a cake 'in the pan' from the last person in church who had a birthday. They take the pan home and get the name of the next person having a birthday in the church. Then they bake that person a cake and give it to them in the same pan and it continues on and on. They said you never know who will be bringing you a birthday cake. What a great idea. I think that would be a fun tradition to start.

Rachel was a very sweet girl and Chanel really had a fun time talking with her. She asked Rachel how they celebrated Christmas. She said they don't have a tree or decorate but they get practical presents. They celebrate birthdays with dinner, presents (not always practical) and cake. Rachel took her over to her Grandma's chickens and Chanel got to hold one of the little baby chicks. They also had a miniature pony. Samuel said the animals were Rebecca's garden.

We were there for over an hour visiting with their family. They invited us back on our return trip home and would like Bob to speak at their children's schools. They said we were welcome to stay at their farm with our RV. Rachel was so excited to think that we might be back. Rebecca had a guest book that she wanted us to sign and put our address in. I've had a guest book in our home ever since we've been married. Maybe I'm more like the Amish than I realize. She gave us all writing pens as a souvenir. I think they really liked us. We said our goodbyes with hugs and handshakes and told them we hoped to be back.

We continued our ride. We stopped at a little produce stand at an Amish farm and visited with John Fischer and his thirteen-year-old daughter, Emma Mae. She was such a sweet blonde girl with a beautiful smile. She had such a cute Pennsylvania Dutch accent. I loved listening to her talk. Bob shared a little with John about what we were doing and a very short version of how he lost his limbs. He seemed genuinely interested and asked if we had a book. When Bob told him that we didn't he said, "Well, if you ever do, I would like one." And he gave us his address so we could send him one and keep in touch. We were *so glad that we stopped and had a chance to meet another Amish family.*

Taking a break in Amish Country.

We passed a sign that read 'Homemade Root Beer.' It was on an Amish farm down a nice country road. Grant had been wanting to try some. So we decided to pedal down the country lane and enjoy some root beer. When we got to the stand we met the hired hand (a young girl) and then all these little children came out. They were such cute little blonde children.

There was a little boy, two little girls who looked like twins (but were not) and then a tiny little girl. She was adorable. They looked over the counter and watched us. We drank the root beer and were on our way.

We stopped at a restaurant called Amish Mennonite Family Cupboard. It was a buffet and had Amish peanut butter and shoofly pie. Yum. After our dinner we began pedaling again. We went down a little country road and stopped to talk with an Amish farmer and his hired hand. They were using machetes to cut down some corn stalks. We thought they were going to cut down the whole field that way but he said they were only doing the corners so that when the horses bring the harvest machine in they don't crush the corners.

Nicole called from Gig Harbor and said that she had just gotten a phone message from John Fischer. He had identified himself as the man we had met at the produce stand. He said he wanted to know if we wanted to get together tonight. Bob and I thought the best way to respond was to ride back to his place (it was the opposite way we were going). So, we began pedaling back to his farm. Grant got a flat tire. We sure don't get as many since Nicole went home. While fixing it, we called Jeanne to meet us at the Fischer's.

Emma Mae was there with a big smile at the end of their driveway. They greeted us and said that we were welcome to stay for the evening. John and his wife, Sylvia, were preparing for a tour group doing something called 'The Amish Experience.' Each Monday evening they open their home for visiting tourists to enjoy a light snack and ask questions about the Amish. I felt funny being there while they were preparing for the tour but they really seemed to want us to stay and join them. All the children came out and met us. There was Sarah, sixteen years old; Emma Mae, thirteen years old; Amos, eleven years old; David, nine years old; Mervin, four years old; and Aaron, soon to be two. The children were very friendly. The boys each took a turn sitting on Bob's bike. They loved it and they looked so cute ... all four of them gathered around Bob.

I told Emma Mae that I had a question I wanted to ask her. I also told her that any answer she gave me would be just fine. I asked her if I could take a picture of her brothers with Bob on his bike. She said they usually don't let people take their pictures because they don't want to be in the newspapers or magazines. I told her that I appreciated her being honest with me and that was just fine. I had never really thought about how much people would probably use their photos for publication purposes. I began to understand why they don't want their pictures taken. It began to make sense to me. I decided then I would not ask again if I could take a picture of one of my Amish friends. Their friendship meant too much for me to jeopardize with a picture. I will always cherish the picture in my mind of Bob and those four little barefoot Amish boys. What a precious sight it was to see.

It wasn't long before the tour bus came with four tourists. We all sat in a circle in their yard under a big maple tree. It was a beautiful warm night with locusts chirping and fireflies flashing. We all took turns introducing ourselves. Mervin sat on my lap and so when it was my turn to say my name I said, "I'm Darla and this is my newest addition to our family, Mervin!" (I got to pretend I was an Amish mom.) He was so cute, with a big smile and his blue eyes were full of life. As it began to get dark, it was so sweet watching the little boys running to catch fireflies. It was fun listening to the questions the other families were asking. We already knew some of the answers but we did learn a few new things.

Sylvia asked the tour guide what else they had done on the tour. She told them they had just gone to the Esh farm! We were so surprised because we had just been to the Esh farm earlier in the day. Also, talking to John we found out that the farm where we got our root beer was his parents' farm that he grew up on. He is the oldest of a very large family. His sister runs the root beer stand. It was his nephew and nieces that we had seen earlier. It is a small world, especially within the Amish community.

After the tour group left, John
and Sylvia invited us to stay longer.
They were all very interested in the
details of Bob's accident. Bob began
his story and they all brought their
chairs a little closer so they could
hear everything he had to say. The baby
began to get a little fussy so Jeanne
and Chanel took him so Sylvia could
listen better. She really appreciated
their help. She told Chanel she could
take him in the house to play with
him. Chanel decided to stay in the
yard and read him some books and
play a game with his little piggys.

Bob took this opportunity to see
how his story was received among
the Amish. You can be sure it was
received very well. It was getting so
dark that all I could see was the
glistening of John's tears. I could
not see Sylvia very well but she later
said, " I was crying through your
whole talk." Bob asked each of the

children, "If there was something you learned, what would it be?" They were shy about answering. Bob realizes that question and answer time may be a little quiet in the Amish schools.

Bob had told the kids that they could see how he drives the truck. They wanted to learn as much about us as we wanted to learn about them. When it was time for us to leave they all (including John and Sylvia) were there to watch. It was another beautiful picture that I will keep in my heart. They were all gathered around and little David was standing on the truck running board. They did not want to miss this opportunity!

Sylvia came over to me and shared some personal tragedies. She told me about her twelve-year-old brother who had burned to death from a propane leak. He had been sorting potatoes by lantern and the barn caught on fire,

he was not able to get out. She told
me her mother watched everything
go up in flames and there wasn't
anything she could do. It was a
horrible accident. She also told me
about their baby boy, Jonathon, who
had died after he lived twenty short
minutes. She shared with me that
she had suffered six miscarriages.
And I shared with her about my
two miscarriages. Our common
loss bound us closer together.
She said heaven was getting fuller
of her loved ones. I understand.

We had a precious time together.
They are a very sweet family. We
really enjoyed our evening with them.
We were there for a couple of hours.
They invited us to come back on our
way home and visit their children's
school. They would also like us to
come back another time and minister
to their youth. John said they would
make up flyers to get the word out.

303

We are so amazed at how many Amish we have met and how they seem to welcome us into their communities. Lancaster is the second largest Amish community in the world and Shipshewana is the third. It is such a blessing (and I believe rather rare) that we have been so well received. I really feel that if we were not pedaling our bikes and coming into their towns at a much slower pace that these most wonderful opportunities would not be given to us. Once we started to visit with them, we all realized we share a common God and a common love for family. Thank You, Lord, for this unique experience. What a huge blessing this has been for me.

I am loving the gift of getting acquainted with the Amish. I admire them as friends and don't look at them as 'postcards' anymore. Bob said he did not want to come into their community as a tourist anymore. Instead, he wanted to come and minister as a brother.

When we began our day of pedaling, Bob told me, "This is your only day in Lancaster. Enjoy it, and we can always make up more miles on another day." I am so thankful he gave me that gift. We rode through the Amish community at a slower pace and took the time to meet some wonderful new friends. When following Jesus ... He gives you beautiful blessings along the way.

Not all of God's messages are subtle.

Chapter 25

On Tuesday, we moved our camp near Valley Forge. I am sure our accommodations at Valley Forge were much more hospitable than George Washington experienced back in 1777. We had a very pleasant RV park. It would be our base for the next five days. Our favorite ride through the area started at Valley Forge National Historical Park. It continued on a bike path that went along the Schuylkill River. How'd you do on pronouncing Schuylkill? I am sure you did better than I did at first. Just in case you are in a situation where you have to say it out loud, the correct pronunciation is SKOO-kel. You'll thank me later. We have been trying to use bike paths more in the eastern part of the country than we did in the west. The east is crowded and good cycling roads are harder to find. The paths are safer and let us keep Chanel riding with us more.

This path went along the river and entered Philadelphia from the north. It was a wonderful blend of parks, suburbs and city. Our backgrounds varied from wooded riverbanks and manicured lawns to urban graffiti. All of them were beautiful. Including the graffiti. Our cities have some very articulate and artistic youth. The murals and signatures were colorful but I liked the words best of all. Modern day proverbs painted on a concrete canvas. My favorite was a single word sprayed on a huge block of cement next to a decaying neighborhood … HOPE. Neither King David nor his son, Solomon, could have written it better.

We had been in Pennsylvania for the last eighteen days. Pennsylvania is a beautiful state filled with wonderful people but eighteen days is long enough. We were ready to leave the area and head to New York (New York State, not New York City). Our last Sunday before reaching the Statue of Liberty would be spent at Hopewell Reformed Church in Hopewell Junction, New York. How does a journey called Hope and Courage Across America travel four months and end up giving its last message at Hopewell Reformed Church in Hopewell Junction? Don't ask me. The schedule and plan have been out of my hand since May. I am not in charge. Ask God if you want answers.

We were not the only event to travel a long distance to reach New England this weekend. Hurricane Hannah had finally come ashore in the Carolinas and was racing up the Atlantic Coast. The radio warned of heavy rain and high winds from the coast and inland. I must admit, hurricanes had rather slipped my mind when I was making my "weather we might encounter" list. The air was thick, muggy and very still. It was the proverbial calm before the storm. We quickly broke camp and pulled onto the highway as the first raindrops started to fall. I had found the only campground on the map near Hopewell Junction. It would have to do. I plugged the address into the GPS and headed north. The winds picked up and blew sheets of rain at the side of the truck and RV. I kept my hand tightly on the wheel to counter nature's attempts to push us out of our traffic lane.

Grant, Chanel and Aunt Jeanne sat in the back seat. The kids were reading while Jeanne worked on some project. Darla sat up front with me and wrote in her journal. I figured they were either really comfortable with my driving in this storm or they were keeping busy so they didn't have to think about it. The GPS took us off the main highway to smaller tree lined roads. The wind swayed the trees closer to the road than they belonged. Small branches blew past the windshield as I strained to see through the wipers. It was getting later and I wanted to pull into the campground before it got dark. The GPS brought us right to the address of the map. The only problem was there was not a campground. There was no sign, no driveway, nothing. I checked the address and it matched. I searched the guide and it said this is where it should be. I drove around in hopes of stumbling upon it. There was no campground and now there was no daylight.

Where's one of Darla's 'angels' now? I was just about to say it out loud when our cell phone rang.

Darla answered it, "Hello." I could hear the conversation from the other end.

"This is Pastor Taylor Holbrook from Hopewell Reformed Church. I'm just calling to see how you guys are doing and where you're at."

"Well, funny you should call. We are not really sure where we are. We're supposed to be at a campground but we can't find it."

"That's not good. What road are you on?"

I looked at the GPS and told Darla the name of the road and she repeated it over the phone.

"You guys aren't too far from the church. Why don't you park in our lot? We can open up the youth building and you can use whatever you need in there."

"Hon, tell him that's a great idea. It's better than driving around in this storm."

Darla wrote the address down and got the directions.

I heard Pastor Taylor say, "I'll go unlock the door and turn the lights on for you. You should be there in five minutes."

"Thank you. Your call came just at the right time. You are our 'angel' today. See you soon."

I just kept my mouth shut and drove. The directions led us right to the church. Pastor Taylor was there to greet us and point to a good spot to park the RV. Next to the church was the parsonage that was now converted into the youth building. We hurried into the building through the wind and rain. Pastor Taylor was a very warm man with a bright smile and friendly voice. A white board on an easel greeted us with a handwritten note, "Welcome, Hope and Courage." Obviously, Pastor Taylor also knew how to improvise quickly.

While the girls were given a tour of the place, Grant and I focused on hooking the RV up to whatever utilities were available. We knew a sewer hook-up was not available. We didn't really need water but electricity would be nice. We figured we could plug into an outlet in the house if we could find a long enough extension cord. With Pastor Taylor's help, we searched for an appropriate outlet and cord to no avail.

Finally, he said, "I know who can help us. I'll call Norm. He knows more about this place than anyone."

"We hate to bring him out on a night like this. Do you think he'll mind?" I asked.

"No. He won't mind. Norm lives for stuff like this. Wait 'til you meet him."

We didn't have to wait long. The time between the phone call and the headlights pulling into the parking lot was extremely short. The door opened and in came Norm. He was a sturdy man in his seventies with a deep tan from outdoor work. He wore jeans that were smudged with traces of today's projects. A red bandana hung from his belt. This was definitely for function, not fashion. Norm is a handyman's handyman.

"What do you need?" He said it with such confidence I was sure that whatever I asked for he could get.

"We'd like to get electricity out to the RV. We need to find an extension cord that will reach and an outlet."

"That shouldn't be a problem. Let me look around."

Before long he was back with a cord in hand. "We can plug into the garage on this end. Show me where you want it to connect to the RV."

Grant led him out and finished connecting the power. When they returned, we had time to visit. Norm had been a part of this church for a long time and knew quite a bit of its history. He wasn't around when the church started. None of us were around then. The church was organized in 1757 when England ruled and this state was called a colony. The first building was built in 1764. That is not the building that is here now. The structure we were parked at is the new building. It was erected in 1833. The depth of history in New England amazes me.

I commented to Pastor Taylor, "The congregation of this church has been gathering on this spot steadily since before America became a nation."

"That's true," he said. "But we're not meeting here tomorrow. Our church actually consists of a few congregations that meet at different sites. We wanted to offer an opportunity for worship and fellowship to people who may not be comfortable with established church settings. One of our groups meets at Tymor Park. Tomorrow all of our groups are meeting there for your message and a picnic afterwards."

"That'll be great," I replied.

I was truly impressed. This church was sensitive to the needs of people that had a problem with 'established church settings.' This church, Hopewell Reformed Church, has been meeting since 1757. How much more of an 'established church setting' can you get? These guys really know how to think out of the box. We bid farewell to our hosts and settled into the RV. The edges of Hurricane Hannah roared all around us. That was okay. We had found our port in the storm.

We woke up to clear blue skies, warm temperatures and a mild breeze. It is then that we realized the beauty of our parking spot. The church was a stately white building. The kind you see on New England postcards surrounded by autumn foliage. The director of outreach for the church came by to guide us to the park. He introduced us to his wife and their three young children. Chanel immediately made their ten-year-old daughter, Courtney, her new Best Friend Forever.

Tymor Park has the distinction of being the largest municipal park in New York State. It is a 500 acre farm converted to public use. The festivities at Tymor Park went great. I shared a brief message to the children in the morning and a longer message to the crowd in the afternoon. All of this was done to the background of great food and fellowship.

We were able to leisurely visit with people all day. I enjoyed sitting around the table with the men. Not that men and women sat at separate tables because of tradition. Remember, there was a concentrated effort to avoid tradition. It is just the dynamics of large group communication. Give a large group of people the freedom to just sit and visit and they will naturally break into smaller groups of similar interest. I comfortably found myself with a bunch of guys. Many of them were from the same family and represented four generations. The most senior member was ninety six years old. Where I come from, you line them up and take pictures when four generations get together. Not here. They act as though it happens every week. As I said, the depth of history in New England amazes me.

During my various conversations, I kept being asked two questions: "Do you think you will reach the end of your ride on September 11?" And, "Where exactly in New York City will you finish the journey?" We had asked these questions ourselves many times over the last several months.

We had always intended on making September 11 the ending date of our journey. It is a very symbolic date and connects well with our Hope and Courage message. Just this past week I learned something that made me rethink that plan. We are two months away from the national elections and both presidential candidates, Senators McCain and Obama, are in full campaign mode. Both of them have scheduled to be at Ground Zero in New York City on September 11 to be a part of the memorial services. The security, crowds, and activities are going to be huge. Our route goes right past Ground Zero. Maneuvering our bikes and support team through that event could be a real mess.

We decided it would be best if we waited until September 12 to ride into the city and finish our journey.

As for where we would end our journey, that had complications, also. The Statue of Liberty had always been our plan. It, too, is very symbolic and fits well with our Hope and Courage message. I figured we could pedal to Battery Park, put our bikes on the ferry to Liberty Island, and pedal to the statue. I called the ferry office and explained what we wanted to do. You know, we are ending a ride on bikes from Washington State to New York, our ride is called Hope and Courage Across America, and we want to end our ride at the Statue of Liberty. The person was impressed with our effort and admired what we were doing. The only problem is that bicycles are not allowed on the ferry to Liberty Island. The security is very much like airports. You can't even take large bags onto the island. Bicycles were out of the question. Okay, this must be another one of God's roadblocks and I am not going to argue, I will adjust. We will end our ride at Battery Park and wave at the Statue of Liberty across the bay. I was explaining this to one group and one of the men, Mark, asked me to clarify why we could not go to the Statue with our bikes.

I went back through my story and he said, "Interesting. Do you have a number where I can reach you?" I gave him my cell phone number. The conversation soon turned to other topics and ended with the art of grilling the perfect burger. I really love sitting around the guys' table.

We were told of a of a bike path that we could catch in Carmel, New York, that would take us into the city. This information was priceless. Finding a bike route into New York City had been haunting me for quite a while. Pastor Taylor, an avid cyclist, said he had ridden the trail and would be glad to meet us Monday morning and ride with us. A few more men said they would like to ride, too. We had not had guest riders since Indiana. The company and the guidance would be a welcome blessing. Pastor Taylor gave us directions to the trailhead and we set a start time.

Before we left, the Elders of the church called our team together. They wanted to pray for us. Their prayer was different from the ones we had in other places. They didn't pray for this journey. Their prayer was for our next journey ... that God would show us where He wanted our ministry to go ... and to direct the next chapter of our ministry. Our Sunday at Hopewell Junction was ideal.

Monday morning we drove to the meeting point and unloaded our bikes. Pastor Taylor arrived with his bike and before long Tom and Pat joined us. Tom and Pastor Taylor had nice road bikes with proper gear. Pat had a slick recumbent bike. These men were obviously experienced cyclists. The next person to arrive was a different story. Norm arrived dressed just as he was the night we met him at the church. He was wearing jeans, a T-shirt, work boots, and his ever present bandana hanging from the belt. He explained later that he hung the bandana from his belt because he didn't want to put it back in his pocket wet after wiping his sweat. Norm is an extremely practical person. I like him.

Darla greeted him with a smile and a hug. "Norm, it is great to see you."

"I thought I would drive over and see you guys off. I tried to get a bike together but couldn't find one."

"Would you like to ride Nicole's bike and come along with us?" Darla asked, pointing to Nicole's bike on the rack of the truck.

You would have thought you just asked the little brother if he wanted to go play ball with the big kids.

His eyes watered up, "I would love to. I haven't ridden since I took the Boy Scouts on a bike ride."

"Really? When did you do that?"

He put his hand to his chin and looked up toward the sky. I am not sure what type of filing system he had for memories but he eventually found what he was looking for.

"1985 … it was 1985 when I took the Boy Scouts."

"1985?" Now I got involved in the conversation. "Norm, that was over twenty years ago. What kind of bike did you have?"

"It was a girls' bike. I borrowed it."

I am sure the girls' bike he borrowed in 1985 had big tires and a step-through frame. That is quite a different bike than the one-inch tire, twenty-four gear, light framed piece of equipment he was borrowing today. Grant got Nicole's bike down and brought it over.

"Do you think you can ride this one?" I asked.

Norm proving you never forget how to ride a bike.

"I don't know why not."

I looked at his outfit and tried to think if we had any extra gear he could use. No such luck.

"Would you like to run home and change?"

"No. I can wear this." He really did not want to miss out or hold us up. I could tell it was a huge treat for him.

"At least roll the pant leg of your jeans up so it doesn't get caught in the chain."

I wasn't sure how long he would be able to pedal but that wasn't a problem. Chanel was riding with us and she was good for ten miles or so. If Norm wanted to stop then, Jeanne could pick them up in the truck. We were not planning to make it all the way to the city anyway.

We made plans for Jeanne to meet us in a community down the trail. Everyone was in good spirits. We gathered for a group prayer and started pedaling. Darla stayed next to Chanel for the first few miles. After a while I held back to ride with Chanel. Darla and Grant pulled ahead and joined Norm. He was definitely giving his bandana a workout. We had gone up a few inclines and Norm struggled pushing to the top. I totally understood. Being off a bike for twenty-three years or using just one limb both take an adjustment period.

"How are you doing, Norm?" Darla asked.

"Pretty good. I have a hard time keeping my feet on the pedals. And this bike rolls a lot harder than the one I rode before."

"Your work boots make it hard to keep your feet on but it shouldn't be pedaling hard. How many gears did the last one have?" Darla asked.

"Gears? I don't know. One I guess. Where are the gears on a bike?"

"Your shifters are up there on your handle bars. Right next to the brakes," Darla pointed out.

"Oh. I figured out the brakes but I wondered what those other things were."

Grant glanced down at the position of the chain on the sprockets of Norm's bike and saw right away they were in a very difficult gear.

"Mom, he's got that bike in a real hard gear."

"Norm, you need to shift to an easier gear. Let me show you how to do that."

Darla gave him a quick lesson about shifting. Norm's face lit up as his legs immediately felt the benefit of the easier gear.

"Wow. That makes a big difference. This is the nicest bike I've ever ridden. Statue of Liberty here I come!" Having Norm along blessed everyone.

Thirteen miles into the ride, we met Aunt Jeanne. Chanel was done for the day. She was hanging up her cycling helmet and putting on her support team hat. Norm decided thirteen miles was far enough for him, too. Jeanne could drive him back to his car while the rest of us continued on the trail. We set a goal of forty miles and settled into our ride. I joined Pastor Taylor and Pat up front and Darla and Grant rode with Tom behind us.

The path meandered through towns and villages. You could hear the children, dogs and traffic through the greenbelt of trees that sheltered us most of the way. Under the canopy of trees, other critters scurried, hopped and slithered as we pedaled past. They presented no danger to us. These weren't the rattlesnakes and dogs we faced out west. We rarely saw them and only knew of their presence by the rustling noises they made in the bushes. Occasionally, a chipmunk or squirrel would dart out in front of a bike as if playing some sort of game. Chipmunks played the game better than the squirrels.

Thirty miles into the day a squirrel ran in front of Darla. She was going too fast to stop or swerve. Her front wheel went right over the squirrel and her rear wheel did the same. She immediately stopped and Tom and Grant did the same. They went back to look at the damage done to the squirrel. The bike tires had killed it. Darla felt horrible and was upset. The guys assured her there was nothing she could have done. There was just not enough time to react. Tom pointed out how fortunate Darla was the squirrel didn't get tangled in her spokes. She could have gone over the handlebars and gotten seriously hurt or worse. Darla thanked the Lord for protecting her and said a little prayer for the squirrel, too. Maybe squirrels are just as dangerous as rattlesnakes and dogs, after all.

The rest of the ride was uneventful. All in all, it was a beautiful day and the trail was excellent. The company proved to be excellent, also. Being on a bike path allowed us to visit more than if we had been on a road. We would take turns riding next to each other. This made a good environment for one-to-one conversation. As the miles clicked away, we got to know more about our travel companions. Darla would ask about their families, the ones they came from and the ones they raised. If you have ever had a conversation with Darla, I am certain you talked about your family. It is what interests Darla most. She is truly interested in your mother, father, sisters, brothers, children and grandchildren. She will remember their names, their age, and even their birthdays if you tell her. I, on the other hand, would talk about careers and journeys, where they worked and how they got here. These men were all good men. The journey of their lives had been filled with mountains, valleys and detours but they never gave up. They pressed on through it all and continue to do so today. The journey of Hope and Courage is all about pressing on. So is the journey of life.

Chapter 26

September 9

It was time for Hope and Courage to press on. Pedaling had taken us to the edge of the city. Now we had to move camp. Our next stop would not be a camp at all. We had rooms reserved at a hotel near the Newark Airport. There were several people flying in on September 11 to be with us at the end. Jeanne's kids, Robby and Jenny, were coming. Robby's new bride, Marlo, and Don were not able to make it. Our best friends, Todd and Media, were coming in from Oregon. They were with us at the start and wanted to be with us at the finish. The depth of their friendship has always been a blessing to Darla and me.

We wanted Nicole to join us but she had just started her senior year at Northwest University. Her nursing studies were intense. The school has strict grade standards and several of the students had already fallen out of the program. Nicole is an excellent student. Keep in mind, she just turned twenty this summer and is in her senior year of college. I personally don't think missing a few days would have a negative effect on her overall grade. However, I am not the student or the dean of medicine. I tried to get involved. I called the dean and asked him what he would recommend. He did not suggest she leave. I asked Nicole what she wanted to do. She did not want to do anything to jeopardize her nursing degree. In the end, she chose to stay back. We were all disappointed. She is part of our team, part of our family. It did not seem right for her not to ride the last stretch with us. Nevertheless, this journey has taught us all to make tough decisions.

Our drive brought us to the interstate that would lead to Newark. Driving the truck while pulling a thirty-five foot trailer took all my concentration. I relied heavily on the GPS for turn-by-turn directions. Traffic got heavier as we headed into the afternoon commute. I kept an eye on my mirrors and hoped for as few lane changes as possible. I did not have to worry about making quick decisions. The freeway had slowed to a crawl. The sign above the lane we were in read 'New York City.' I glanced at the GPS to make sure I was on the right road. I was. Our route was taking us through New York City during rush hour. Don't get me wrong, I'm not afraid of driving in the city. In fact, if these people in these cars around me knew that a man with no legs and only one arm was driving this big truck pulling this huge RV, they would be afraid. I just kept my position in my lane and followed directions. We nudged on to the George Washington Bridge toward Newark. I could not help but notice in this huge mass of vehicles that we were the only RV.

We made it to the hotel in Newark before dark. They said we could park right in front. This would be the last stop for the Hope and Courage Across America RV until we headed home. It was a relief to climb out of the driver's seat and into my wheelchair. It had been a long drive for all of us. We settled into our rooms and my cell phone rang.

"Hello, this is Bob."

"Bob, this is Mark. We met at the church picnic Sunday."

"Yeah, Mark. How are you doing?"

"I'm fine. Hey, I made a few phone calls about the end of your ride. When you get down to Battery Park, go to the Park Service office, and knock on the door. Ask for Pat, he is a park ranger, and tell him who you are. He's going to put you and your bike, with your team on a ferry and take you over to the Statue of Liberty."

"You're kidding. Really?"

"No, I'm not kidding. It did not seem right that you would ride your bike all this way and not be allowed to finish. I knew some people who could help. Unfortunately, they will only let you take your bike on the ferry. The others will have to leave theirs back. Is that okay?"

"I wish everyone could take their bikes over but this is better than what we had going this morning. Thanks Mark, this is really a blessing. You've been our angel today."

I could not believe I actually used the word 'angel.' Now Darla has me doing it, too.

September 10

We got ready and went out for a day in the city. And when I say the city I mean the city ... New York ... the Big Apple. I had scheduled to speak in two schools in Brooklyn for my friend, Kevin Young. Kevin is part of Student Ventures, a Christian group that helps mentor teens. We have worked together for several years. I had called him last spring to offer my services when we got to New York. Kevin gladly accepted.

We dropped Darla, Chanel and Aunt Jeanne off in Times Square. The stores were just opening and they planned a day of window shopping and afternoon tea. Grant and I drove across town to Brooklyn. Driving the truck through the city without the RV was almost like driving a sports car. Almost.

We met Kevin at our first school. It was a middle school. After that, we went to speak to a high school football team that was on a long, hot losing streak. I talked about crossing a mountain with one arm and not quitting even when you don't think you can win. I told them about the first time I met Kevin and how he took me to speak to the New York Giants NFL team. Moreover, I told them the Giants were no different from them ... everyone needed hope and courage.

Kevin has brought me to some of my favorite schools over the years. There are more than one million high school students in the city. It has both the most multi-cultural and the most mono-cultural schools I have ever visited. I have gone from a school that had armed guards visible in every corridor directly to a performing arts school that had students performing on Broadway. New York City is a world unto itself. The full spectrum of humanity lives within its boroughs. From the over-privileged to the under-privileged ... from those relying completely on hope to those not knowing how much they need it. It is a great place for a message of Hope and Courage.

We picked the girls up later in the afternoon. The favorite part of Darla and Chanel's day was having afternoon tea with Aunt Jeanne at the American Girl Doll Place. This was the third American Girl Place they have visited. The other two were in Chicago and Los Angeles. Each one had its own unique style. After tea, they had a great time browsing in the stores, especially Saks Fifth Avenue. They saw a $2,500 purse and a $1,400 pair of shoes. Boy, was I glad they were just window-shopping.

Traffic was thick getting out of the city so we drove through Manhattan to look at the sights. We went to Battery Park to get a look at where we would catch the ferry to the Statue. It was smart to get a little familiar with the area. There was a lot of hustle and bustle in preparation for the 9/11 events the next day.

Seeing all the activity confirmed to us that our decision to wait until September 12 was a good one. We would rather finish our journey on a quieter day. We stopped for something to eat and headed back to the hotel.

September 11

We had said "September Eleven" hundreds of times in the past year. It is hard to believe it is actually here. And like so many other aspects of Hope and Courage Across America, it is not how we imagined it would be. That is all right. We have come to learn there is a difference between our plans and God's plans. God's plans are always best, even when we don't know why. If that is all we learned on this journey, it is enough.

We all busied ourselves with chores. Our hands were busy doing the task in front of us but our minds were on tomorrow. Grant and Chanel did school work. Classes started shortly after Labor Day. They do their studies through Internet Academy. Internet Academy is a school that has the curriculum online and teachers on the other end to guide their studies. It has been a blessing to our family. Because they can study anywhere and anytime, we have been able to bring them on many ministry trips. That is important to me.

I would never have traveled as far as I have in the past twenty years if I could not bring my family with me at times. Not because I need my family to be with me, it is because I do not need to be away from my family. My first priority is to my wife and children. This stuff I do as an evangelist and motivational speaker is further down the list. Don't get me wrong. I enjoy being a speaker; I think I am a good communicator. However, many people can communicate as well as I do and better. They can have my job. I can live with that. However, there is no one that can be a better husband to my wife or a better father to my children. If I do not make them the priority of my life, someone may come and take my place. I cannot live with that. From the beginning, Hope and Courage Across America has been the journey of a man and his family. I would not have done it any other way.

Jeanne busied herself cleaning out the truck. Robby and Jenny were arriving very late tonight on the same flight with Todd and Media. She was looking forward to seeing her two children. She had spent so much time with ours that I am sure she would cherish the time with her own. I cannot adequately express how important Jeanne has been to this journey. She is our unsung hero. Newspapers and TV stations have not turned their cameras in her direction. She does not get pats on the back as she climbs off a bike. No crowds applaud as she comes to a microphone. But every time those things happened for the rest of us, Jeanne was right there. Standing out of the spotlight, she arranged the media, drove the truck to pick us up, and told our story ahead of us. She was always encouraging, even in the

Aunt Jeanne and Chanel – BFF

midst of our hardest days. Her greatest contribution, though, was watching Chanel so the rest of us could ride. There is absolutely, without question, no one we could have trusted more with that role than her. On top of that, there is no one Chanel would have wanted to spend the summer with more than Aunt Jeanne. She not only did all of these things, she always did them willingly and with a smile on her face.

Darla took advantage of the hotel laundry room to get our clothes washed and dried. On one of her many trips between the RV and laundry room she met a family. There was a grandma, a mother and two daughters. They talked about family, and the tragedy of 9/11, and our trip across America. Darla gave each of the sisters a Journey Bible.

When she came back in the hotel, she told me, "It was special for me to give the Journey Bibles away on 9/11. So many Americans were remembering what we lost ... I wanted to be sure and give an American something they could find ... salvation." Darla has become quite the evangelist on this journey.

Grant and I checked the bikes and gear in preparation for tomorrow. It was only an eleven-mile ride but it was an important eleven miles. I sent a notice out to everyone on our email list last week about the finish. I told them we would end our journey at Battery Park on September 12 around 1:00 p.m. This was before we had access to the Statue of Liberty. I invited anyone who could to be there to greet us. We don't know who to expect, we just know we don't expect many. Our buildup to the finish was not as extensive as our buildup to the send-off.

There was actually more media interest back home about the end of our journey than there was in New York. The Seattle station, KING-5, was going to rebroadcast the "Evening Magazine" episode about Hope and Courage. They called for an update and some photos they could add to the original show. Ichabod and the Morning Crew at KMPS scheduled a live radio interview when we reached Battery Park. I have truly enjoyed the weekly sessions we have done every Thursday morning at 8:00 a.m. Pacific Standard Time. I have had to be aware of my time zone to be ready for their call. I look forward to talking to them tomorrow. We ordered New York style pizza delivered to our hotel. It seemed appropriate even if we were in New Jersey.

As the hours between today and tomorrow grew shorter, we settled into our own rooms and into our own thoughts. Darla made her final journal entry before reaching Lady Liberty.

September 11, It is the
seventh anniversary of 9/11
and we are in New York.

I am not quite sure how I feel right
now. We will begin the final miles of
our Hope and Courage Journey across
America in a few hours. I was asked
earlier today how I felt about finishing
the trip. I said it was a bittersweet
feeling. I was happy that we actually
were able to achieve our goal but I
was sad because the trip was coming
to an end. This trip has been such a
blessing in so many ways. I am not
really sure if I will fully be able to
describe in words how amazing the trip
has been. I would be lying if I were to
say it was a bed of roses out here and
that everything went as planned because
actually hardly anything went as planned.
But even though we were not able to
pedal each mile or have the leisure time
that we had anticipated, the trip itself
was much more rewarding. I never

imagined all the nice people we would be meeting and the encouragement we would be receiving from total strangers. There were countless times when we would be talking with someone, and as we were telling them what we were doing their eyes would well up with tears. We seemed to stir their emotions. Lord, I just pray we were helping to stir their emotions toward You. I hope that we were good stewards of the finances and blessings You provided, and I pray that we were faithful to the message we were giving. We hope we were able to guide many toward You. We hope and pray that we did not bring any shame to You and that we were good and faithful servants for You.

Thank You, Lord, for this incredible journey. It will be a lifetime memory for our family. We do look forward to see what path You will guide us to next. It will be hard to top this one!

Chapter 27

The only thing between the Statute of Liberty and us was Manhattan. A mere eleven miles. Starting in Harlem and going down past Central Park, past the Theater District, past Times Square, past the Empire State Building, past Wall Street, past Ground Zero, down to Battery Park, and the raised torch of the Statue of Liberty with her welcoming words.

"Give me your tired, your poor; Your huddled masses yearning to breathe free; The wretched refuse of your teeming shore. Send these, the homeless, tempest-tost to me; I lift my lamp beside the golden door!"

There is a beacon of Hope and Courage. Since last May, we have crossed America with one message. Hope in Christ and courage to do something with that hope. I cannot remember most of what we have seen or done. There were so many faces, so many miles. Nevertheless, today, September 12, 2008, our journey will reach its destination.

We awoke early, fully awake. Even Grant and Chanel were eager to get up and get going. Todd and Media were in the room next to ours. They had come in late and taken the airport shuttle to the hotel. I called their room to welcome them and set a meeting time in the lobby for breakfast. The hotel provided pastries, cereal, fruit, coffee, juice and such for the guests. After talking to Todd, I called Jeanne's room. Robby and Jenny had flown in with Todd and Media. They were all excited for today and would meet us for breakfast. It didn't take anyone long to get ready. We had done most of the preparations yesterday. Grant and I headed down to the lobby and met Todd. It was great to see him.

"Todd! Good to see you. It has been a long time."

"Yeah, it has. The last time we saw you guys was when you left Washington in May."

"Well, we've come a few miles since then," I replied while giving him a hug. "I can't believe you and Media flew to New York to be here with us at the finish."

"We wouldn't have missed it for the world," he said with unquestionable sincerity.

We found the largest table available and caught up on each other's summer. Actually, Todd did not want to talk about the summer. He wanted to talk about today. He wanted to know what he could do to help us reach the end of our journey.

"Having you and Media here is a great support to us. I can use you to drive the truck. This time you won't have the RV attached. How about riding with us? We have an extra bike and helmet. We thought Nicole would be here but she couldn't come. Do you want to take her place?"

"You bet I want to ride with you. It would be an honor."

"I don't know about the 'honor' part but we would love to have you with us. You're wearing the Hope and Courage T-shirt we gave you in May so you are officially part of the team."

It wasn't long before Jeanne came down with Robby and Jenny. It was good to see Jeanne with her kids. Darla and Chanel joined us. Our team of nine outgrew one table and spread into another. Darla took a seat next to Media to catch up with her best friend. We all grabbed a bite and started going over the logistics of the day. Our first challenge was getting us all to our starting point in the city. There was no way we could transport nine people and five bikes in the truck. It would take two trips. Todd could drive the bikes and some of the people over first, then come back and get the rest. In the middle of working out the details, a familiar voice interrupted us.

"Hope and Courage, here we come!"

Brett, our nephew, came bounding into the room with a big smile. His exuberance filled the lobby. Grant and Chanel were so surprised they sat frozen in their seats, their mouths stuck in an open position.

"Brett! What are you doing here?" Darla quickly got up and rushed over to give him a hug.

"I came to see you guys finish the ride. And look who I brought with me," he said stepping aside.

Chuck and Nick stepped into the room. They both had ridden with us on our very first Sunday after we spoke at their church, Riverview Community in Kent. Brett is the pastor there.

"We didn't want to miss this," Chuck said.

"We wouldn't miss this," Nick added.

"I cannot believe you are here. When did you decide this?" Darla sounded as though she was in shock.

"We had it planned for quite a while. I didn't have to do anything. Chuck and Nick said they really wanted to be here and put it all together. I just get to come along."

"Well, we're glad you did," Darla said while hugging Chuck and Nick.

Chuck replied, "You had us worried there when you changed your date from September 11 to September 12. We had already bought our tickets but fortunately we don't have to fly home until tomorrow."

"So, what did you do yesterday," I asked.

"We went into the city and watched the events going on at Ground Zero. It was really emotional," Nick said.

"I'm sure it was. I can only imagine what everyone was feeling." Darla paused, "I still can't believe you guys are here."

"Well, we are. What can we do to help?" Brett asked.

"Do you have a car?" I asked.

"Yeah, we rented one."

"Do you have room for a few more passengers?"

"Sure, we can take a two more with us," Nick figured.

I smiled, "Great. You have already solved one of our problems. Now we can get to the city in one trip. We'll take seven in the truck and you can take five in your car."

Our team had grown to twelve. Having the others with us made us feel closer to home. We loaded bikes, gear, and people into the vehicles and headed up Interstate 95 to New York City. We crossed the George Washington Bridge and exited the freeway to the city streets below. Both vehicles stuck close together as we wound our way to the Hudson River Greenway. The HRGW is a walking/bike path that goes down the west side of Manhattan along the Hudson River. We unloaded the bikes and attached our packs. The sky was slightly overcast and the temperature was warm and pleasant. A perfect day for a bike ride.

Our destination was only eleven miles but the significance of those miles made it feel like a much longer ride ahead. Darla, Grant, Chanel, Todd and I would be pedaling. The other seven would be the support team and wait for us at Battery Park. We gathered in a circle for prayer. Every one of us was together in a similar circle on May 18. Our prayer included a big "thank You" for bringing us safely from that circle to this one. We posed for one last round of pictures and started on our way.

We got on our bikes in Harlem and started down Manhattan. The Hudson River was on our right and the city was on our left. We shared the bike path with a lot of people. The Hudson River Greenway is the most heavily used bikeway in America. That does not surprise us. We are in New York City, after all. We smiled, waved, stopped to talk, and took pictures. We attracted attention. Even in the Big Apple we stood out as unusual. We stopped along the path to enjoy the scenery. We were in no hurry. This was time just for the riders. We reminisced about the miles and the months that had brought us to this spot. Darla and I told Grant and Chanel how proud we were that they did this. They have been amazing. I told Darla how much I loved her and appreciated her staying beside me. Not just on this journey but on every journey.

We passed artists painting in the park, lines of schoolchildren escorted by their teachers, mothers with strollers, people with dogs, bicyclists, skaters, and runners. Luxury apartments and high-rent office towers stood on one side of the path. The homeless and downtrodden claimed the benches on the other side next to the river. I watched Chanel maneuver her bike around the few who still lay on the path. The contrast of New York seemed to be a condensed version of the whole nation. It is made up of people from every aspect of life. They are all incredibly different and incredibly the same. The point is no matter how different or how similar we are, we all need Hope and we all have Courage.

"Hope in Christ and the Courage in yourself to do something with that Hope."

I cannot tell you how many times we have said those words over the last four months. Our path went past Central Park, Times Square, Broadway, and Wall Street. We stopped for a break on a spot overlooking Ground Zero. There is an example Hope and Courage. A lot of cleanup work is still going on there. Two construction workers turned and noticed us as we paused and took pictures.

"Whoa, nice bike!" one worker shouted.

I told them we were moments away from finishing a journey we started last May in Gig Harbor, Washington.

"What's the ride about?" they asked above the noise.

The words rolled out of my mouth again.

"Hope and Courage ... Our Hope is in Christ and the Courage is in us to do something with that Hope."

This would be the last time I said those words before we reached the end. It seemed appropriate we were at Ground Zero. There are more stories of Hope and Courage in the ruins of the World Trade Center Towers than we will ever know.

We were fewer than ten blocks away from Battery Park.

I said, "Tighten up on our riding. I want us going in as a group. We started together, we are finishing together."

I can't believe we made it!

We reached Battery Park amid a sea of American flags and the sounds of bagpipes playing. We knew they were not for us. They were part of the 9/11 ceremonies carried over from the day before. It did make an appropriate background, though. Our support team met us with applause and cheering. They rushed to us with hugs and congratulations. Nick gave Darla a bouquet of red roses.

Kevin Young came up. "Hey, Bro. Congratulations."

"Kevin, what a surprise. Thanks for coming."

"I couldn't let you pedal a bike from Seattle to my town without stopping by to say hello. And thanks for talking at those schools the other day. I really appreciate it."

A large group of boys wearing Hope and Courage T-shirts stood together and cheered our arrival. Our friend Bill Beatty had driven them down from Danbury, Connecticut. Bill has an organization, Pathways, for mentoring youth to live successful lives. I speak to the boys every time I am in the area. Seeing forty young men wearing T-shirts with Hope and Courage printed on them made us all feel great.

An unfamiliar man walked up to us wearing a familiar vest. "My name's Joe. I heard through the grapevine you guys were finishing an epic journey today."

His vest had the Christian Motorcycle Association crest on the back. The CMA is the biker club that roared away from city hall with us on May 17. It wasn't a coincidence one of their East Coast members would be waiting for us in New York City. Even strangers got caught up in the excitement, shook our hands and took pictures.

I pedaled to a quieter spot to make a phone call. There was one team member who needed to be a part of this moment. I waited for the voice on the other end.

"Hello, Daddy."

"Nicole, we have made it to Battery Park."

"You hoo!" Her enthusiasm was genuine. She was truly thrilled that we were there even if she could not be with us.

Jeanne came over, "Bob, look at the time. Ichabod will be calling any minute to put you on the radio."

"Nicole, I gotta go. Mom will call you later." I did not wait long before the phone rang.

"Where in the world is Bob Mortimer?" Ichabod's voice filled my ear.

"Guys, I am sitting on my bike looking at the Statue of Liberty."

"You made it?"

"We made it!"

"Do you hear that, listeners? Bob Mortimer and his family have made it to the Statue of Liberty. Hope and Courage has made it across America." I could hear the whoops and hollers from the crew.

I spent the next few minutes describing our ride down Manhattan, explaining our feelings and impressions of the day. I expressed the impact Ground Zero had on us as a true example of Hope and Courage. The interview carried on as long as the station could allow.

Before signing off, Ichabod said his familiar, "Thank God for Darla."

I said, "Amen."

We contacted the park ranger to arrange to get on the ferry for Liberty Island. He explained only my bike could go on the ferry and the rest would have to go on foot. Chuck and Nick volunteered to stay back and watch the other bikes while we were gone. We hated to see them stay back but so appreciated them doing so. I don't know what else we could have done with the bikes. If we left them unattended in the city, there is a good chance they would not be there when we returned. The ranger asked me how many were in our party.

I said, "We have about a dozen. I'll send someone to the ticket booth to pay our fare."

He said, "You don't need tickets. Everyone follow me and stay close."

He led us past the ticket booth, into the short security check line, and onto the ferry.

"Congratulations on the end of your ride. Enjoy the Statue."

We all got on the ferry. Even the boys from Danbury got tickets and joined us. There was an atmosphere of celebration on the boat. We visited with all the wonderful people who took the time and effort to share this day with us. The ferry eased up to the dock and dropped the gangway. We let most of the passengers off first before maneuvering my handcycle to go ashore. As we got off the ferry, we had another surprise. Darla's sister Betty and her husband, Dave, along with her brother Paul and his wife, Karen, were waiting for us on the dock. Darla's face lit up like fireworks. Chanel and Grant looked just as amazed as they did when Brett showed up. They couldn't believe their aunts and uncles were in New York at the end of their ride.

Betty and Dave had flown to Paul and Karen's home in Harrisburg earlier in the week. Then they all drove to New York to surprise us when we reached the Statue of Liberty. And they really did surprise us. This was the second time Betty and Dave showed up unexpectedly. The first was in Columbia Falls, Montana, back in June. Having those four waiting on the dock was the icing on our cake. What a treat.

Darla and Betty ... Sisters

I pedaled my handcycle away from the dock and toward Lady Liberty. We stopped at the base of the statue. We had made it. Our bikes had carried us over Snoqualmie Pass and the struggle of that first mountain and through the snowstorms and rattlesnakes of Montana. We raced ahead of dogs crossing the prairies of North Dakota and lingered on the Amish farms of the Midwest. We rolled up and down the hills of Pennsylvania and finally through the city streets of New York. Hope and Courage Across America could pedal no further. The emotions of the day hit us in waves. Had we been alone we would have cried. And at times we did.

Chanel, Grant, Darla and I moved over to the railing surrounding the island and looked back at the skyline of Manhattan.

Swallowing the lump out of my throat, I said, "Hard to believe we got here, isn't it, Family?"

"It sure is," Darla replied as she wrapped her arms around Grant and Chanel.

We enjoyed the solitude of our own thoughts for a moment and then Darla asked, "Is there anything special you kids learned along the way?"

Chanel thought a while, "I learned America is made up of a lot of different people and I can be a friend to all of them."

"Yes, you can, Sweetheart." She had made new friends from sea to shining sea.

"How about you, Grant? What'd you learn?" I asked.

"I don't know." He paused. "I think I learned to be adaptable."

"That was a good lesson for us all," Darla added. "Anything else?"

"Yeah, I guess if you keep at something long enough you'll finally get there." I must say, for a young man that does not talk much he sure says a lot.

I looked at Darla and said, "What about you, Hon? Did you learn anything unexpected in these last four months?"

She thought awhile before answering. "I know we left home to bring a message of hope and courage to people but I realize something else happened. Not only did we share hope and courage, we also received it. If it wasn't for the prayers and encouragement from everyone we met along the way, I don't think we could have made it."

I agree with everything they said. As for my thoughts, the welcome we received at the end of Hope and Courage was greater than I expected. I must admit, there were times over the last four months that I imagined a grand finish in New York. I pictured TV stations and newspapers recording our arrival with large crowds cheering us on. I also knew those thoughts were rooted in my vanity and pride. The farther I progressed on this journey, the less room there was in my heart for such fantasies. If it were only Aunt Jeanne waiting for us at the end with her encouragement and hugs, that would have been enough. Hope and Courage Across America was not about fame and glory.

I led my family on an adventure that covered four months, a dozen states, and a couple of thousand miles on bicycles to learn two simple truths. One ... life is experienced in the journey. And two ... it's not about the miles, it's about the Message.

Family and friends soon ended our private moment. We enjoyed the rest of our time with them as we toured the Statue of Liberty. The weather went from slightly overcast to cloudy and it soon began to rain. It was not a downpour. It was a Pacific Northwest rain, just a constant drizzle. It was as though the sky was saying it was time to go home.

The Hope and Courage Team had reached their goal.

Chapter 28

THE JOURNEY HOME

On the Monday after reaching the Statue of Liberty, our 'finale team' broke into smaller groups and went their own ways. Todd and Media flew home early in the morning. Robby and Jenny took a later flight with Jeanne. Saying goodbye to Jeanne was the most emotional parting we had all summer. She was the underlying support of our team. While America was our mission, we were her mission. Chanel felt the impact of her leaving the hardest. Aunt Jeanne was her Number One Best Friend Forever all summer long. I do not know how long Jeanne's tears lasted. I just know it was hours before Chanel's tears stopped. After they left, Grant and Chanel found their places in the backseat of the truck, Darla settled into the passenger seat, and I drove the RV onto Interstate-78. This time we followed the signs that read 'West.' Hope and Courage Across America was on the way back home.

We made it as far as Lancaster County, Pennsylvania, and found a campground. Our schedule allowed us to spend the next day with our new Amish friends, the Eshes and the Fishers. They arranged for me to speak in four Amish schools.

Jacob Esh rode with us to the first school. We drove past farms and down a gravel lane to a white, one-room schoolhouse and parked our truck next to a horse and buggy. The children were at recess when we arrived. When Grant lifted my wheelchair out of the back of the truck and brought it around to the driver's door, they stopped playing and gathered to watch. I have always said that I am a pretty interesting guy until you get to know me. The teacher rang the bell on top of the schoolhouse and the children quickly went inside. On our way in, we passed the cloakroom. The boys' black hats hung neatly on pegs.

Darla and I were aware of the great tragedy that had happened two years earlier a few short miles from here. The one I mentioned in a previous chapter where a disgruntled truck driver entered a school just like this one and held the students hostage. Releasing the adults and the boys, he shot the ten remaining girls before turning the gun on himself. He killed five of the girls and critically wounded the others. Worldwide media attention shattered the quiet, private lifestyle of this community. Within a day, the Amish families had already begun the process of forgiving the shooter and bringing comfort to his widow. News stories quickly shifted from the senseless horror of the shooting to the amazing grace of the Amish. WWJD (What Would Jesus Do) is not a bumper sticker in the Amish community; it is a way of life.

That evening I presented my testimony to a group of adults in a cleaned out shop building on the Esh farm. One of the men removed his hat, put a bill in it, and handed it to the person next to him. The hat went around the room and they gave us the contents to help our ministry. We appreciated the offering but an equal blessing was seeing someone actually 'pass the hat.' We would have stayed longer but I had 1,200 middle school students expecting me the next day in Austintown, Ohio.

From Ohio we headed to Fort Wayne, Indiana. A church was having a Disability Awareness Sunday. They asked me to be their keynote speaker. They have a great outreach to the disabled community (mostly developmentally challenged) called One Heart. It was an honor to be a part of their day. After the service, we went to the hospital to visit a One Heart member. He recently had his leg amputated below the knee due to a moped accident. He had a wonderful attitude along with solid support from his family and One Heart. I was able to assure him the phantom pain would go away and his coworkers (he had a dishwasher job) did not think he was letting them down. I also told him to make sure he orders his prosthetic foot the same size as his other one. He will save a lot of money on shoes that way.

From Fort Wayne, we moved up to Shipshewana, Indiana. We arrived on Monday and set camp for the coming week. We had made friends in this Amish community when we pedaled through in July. There were already several Amish schools on our schedule as well as a Sunday service at Waterford Mennonite Church in Goshen. Monday evening Darla and I took a short bike ride through the area before the sunset. It was beautiful and peaceful. You could hear the clop-clop-clop of horse drawn buggies just about all the time. Tuesday morning we went to the Amish school where Marilyn Miller was a teacher's assistant. We had met Marilyn and her mother, Ruth, in July and became quick friends. Marilyn is fifteen years old and has a twin brother, Marlin. After school, we went to their home for a meal and fellowship. They invited us to go on a horse and buggy ride before supper.

A pleasant afternoon, quiet country roads, an Amish buggy ride ... what could go wrong? Well, if you read the first chapter of this book, you know what could go wrong. A feed truck hit our horse and cart. I never finished that story for you. If you do not remember where I left off, feel free to go back and reread the details. I will wait …

Anyway, after the first paramedic arrived, the ambulance pulled up with the rest of the EMT crew. They split their attention between Marilyn and Marlin. A crowd of Amish started gathering behind the yellow tape. Many were children from the school we had spoken at and their parents. We saw "Hope and Courage" buttons on most of them. The Amish community is amazingly geographically and socially close.

As the EMTs took over, we were able to relax. Chanel came and sat next to me on the ground.

"Daddy, my leg really hurts."

"Oh, Sweetheart, let me get someone to look at that." I motioned an EMT to come over. "You should have said something."

"I didn't want to say anything until they took care of the twins."

I pulled her close and choked back my tears. I looked over at Darla comforting Ruth and saw blood around her left knee. I glanced around and found Grant standing near Marlin as they loaded him onto the stretcher. From where I sat, I could see that Grant had a gash on his heel. My family had just been hit by a truck. They should be sitting in the grass crying. Instead, they were up and tending to the injured people lying on the road. They did not just share hope and courage this summer, they learned hope and courage. I was watching them put it into practice right now.

The EMT came over and I said, "My daughter says her leg hurts. Can you check it out?"

"Of course. How'd did she hurt it?"

"In the crash when she fell out of the cart," I replied.

"She was in the buggy crash?" he asked, surprised. "Who else was in the crash?"

"All of us," I said.

"All of you? You were all in the buggy?" He assumed the Amish twins were the only passengers in the cart and we had just stopped to help.

"Yes, my wife, our two kids and I were all in the cart with the Amish. I think my wife and son got hurt a bit, too."

"Well, let's have a look at them. Your daughter's leg isn't broken or bleeding but you might want to get it checked out at the hospital."

He examined Darla and Grant. Darla had a pain in her knee and chest. Grant had a laceration on his heel.

Another EMT said, "Typically when a buggy crashes with a big truck, the buggy passengers sustain very serious injuries and need to be flown to distant hospitals. This is a miracle."

We were not surprised. We have become accustomed to miracles. The ambulance prepared to take Ruth and the twins to the hospital in Goshen. We told Ruth we would be at the hospital and would help see her through this. We contacted Vic and Marie Stoltzfus. They lived nearby and said they would meet us at the hospital. They have been a part of our journey since I was a little boy. It is no surprise they are with us on this day, too.

We decided I would drive my family to the hospital for x-rays. A police officer took Darla back to the farm to get our truck and my wheelchair. They returned shortly and brought my wheelchair to me.

As I was positioning myself to climb into my wheelchair an EMT asked, "How about you? Did you get hurt in the crash?"

"I don't know. I fell hard on my shoulder blades and they hurt a bit. Take your fist and press it hard into my shoulder blades and I will tell you if anything feels broken."

He pushed hard and I did not feel unbearable pain.

"No. I don't think I broke anything."

I reached ahold of the back of my wheelchair and pulled myself up in the seat with my arm. I turned around to face the front and saw a crowd of people staring at me with their mouths open. I am assuming they do not get to see a man with no legs and one arm get into a wheelchair very often.

The EMT said, "If you can do what you just did, I don't think you broke anything, either."

We loaded into the truck and prepared to leave. The EMT that had arrived on the scene first came over to my window.

"Before you leave, Mister, I have to tell you something. When I got out of my truck and saw you sitting on the road I thought, 'This is really bad. That guy has lost at least one limb ... maybe three. I better call the Medevac helicopter right now.'"

I laughed, "You were going to start looking for limbs in the bushes, weren't you?"

He said, "Yes, I was! That is what we are trained to do. It was surreal, though, because I didn't see any blood."

"Don't worry. I was in this condition when I arrived at this crash."

We spent the rest of our day at the Goshen Hospital. Marilyn was released with some serious bruises and a lump on her head. Marlin was kept overnight to watch a cracked sternum. Chanel was bruised but not broken. Grant did not require stitches. Darla fractured her kneecap. It was swollen and tender.

We took the next day off to comfort our family. In the following five days we spoke in seven more Amish schools, one Mennonite school, preached at a Mennonite church, had supper in three Amish homes, and made several visits to the disabled in the Amish community. We feel very close to the people in this area. I do not know what all of this means. I just know that Hope and Courage Across America did not end when we got off our bikes.

We are driving through Nebraska now. Nebraska is a good bike riding state. It is mostly flat and with the wind in the right direction, you can really sail. I am just guessing, really, because we have never ridden bicycles in Nebraska. We have not ridden bicycles since the buggy crash. Darla's knee will not tolerate the strain. I am driving the truck with the fifth wheel faithfully hanging on for the ride. Sometimes I forget the RV is back there and when I look in the rearview mirror and see it three feet from my window, it startles me. I have been using the cruise control for the last fifty miles. The drone of the diesel engine has lulled Darla and the kids to sleep. The billboard along the freeway reads, "Cabela's: the world's foremost outfitter of hunting, fishing, and outdoor gear. International Headquarters Next Exit. Sidney, Nebraska."

That would be a fun place to stop, I thought. *But they just fell asleep. I better not wake them up. I wish I had someone to talk to.*

The next sign read, "US 385 North – Rapid City, SD Next Exit."

Remember Rapid City? It was a familiar, internal voice that I had not heard for a while.

Hello, God, so good to hear from you.

I have missed our conversations, Bob.

Me, too. I have been so busy lately, I haven't had the time to stop and talk.

Do you have the time, now?

Oh, yeah, God. I have lots of time now.

Do you remember Rapid City? He repeated.

My mind rewound thirty-seven years to 1971. As I mentioned before, my dad died in Rapid City, South Dakota when he was forty-one. We had just moved there from Ohio nine months earlier. His journeys in this world always seemed too short. Mom, Reenie and I were left in South Dakota alone. Our journeys were far from over. Thank God (literally), Mom is a strong person.

Her father was dying of cancer in Olympia, Washington. Instead of moving back to Ohio, she decided we would go west. We loaded everything we owned in the back of a pickup truck and moved to the Pacific Northwest, the great state of Washington. Grandpa died a month later.

Mom said, "We're not going back."

Who could blame her? She was forty-six years old, widowed, orphaned, and still had two teenagers to raise.

She buried the past and looked the future right in the eye, "We're going to make this our home." She didn't even blink. I told you she was strong.

The first thing I noticed about Washington was that it rained … a lot. That was not enough for my mother, though. She moved us to Hoquiam. There are two things you need to know about Hoquiam. First, how to pronounce it, HOE-kwee-um. Because if you are sixteen years old and your mother moves you to Hoquiam and you don't know how to pronounce it, the other children will laugh at you. The second thing you need to know is that in the state of Washington it rains a lot. But in the town of Hoquiam it rains a lot … more.

Do you remember the road you chose when you got to Washington? God asked.

You were there?

I have always been 'there,' He reminded me.

I became defensive. *If You were always there, why didn't You stop me?*

Hey, you are an independent man and have to choose your own road. Do I need to refer you back to, 'I have a schedule, I have a plan, and I am in charge'?

Okay. Okay. I get the point.

Let's get back to Hoquiam. I was sixteen years old and walking rainy streets. Seeking the same things we all searched for at sixteen. The same things teenagers are searching for today. Sixteen years old, walking rainy streets, seeking acceptance. Somewhere I can go, take off my mask and just be myself. And myself is good enough, people will like me.

Sixteen years old, walking rainy streets, seeking someone to listen to me. Because at sixteen, I was filled with dreams. Chock-full and bubbling over with 'who I want to be, what I want to do, where I want to go' dreams. And I wanted to tell somebody about those dreams. It couldn't be just anybody. I did not want them to judge me. I did not want them to laugh at me. I did not want them to take my innermost thoughts and use them against me later. I was seeking someone who would just listen.

I was sixteen years old, walking rainy streets, seeking someone to say 'I love you.' Oh, I heard the words a lot. The teen culture of the 1970s was throwing those words around like Frisbees. I wanted to hear the words without someone trying to manipulate me. I wanted to hear the words without a bunch of conditions attached.

I was sixteen years old, walking rainy streets, seeking the same things we all searched for at sixteen: acceptance, someone to listen and someone to say 'I love you.' Maybe you are still seeking. When we do not find those things in healthy places, sometimes we will compromise and look in other places. I started to go to parties and I started to drink. Drugs soon followed. When you get on that road (parties, drinking and drugs), that road never spirals up. It only spirals down.

Thus began a ten-year journey on a road I should have never been on. I followed that road to Ohio with my two brothers and back to Washington with Tom. I followed that road to downed power lines on a dark night. I lay on that road as three limbs were amputated from my body. After six months, I left Harborview Medical Center and got right back on that same road. Back to the parties. Back to the drinking. Back to the drugs. How could I do that? At the age of twenty-one, I was in a crash and lost three limbs while coming home from drinking. How could I get out of the hospital and go right back on to the road that brought me in there?

Well, the answer is simple. I looked in a mirror. I looked in a mirror and saw stumps where I used to have limbs. I saw scars where I used to have skin.

I thought, *nobody is going to accept me. Nobody is going to listen to me. Someone to say 'I love you'? Maybe in my dreams but not in reality. Nobody is going to want to sit next to me when I look like this.*

I went right back onto the same road hoping I would find what I was seeking. But the road hadn't changed its direction. It still spiraled down. This meant I spiraled with it. I tried to make progress with my life. It seemed like I would take one step forward and two steps back. Most people thought I was doing great. However, to be honest with you, when you are missing three limbs it does not take much to impress people. They didn't realize, it wasn't my limbs I was missing because it wasn't my limbs I was seeking.

Reminiscing opened up old wounds and I felt the pain again. I lashed out, *Hey, God, where were You during all of this?*

It is okay. The pain you feel right now is expected. When you pick at your scars, they will bleed again. I could not choose your road, but I never left you. What happened next?

He is right. He is always right. And God doesn't have to ask me 'What happened next?' He is omniscient. He knows everything about that road I was on. But you don't, so let me get back to my memories.

I do not know how close I was to the bottom of that spiraling road when the phone rang.

"Bob," it was my sister, Jeanne. "I've got a favor to ask you. Darla, our babysitter, is watching Jenny and Robby tonight and we didn't make plans for their dinner. Could you pick up some chicken and bring it over to the house?"

Meeting Darla was wonderful but Darla was not what I was truly seeking, either. However, she knew where I would find what I was seeking. She took me to her church. Calvary Temple in Auburn, Washington, to be precise. Now, those of you readers who are church attendees, do not be offended by what I write next. Stick with me.

Darla takes me to church and we enter the sanctuary through the big doors in the back.

I'm thinking, *This is a joke. Seriously, what kind of help am I going to get in a place like this?*

I got to the back row and said, "This is far enough. I'll sit here."

I got out of my wheelchair and sat on the pew. Darla just sat down next to me. You see, Darla knew God was actually powerful enough to reach the back of a church. In fact, I have some good news for all of you. God is powerful enough to reach wherever you are. I do not care how many times you have fallen. I do not care how many wrong roads you have been down. I do not care how dark it is around you right now. God is powerful enough to reach you.

We have seen this all across America. We have seen this in places most people consider the darkest. Part of our ministry takes us into prisons. The first time I went into a prison was a little unnerving. I was aware of every door that I went through into deeper levels of security. I actually heard the locking mechanism fall into place behind me. I did not let that stop me from going back. The next time I didn't notice the doors as much. I kept going and now I don't notice them at all. In fact, it is almost like you are visiting Grandma. Unless Grandma is serving time, then it is just like visiting Grandma.

Even in prison, God reaches people. I have been visiting a prison on the east coast quite regularly over the past years. The chaplain schedules me to speak to the guys when I am in town. After a few years I noticed many of the same faces were still there. Joe comes to mind. He plays guitar in the chapel worship band. Joe is a strong, bushy haired man. He looks like his hands belong on the handles of a Harley more than the strings of a guitar. Before the rest of the inmates came in I had a chance to talk to him.

"Joe, I keep seeing you every year I come here. If you don't mind saying, why are you in prison? What'd you do?"

He told me a tale of a fight in a bar that cost a man his life. I could tell he was sorry for what he did. He knew he deserved his punishment.

"How long will you be here, Joe?"

"I've got twenty-five down and life to go."

One man died that night in the bar but two men lost their lives. Even in the prison where Joe lives, God was able to reach him. You should hear him play guitar in the worship band. God's light shines brightest in the darkest places. God can reach you wherever you are.

Darla knew the back of the church was more than close enough to God. I sat in the back row distracted by the Sunday morning congregation. It had been a long time since I had seen that many people with clear eyes and smiling faces after Saturday night. Pastor Dave Tonn was preaching. I told you about Dave Tonn back when we were pedaling through Columbia Falls, Montana. He said something that focused my attention away from the people and onto his words.

He said, "God loves you and accepts you ... just as you are."

Excuse me? God loves you and accepts you just as you are?

Now, I had read the Bible back when I was going to the Mennonite church. I liked reading it. The Bible is an exciting book. I really liked the New Testament, especially the miracles. I read about Jesus walking on water. This was long before special effects. If they saw Jesus walking on water, He was really walking on water. I read about Jesus healing all the sick. Not one of the sick or some of the sick. Look at the small words in the Bible. "When evening came, many who were demon-possessed were brought to him, and he drove out the spirits with a word and healed all the sick" (Matthew 8:16, NIV). Jesus raised the dead. That one makes the hair stand up on my arm. The Bible is full of amazing miracles.

Nevertheless, in my mind, the most amazing miracle I had ever heard was what Pastor Tonn just said. "God loves you and accepts you just as you are." That is amazing. Not that God could love and accept all those other people in that church. Have you been to a church on Sunday morning? Take a look at those people. Those are very lovable people. Anybody on this planet can love those people. But to love me? That is a different story. That is a miracle.

Everything I lost, every scar I had, every wrong road that I had ever been on, God knew about … and He loved me anyway. He loved me so much He sent His only son, Jesus Christ, to come to this earth, take the form of a man, walk in the dirt of this world, and live a sinless life. That 'sinless life' part is a key theological point. I do not have time to go into all the details of that point now but if you visit a church, I am sure it will come up in a sermon before too long. He had to live a sinless life because He was going to go to a cross as a pure and spotless sacrifice for my sin.

I am sitting in the back row of a church and I do not want to hear this stuff. But do you want to know something rotten about only having one hand? When you only have one hand, you can only cover one ear. It did not matter. I had quit listening with my ears. I started listening with my heart. Pastor Tonn asked a simple question.

"Is there anybody here who needs to be forgiven of their sins? Washed by the blood of the Lamb? Reconciled with a heavenly Father who loves them more than they can understand? Set free? Is there anybody here who needs to give their life to God? If that's you, just raise your hand."

I am sitting on the back row and I am thinking, *"Why is this man being so vague? Why doesn't he just say 'Bob'? Who else could he be talking to? There's nobody else in this place like me."*

I looked at my life. I had run it into the ground, burned it up and left pieces littered behind me.

If God wants this life, He can have it.

Do not think too highly of me, folks. I was not giving Him much. I raised a shaky hand in the back of the church.

Yes, sir. That's me. I need Jesus.

Pastor Tonn said, "If you raised your hand, come down front here … down to the altar. We want to pray with you."

My mind raced, *"Wait a minute. I thought all I had to do was raise my hand. Nobody said anything about going down in front of all these people."*

It is one thing to sit in the back of a church with everybody in front of me, nobody looking, and raise my hand to say 'I need Jesus.' What does that take? All that takes is common sense. Of course I need Jesus. However, to get out of my seat and go to the front of the church takes something more than common sense. It takes faith. Faith that something will happen between the back of the church and the front of the church that will change my life forever. Faith that by having the courage to take one step, God would rush forward to meet me. It takes faith. But thank God it doesn't take much faith, because I had very little. But it was enough to get me out of that seat.

I pulled my wheelchair next to me and got off the pew. I started to roll to the altar.

Why did I sit so far from the front?

I tried to ignore the people I rolled past. The pastor had said, "Every head bowed, every eye closed" while calling people forward. I heard him say it three times. I counted how many times he said it because I was depending on it. But do you know what? They peeked. Not a furtive glance either. They held their heads up and looked. These people fully believed in miracles. Many of them had seen miracles. A young man with no legs and one arm was rolling down to the altar, the place of miracles. I am sure some of them had interesting ideas about what kind of miracle they might see today. New legs? An arm? Who knows what God might do? They just knew they were going to see it with their own eyes.

Let them stare. I am not going down to that altar for them. I am not going down to that altar for Darla, either. But I am going down there for a miracle.

Have you ever thought about miracles? God gives them all the time. What if you knew God would give you one miracle right now? Just one. Right now. What would you ask for? Take your time. It is an important decision if you think you can only have one miracle. This is what was on my mind going down that aisle. I was confident God would give me a miracle.

My faith increased every foot of the way. I could ask God to deliver me from my life of alcohol and drugs. That is a good miracle, well within the power of God. I could ask him for legs and an arm. That would be a good miracle, too. God designed and created the human body. I am sure He could find a few spare parts. But I didn't want to waste my miracle on something that was just good when I knew I could have the greatest. I bowed my head and asked God for the greatest miracle He could perform. I asked Him to forgive me of my sins. That is His greatest miracle. It is His greatest miracle because it required the greatest sacrifice … the blood of His Son.

I bowed my head and did not know what to say. Someone came over and helped me with words. I do not remember the exact prayer but it went something like this:

"Father, I know that I am a sinner. And I know You sent your Son, Jesus Christ, as a sacrifice for my sin. I am sorry I made You do that. But I ask now, in the name of Jesus, please forgive me, wash me, and set me free."

As I said the words, I literally felt a weight lifted from me. A burden I had carried for so long that it felt normal, finally disappeared. I began to sob and when I uttered 'Amen,' I became a whole man. A whole man. I know I still only have one arm. And I know I don't have any legs. But I also know this: What makes me whole is not in my shoes. What makes me whole is in my heart. There is a place in my heart, just like yours, that only Jesus Christ can fill. Only Jesus Christ. I had spent many years putting other things where only Jesus belonged. And every one of those things let me down. Jesus has never failed me.

I sat at that altar and realized I did not want to go back out onto the same muddy road I was on before. I wanted to change. I wanted to follow Jesus.

Thank You, God.

You're welcome.

He interrupted my memories and brought my attention back to driving a truck through Nebraska.

I'm sorry. I forgot you were still there, God.

I told you, I am always 'there.' So, you met my Son. How's following Him working out for you?

It hasn't always been easy and I mess up a lot. But He sure is patient with me.

Well, patience is one of His many strong points. Did you ever find what you were seeking?

Do you mean, did I ever find someone to accept me as I am, listen to my dreams, and love me unconditionally? Yeah, I found an abundant portion of all those things. And it all started with You, God.

You said a true word there. Tell me something, Bob, do you ever regret not asking for two legs and an arm back at that church?

His question got me to thinking. It has been almost three decades since I rolled down the aisle of that church. (Six months later, I rolled down that same aisle again to the same altar. That time, I brought my friend from the back row with me and I married her. She is sleeping in the seat next to me in the truck right now.) I wonder where we would be and what I could have done with my life if I had gotten my legs and arm back.

Good question, God. What do You think I could have done? You know everything.

I know what was, what is, and what is to come. Knowledge of the road not taken is always a little sketchy. Maybe with two legs and two arms you could have found a wonderful woman and got married.

No, I did that anyway. I looked at Darla and smiled.

Well, maybe you could have had kids and been a good father.

I glanced in the rear view mirror to see Grant and Chanel sleeping. *No, I think I am covered there, too.*

How about getting a job that fulfills your purpose on this planet? Did it. Doing it.

Okay, maybe with two arms and two legs you could have done some amazing physical activity like ride a bicycle across America.

C'mon, God, I did all that stuff. Can't You think of—Oh, I get it. You're being ironic. Having only one arm and no legs has not kept me from any of those things. It would have made no difference.

You are right, Bob. The best decision you made that day was to give your life to me. Your greatest victory came when you surrendered. Now, that is ironic.

I was scared that day. It took a lot for me to raise my hand and admit I needed Jesus.

You found hope. If you would not have had the courage to raise your hand, you would never have had the courage to lead your family on this journey across America.

I believe that, God. I could not have done any of this without You.

Glad I could be there for you. Oh, and by the way, that road you chose at the altar ... that is a good road. Keep following it and it will lead you home.

Darla opened her eyes and looked out the window. Nebraska had become Wyoming but you could not tell that by looking at the landscape. She reached across the seat and rubbed my neck.

"Are you doing okay, Honey? How's the road?"

I could not help but think of the conversation I had just finished with God.

"I'm doing just fine, Babe ... and the road we're on is perfect." *Just perfect.*

Amazing grace, how sweet the sound
That saved a wretch like me.
I once was lost, but now am found.
T'was blind but now I see.
(John Newton, Amazing Grace)

The journey never ends.

Afterword

We got home and tried to go back to life the way it was before the ride. But things had changed, or to be more precise, we had changed. The summer of 2008 had tested our bodies, minds, and spirits. We were stronger people than before. We were a stronger family.

Nicole finished college, became a Registered Nurse, and married Justin. Grant finished high school and started his college studies. Chanel is a teenager now and makes even more friends everywhere. Darla and I continue to travel the gentle rolling hills of our lives together.

Since Hope and Courage Journey 2008, that's what we call it now, we have ministered throughout the United States and Europe. Several times, we have visited our Amish friends to continue our message of hope and courage. But we missed sharing the message at that slow pace that only comes from the seat of a bicycle.

So, in April 2011, we loaded the bikes into the back of the RV again. Darla, Grant, Chanel, and I pedaled a combined 4800 miles from Long Beach, California to Jacksonville, Florida. We finished August 5, 2011. It was Hope and Courage Across America – Southern style.

We aren't concerned with the distance or how much we ride. We love to ride and will always ride as much as we can. We are more interested in the opportunities we have to present a familiar message. Our hope is in Christ and the courage is in us to use that hope to face mountains.

It's not about the miles, it's about the message.

More About Bob

Bob has a message perfect for you.

Executives have recognized Bob Mortimer's unique style of communication as a valuable motivational tool for their corporations. Schools have used Bob to inspire students to be their best. Churches appreciate his clear testimony of redemption. His topics include…

Facing Mountains –
Bob teaches how the character traits of hope and courage can help individuals persevere through current challenges.

Being Our Best –
The only handicap you have is the one you put on yourself. Bob will help your audience identify the handicaps that are hindering them from having an extraordinary life.

Overcoming Tragedy –
Bob shares three tools you already have to face the trial you are going through at this moment.

Bob is available to your group through Bob Mortimer Motivational Ministries.

Bob Mortimer Motivational Ministries
253.851.2589
www.hcjourney.org
bob@hcjourney.org

34091768R00210

Made in the USA
Middletown, DE
08 August 2016